International Library of Psychology

Cognitive and Computational Aspects of Face Recognition

Explorations in face space

Edited by Tim Valentine

London and New York

First published 1995
by Routledge
11 New Fetter Lane, London EC4P 4EE

Simultaneously published in the USA and Canada
by Routledge
29 West 35th Street, New York, NY 10001

Typeset in Times by Florencetype Ltd, Stoodleigh, Devon

Printed and bound in Great Britain by Biddles Ltd,
Guildford and King's Lynn.

British Library Cataloguing in Publication Data
A catalogue record for this book is available from the British Library

Library of Congress Cataloguing in Publication Data
A catalogue record for this book has been requested

ISBN 0-415-11493-4

*This book is dedicated to my mother, Mollie Valentine
and to the memory of my father, Randell Valentine.*

Contents

Illustrations

FIGURES

TABLES

Contributors

Hervé Abdi is a Professor at the School of Human Development, GR41, The University of Texas at Dallas, Richardson, TX 75083–0688, USA. He is also jointly appointed as a Professor of Psychology at the Université de Bourgogne a Dijon, Boulevard Gabriel 21000 Dijon, France.

Philip J. Benson is a Medical Research Council Research Scientist at the University Laboratory of Physiology, Parks Road, Oxford OX1 3PT, UK.

Vicki Bruce is Professor of Psychology at the Department of Psychology, University of Stirling, Stirling FK9 4LA, UK.

A. Mike Burton is Professor of Psychology at the Department of Psychology, University of Glasgow, 56 Hillhead Street, Glasgow G12 9YR, UK.

Patrick Chiroro is a Lecturer at the Department of Psychology, University of Zimbabwe, P. O. Box MP 167, Mount Pleasant, Harare, Zimbabwe.

Ian Craw is a Senior Lecturer at the Department of Mathematical Sciences, University of Aberdeen, Dunbar Street, Aberdeen AB9 2UB, UK.

Kenneth A. Deffenbacher is Professor and Chair at the Department of Psychology, University of Nebraska at Omaha, Omaha, NE 68182–0274, USA.

Ruth Dixon is a postgraduate student at the Department of Psychology, University of Durham, Science Laboratories, South Road, Durham DH1 3LE, UK.

Hadyn D. Ellis is Professor of Psychology at the School of Psychology, University of Wales College of Cardiff, Cardiff CF1 3YG, UK.

Peter J. Hancock is a Research Fellow at the Department of Psychology and Centre for Cognitive and Computational Neuroscience, University of Stirling, Stirling FK9 4LA, UK.

Judith A. Hosie is a Lecturer at the Department of Psychology, University of Aberdeen, King's College, Old Aberdeen AB9 2UB, UK.

Robert A. Johnston is a Lecturer at the School of Psychology, University of Wales College of Cardiff, Cardiff CF1 3YG, UK.

Alan B. Milne is Computer Systems Manager at the School of Psychology, University of Wales College of Cardiff, Cardiff CF1 3YG, UK.

Alice J. O'Toole is an Assistant Professor at the School of Human Development, GR41, The University of Texas at Dallas, Richardson, TX 75083–0688, USA.

J. Don Read is Professor of Psychology at the Department of Psychology, The University of Lethbridge, Lethbridge, Alberta T1K 3M4, Canada.

Gillian Rhodes is a Senior Lecturer at the Department of Psychology, University of Canterbury, Private Bag 4800, Christchurch, New Zealand.

Sarah V. Stevenage is a Research Demonstrator at the Department of Psychology, University of Southampton, Highfield, Southampton SO7 1BJ, UK.

Dominique Valentin is a graduate student at the School of Human Development, GR41, The University of Texas at Dallas, Richardson, TX 75083–0688, USA.

Tim Valentine is a Lecturer at the Department of Psychology, University of Durham, Science Laboratories, South Road, Durham DH1 3LE, UK.

John R. Vokey is an Associate Professor of Psychology and Chair at the Department of Psychology, The University of Lethbridge, Lethbridge, Alberta T1K 3M4, Canada.

Preface

The origins of face space

In September 1993, Bob Johnston organized an International Conference on Face Processing under the auspices of the Welsh Branch of the British Psychological Society. I was invited to convene a symposium which was held during the conference under the title of 'Facial distinctiveness, race and caricature'. The idea to publish a collection of papers on these topics came from discussions during the conference, and I would like to thank Bob Johnston and the BPS for the opportunity they provided for researchers from around the world to meet and discuss face recognition, and Chris Barrie and Cath Williams for their assistance in organizing the conference.

This book is not simply the proceedings of the symposium, although many of the contributors to this volume presented papers as part of the symposium or on other occasions during the conference. Some contributions from additional authors have been added. Each chapter presents a review written by an active researcher in the area. In this way it hoped to provide up-to-date reviews of the 'state of the art' in an area which is currently the subject of a good deal of research activity. The approaches used are diverse and include formal mathematical modelling, computer simulations using artificial neural networks, analysis of the three dimensional shape of faces as well as experimental investigation of human performance in the perception and recognition of faces. The chapters cover a wide range of topics in face recognition, including development of face recognition skills in children; the perception of caricatures; the perception of faces of different races, and the perception of distinctiveness, attractiveness, sex and facial expression. What all of the contributions have in common is that they explore some aspect of the effect that the structure of the population of faces has upon our ability to perceive and recognize faces. The central idea is that faces are not perceived in isolation. It is only through our knowledge of a large number of faces that we can judge a particular face to be female, attractive, oriental, happy or distinctive.

One metaphor for the way in which a population of faces may be represented, that has proved useful, is to think of a specific face encoded at a location in a multidimensional 'face space'. The dimensions of the space are the features that vary between one face and another (e.g. face width, distance between eyes, etc.) and the location of a specific face defines its value on each dimension. This kind of approach has been explicitly used to generate caricatures of faces (Brennan, 1985) and has recently been used as a model for the mental representation of faces that could account for the effects of facial distinctiveness, inversion, race and caricature on human performance in recognizing faces. Although the role of the categorical structure of the population of faces is a common theme, the reader will find differences of opinion among the contributions on the mechanisms by which the structure of faces influences perception and the nature of the information which gives rise to the structure. Although such debates about the details and limits of the approach are important, what is most striking is that there is much common ground emerging among scientists from a number of disciplines who for one reason or another are interested in how to recognize human faces.

As an 'implicit' theory for the representation of faces, the idea of a 'face space' is not new. One consequence of such a representation (in a linear space) is that it would be possible to move between faces in the space, and at all points in the space the location would still represent a face. Galton (1878) experimented with 'composite portraits' by exposing a photographic plate to multiple portraits, which had been matched for size and angle of view one at a time so that the images were superimposed. He noted that the resulting composites 'have a surprising air of reality. Nobody who glanced at one of them for the first time, would doubt its being the likeness of a living person' (p. 133). Examples of Galton's composite portraits are shown in Figure 1. Galton (1878) also quotes a letter from Mr A. L. Austin addressed to Charles Darwin written in 1877. Mr Austin noted that two portraits of two different people placed in a stereoscope fused into a single composite portrait. He commented that 'the faces blend into one in a most remarkable manner, producing in case of some ladies' portraits, in every instance, a *decided improvement* in beauty' (p. 137). The observation that composite faces appear to be strikingly attractive is a topic of interest to psychologists more than a century later, who now have sophisticated image-processing software at their disposal (e.g. Perrett *et al.*, 1994).

However, Galton's interest in composite portraiture was as a tool to study the inheritance of characteristics rather than to study the processes of face recognition. (For example, Figure 1 includes composites of health, disease and criminality.) Our interest in the idea of a face space (and composite faces) is to understand how the remarkable ability of humans to recognize a familiar face from among the thousands of faces seen can be achieved. Johnston and Ellis (Chapter 1) explore the development of the 'face space' of young children by use of the effects of distinctiveness.

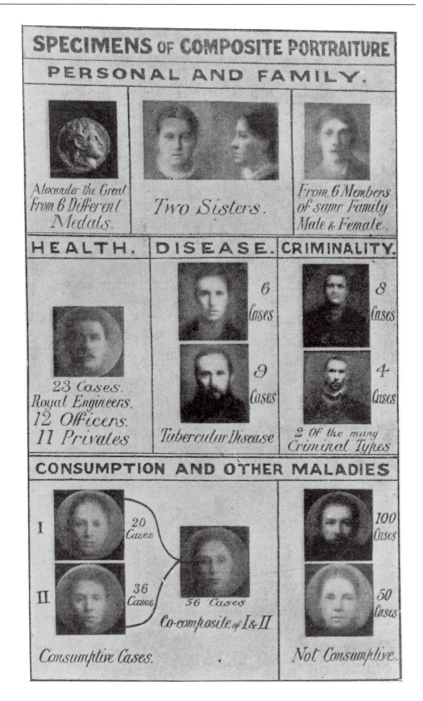

Figure 1 Examples of Galton's composite portraits

Stevenage (Chapter 2) explores young children's face recognition ability by examining the development of recognition of caricatures. Rhodes (Chapter 3) considers what conclusions can be drawn concerning the nature of the information used to recognize faces from studies of the effects of caricature and inversion. My colleagues and I (Chapter 4) consider how the notion of a face space might explain the apparent difficulty people have in recognizing faces of another race and how the ability to recognize other-race faces develops from experience.

Many of the contributors discuss the effects of facial distinctiveness on face processing. Hosie and Milne (Chapter 5) show that distinctiveness effects might arise because a face is distinctive in the population or because it is distinctive in a specific experiment. This observation suggests some caution might be required in the interpretation of experimental results. Vokey and Read (Chapter 6) convincingly argue that the structure of the population of faces gives rise to two psychological dimensions rather than to one. This theme is developed in the chapters by Bruce *et al.* (Chapter 7) and by O'Toole *et al.* (Chapter 8). By use of some sophisticated measurements using lasers, Bruce *et al.* are able to explore the physical three-dimensional characteristics of faces which differentiate males from females and underlie facial distinctiveness. O'Toole *et al.* review their simulations of human face processing using an artificial neural network which receives input from images of faces. In this way, they are able to simulate the effects of race discussed by Valentine *et al.* Craw (Chapter 9) presents a mathematical model of object recognition and its application to face recognition. He provides some much needed mathematical precision to the idea of a face space. Finally, Benson (Chapter 10) argues for an increased role for 'composite portraits' in face processing research and illustrates the case with a discussion of research on the processing of facial expression. Which brings us full circle to the method with which Galton started the exploration of face space.

REFERENCES

Brennan, S. E. (1985) The caricature generator. *Leonardo*, 18, 170–178.

Galton, F. (1878) Composite portraits. *Journal of the Anthropological Institute of Great Britain and Ireland*, 8, 132–144.

Perrett, D. I., May, K. A. and Yoshikawa, S. (1994) Facial shape and judgements of facial attractiveness. *Nature,* 368 (No. 6468: 17 March), 239–242.

Chapter 1

The development of face recognition

Robert A. Johnston and Hadyn D. Ellis

Infants may arrive into what James (1890) described as 'booming, buzzing confusion' but it is apparent that from a very early age they are able to respond differentially to faces. It has been demonstrated that babies aged less than 10 minutes old have a preference for following a moving schematic face rather than a blank head shape or one containing facial features in a jumbled configuration (Goren *et al.*, 1975; Maurer and Young, 1983; Johnston *et al.*, 1992). While there is still debate over exactly to what the neonate is responding, a face *per se* or some more fundamental sensory characteristic of the stimulus (e.g. phase, amplitude, etc.), the early preferential orientation towards such objects is not in doubt. It is clear, however, despite evidence of this early sensitivity, that children's skill and efficiency in processing faces continue to improve throughout the course of childhood. Indeed, over the next forty-eight hours neonates learn to recognize their mother's face – a quite remarkable cognitive feat for such an immature nervous system (Bushnell *et al.*, 1989).

The earliest systematic studies of the later development of face rec nition abilities were carried out by Goldstein and Chance (1964) on schoolchildren of different ages. Their initial experiments required children of 5, 8 and 13 years of age to perform a recognition memory task. Children were first shown a set of unfamiliar faces and then at a later stage were required to select these previously encountered faces from a larger set of unfamiliar faces. Performance in this task improved steadily across the three age groups tested.

Ellis (1991) has also shown that children below the age of 11 years find it particularly difficult to deal with simple age transformations or expression transformations of faces that would be trivial for adults. Children aged from 3–11 years were required to match simultaneous presentations of faces which differed in expression (e.g. smile, grimace or surprise): the performance of the children showed a clear developmental trend. Three year olds performed the worst and 11 year olds the best.

There is some disagreement when the performance of children reaches adult levels. Feinman and Entwistle (1976) reported that after 11 years of age subjects show little improvement in performance. Other workers, however, have shown a dip in performance at around 12 years of age (e.g. Carey *et al.*, 1980; Flin, 1980). This dip in performance has been ascribed to a change in the processing strategies of children when recognizing faces (Carey, 1981). Below this age the processing of faces by children is assumed to be dominated by featural or piecemeal strategies rather than the more predominately configural recognition strategies customarily employed by adults. This idea is supported by a whole battery of experiments which appear to show that young children are particularly influenced by salient aspects of facial stimuli. Different faces may be erroneously judged to be the same if they share the same expression, if they possess the same piece of paraphernalia or if they are subjected to the same size transformations (Diamond and Carey, 1977; Flin, 1980; Ellis, 1990; 1991). This developmental inflection has been observed in the processing of other stimuli (e.g. voices: see Mann *et al.*, 1979), which suggests that a more general developmental change may underlie any inflection in face processing.

There may be several explanations for the phenomena we outline above. Nevertheless, it is clear that strong evidence exists to demonstrate that a child's ability to recognize faces continues to develop steadily across the school age years despite any early, probably innate, attunement to faces.

One potential explanation we would like to explore in the course of this chapter proposes that these effects mainly arise through an increasing ability to discriminate among faces. This may be due either to the way that faces are encoded when they are encountered or because of the way that representations of faces are stored in memory – indeed these options may be impossible to disentangle. It would not be surprising if to an untutored (or alien) eye human faces all looked identical. They all have the same component features, which are juxtaposed in more or less the same arrangement. The differences in the way these components are laid out are so small as to be considered insignificant if we were considering exemplars of another similarly homogeneous category (e.g. markings of dogs). The adult ability to discriminate among faces has been described as the acme of human visual perception (Ellis, 1981). Underlying this skilful perceptual ability must be an appropriately refined and discriminating process for storing representations of faces in memory – perhaps this ability is not present to the same level of sophistication in young children and only develops over time.

Ellis *et al.* (in preparation) have attempted to examine experimentally anecdotal reports of children's tendency falsely to recognize strangers who are similar to familiar people. Parents of young children are often all too embarrassingly aware that their offspring make category-inclusive errors of facial recognition. If Uncle John has a round face and a bald head other men of similar appearance may be mistakenly identified as being him by pre-school children. This is an error typical of young children rather than adults. A diary study conducted by Young *et al.* (1985) analysed almost a thousand misidentifications which were made by adults when attempting to recognize people – very few of these errors were false positive identifications based on spurious facial similarity between the known person and the stranger. Keil (1987) provides a possible theoretical analysis of the way children of different ages make categorical judgements. He claims that younger children use wider boundaries and hence include more items within a category. As a child matures the critical, defining features for category membership become sharpened so that fewer objects are included. Ellis *et al.* (in preparation) propose a particular familiar face as a category and examine the preparedness of young children to accept other faces as versions of the target face (i.e. members of that category). In an experimental test of this hypothesis, distracter faces were selected to be either very similar or very dissimilar to one of two target faces. Ellis *et al.* examined identification performance across a range of ages (5, 8, 11 and 19 years) by looking at response latencies and accuracy for decisions as to whether a stimulus was or was not a specified famous person. As would be expected, accuracy was positively correlated with age and the time to make responses was negatively correlated with age. The interesting aspect of the results, however, relates to performance with similar and dissimilar distracters. While all subject groups produced similar error rates in classifying dissimilar distracters, the youngest group showed a unique difficulty with rejecting similar distracters, a tendency not shown by the other groups. When examining response latencies it was noted that the child groups were slower to reject similar distracters than dissimilar ones, but the 19-year-old group shows no difference in response times to reject either type of lure. Can we provide an explanation for these effects predicated on the manner in which faces are represented in memory for different age groups?

Let us first consider how adult faces may be stored in memory. Valentine has suggested that a useful heuristic for understanding how this is achieved is to view the adult face space as a multidimensional space (Valentine, 1991a; 1991b). Facial representations in memory can be viewed as locations within this multidimensional space. So far it has not been possible to specify the dimensions of this space but it would not be unreasonable to assume that they will be based on those that would best serve to discriminate among faces. Indeed there are many reasonable candidates which include such feature dimensions as face shape, hair length, hair colour, or perceived age derived from multidimensional scaling studies (e.g. see Shepherd *et al.*, 1977).

The origin of the multidimensional face space will be the central tendency of the dimensions and it is assumed that the feature dimensions of faces experienced will vary normally around this point. Typical faces, by definition, are more often experienced than distinctive faces and so the density of points throughout this space will not be uniform (see Figure 1.1a). There will be a higher density of face representations around the central tendency (i.e. the region where representations of typical faces are located). The putative framework which Valentine has suggested allows us neatly to account for many effects described in the face recognition literature (e.g. distinctiveness vs. typicality effects, inversion phenomena and face classification effects).

Using this theoretical framework, Valentine has identified two specific models based on the multidimensional nature of face space. One version he describes as being a norm-based model (however, this label is intended to cover a variety of similar theoretical constructs). Specifically, the theoretical approaches included are the prototype hypothesis (Valentine and Bruce, 1986a; 1986b), the norm-based coding model (Rhodes *et al.*, 1987), and the schema theory (Goldstein and Chance, 1980). All these accounts assume that storing representations of faces in memory entails the abstraction of something that can be called a face norm, prototype or schema. The norm-based model proposes that each individual face is stored in memory according to its deviation from a single, general face norm or prototype. This would be located at the origin of the face space. For an n-dimensional face space, an n-dimensional vector from the origin to a point representing the dimension values of a face would uniquely specify that face. The process of recognizing a face involves encoding the stimulus face as an n-dimensional vector and deciding if the resultant stimulus matches the stored vector of a face already encountered.

This is not the only way in which a multidimensional space could be described of course; for example, alternative formulations may not require a prototype face: instead these could be based on inter-stimulus similarity. In fact Valentine (1991a) has described such versions which he groups under the heading of exemplar-based models. It is appropriate in these models to think of faces as being encoded as points rather than vectors. Here, the origin of the space plays no role in encoding stimuli, it is simply the area of greatest exemplar density.

Valentine (1991a; 1991b) has shown how each of these models (norm-based and exemplar-based) can predict a particularly robust effect in the face recognition literature. Research employing faces in recognition memory experiments has shown that subjects are better at recognizing distinctive faces. A typical experiment would involve showing subjects a set of unfamiliar faces and subsequently asking them to identify these stimuli later when given a larger selection of unfamiliar faces. It has been demonstrated that subjects perform at a superior level with distinctive faces compared with typical faces. This differential performance can be demonstrated in a number of different ways. These include a higher recognition hit rate for previously seen faces if they are distinctive; and also faster recognition latencies. The distinctiveness advantage is also exhibited by the occurrence of fewer false positive decisions to distinctive distracter faces. An overall advantage for the recognition of distinctive as opposed to typical faces can often be demonstrated using a measure of sensitivity such as d' or A' (Going and Read, 1974; Cohen and Carr, 1975; Light et al., 1979; Winograd, 1981; Bartlett et al., 1984; Valentine, 1991a; 1991b; Shepherd et al., 1991). Moreover, Ellis et al. (1989) demonstrated that, although when subjects searched for a target face using FRAME (a computerized mugshot retrieval system) they were as good at retrieving typical faces as distinctive faces; yet when other subjects used a traditional mugshot album to recognize faces there was an enormous advantage for distinctive faces, particularly when they occurred later in a series of 1000 mugshots.

There is some variation in how the above mentioned researchers refer to the faces we label as either distinctive or typical. Some share our nomenclature, while others instead use the labels 'memorableness', 'uniqueness' or 'unusualness'. Vokey and Read (1992) even approach the dimension from the other direction and talk of typicality of faces where distinctive faces are considered atypical. Nevertheless, all researchers mean this to describe the range of variation present in *ordinary* faces. We do not intend the appellation 'distinctive' to conjure an image of a face that is deformed or has one eye or a huge scar.

As we mentioned earlier in this discussion, various workers have shown that the ability to discriminate novel faces from ones already encountered is a skill which improves steadily with age (e.g. Goldstein and Chance, 1964; Flin, 1980). However, compared to the abundance of work which has looked at this task with adult subjects when stimuli are controlled for distinctiveness, there is little research available on the performance of children. Ellis (1992) described some preliminary work on school-age children which suggested that the characteristic adult advantage for distinctive faces was absent in children aged around 6 years of age. He suggested that young children either fail to encode those aspects which make faces distinctive or that they store both typical and distinctive faces in the same manner. Ellis also demonstrated that even by the age of 13 years, subjects were not able to discount distinctive distracter faces more easily than typical distracters. In research employing adult subjects this advantage is a robust effect (e.g. Bartlett et al., 1984; Valentine and Endo, 1992), which suggests that the adult level of performance occurs after puberty.

Valentine's multidimensional face space can readily accommodate the distinctiveness advantage shown by adults in recognition memory experiments. According to either norm-based or exemplar-based models, typical faces are located in the areas of highest exemplar density: so, when a typical face is presented for test it is more likely to resemble another face, which produces a situation with greater uncertainty and hence more opportunity for error: it will be reflected both in longer response latencies to typical faces and in more false positives. Is it possible that this framework can also account for effects observed with child subjects?

In order to answer this question we need to speculate on how the way faces are represented in children's memory may differ from the adult arrangement. It is scarcely controversial to suggest that, in some way, a child's face space would be smaller than an adult's. This claim can be sensibly made on the basis that children have simply seen, and hence represented, fewer faces than adults. What is more contentious, however, is how this 'smallness' might be manifested.

One version is that the face space has the same general framework and parameters of the adult space but that it is less densely populated (Figure 1.1b) than the adult space (Figure 1.1a) and so, consequently, the density gradient of the space may be attenuated. Alternatively, the space might be based simply on a smaller volume than the adult space (Figure 1.1c). In this arrangement, relative difference in the density of face space enjoyed by typical and distinctive faces are preserved and, as the child experiences more faces, the volume of the face space increases to accommodate the additions. It is proposed that the space presented in Figure 1.1c has fewer dimensions than the adult space. (The face spaces displayed in Figure 1.1 are shown in two dimensions for the purposes of illustration only.)

It is not immediately apparent how additional dimensions can be added to the face space. We might propose that faces that are encountered early in childhood are not encoded along as many dimensions by the child's face-processing system. This could occur because s/he is not sensitive to some parameters or because there is no requirement to use them. As increasingly more faces are experienced, greater complexity in encoding will be necessary to distinguish among them and so additional dimensions are invoked that take account of second-order and higher-order features (Carey, 1992). This need not depend on any lack of 'power' or completeness of the child's face-processing capacity and is surely the means by which adult specialists become attuned to discriminating among exemplars that for non-experts would appear undifferentiated (e.g. sheep for shepherds (McNeil and Warrington, 1993); cows for farmers (Bruyer et al., 1983); dogs for canine show judges (Diamond and Carey, 1986); or Bewick swans for ornithologists (Bateson, 1977)). The change in the person's power of discrimination arises through frequent and varied exposure to the exemplars. Valentine (1991a) proposes that it is precisely the implicit knowledge acquired from one's lifetime exposure to faces which leads to the normal distribution of faces in the adult face space.

In a recently completed study we (Johnston and Ellis, in press) have conducted experiments to extend Ellis's (1992) earlier findings and examine differential processing by children of distinctive and typical faces. Our

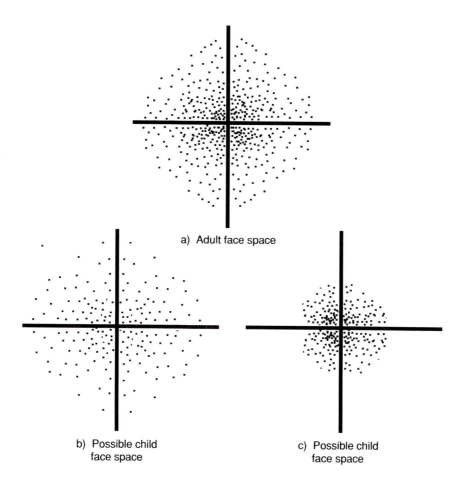

a) Adult face space

b) Possible child
face space

c) Possible child
face space

Figure 1.1 Representations of adult and possible child face spaces
Source: Johnston and Ellis, in press

subjects were recruited across an age range from 5 to 20 years. Several performance measures were used to ascertain how subjects responded to typical and distinctive faces. These included the number of hits, the number of false positives and latencies for correct recognition. Hits and false positives were also combined to yield d' prime scores to permit an overall measure of accuracy. For three out of four of our performance measures (response latencies, d' scores and number of false positives) we were able to demonstrate that the characteristic advantage shown by adults when processing distinctive faces only emerges completely at 9 years of age and was not present at all in our 5-year-old subjects. A graphical representation of our findings can be seen in Figure 1.2.

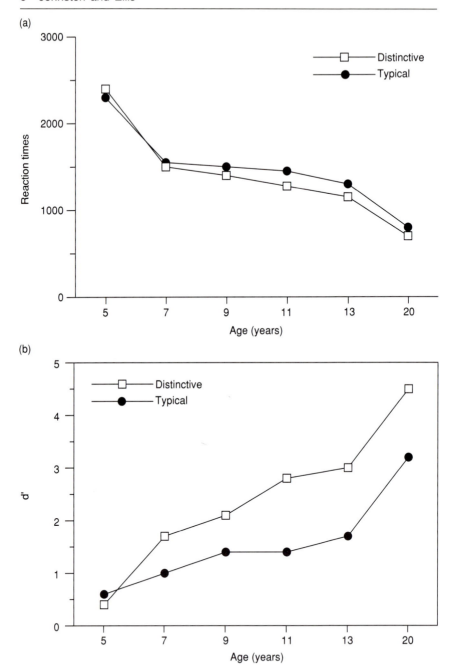

Figure 1.2 Four measures of performance of children and adults in a recognition memory task

Source: Johnston and Ellis, in press

(c)

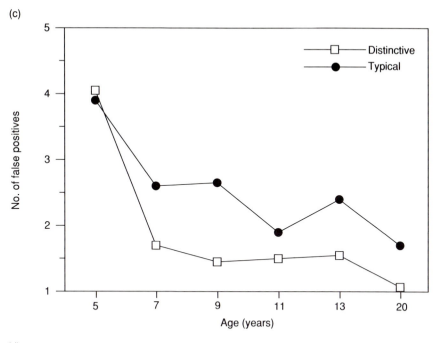

(d)

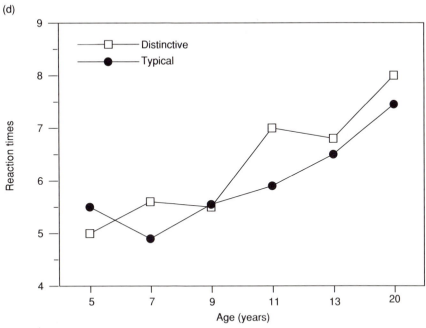

We would now like to consider how these findings can be reconciled with the alternative architectures we outlined earlier for putative child face spaces (Figures 1.1b and 1.1c). In order to do this effectively we need to consider the other possible refinement which Valentine has ascribed to the multidimensional face space. The two architectures suggested for the child face space can be implemented as either a norm-based or exemplar-based model. The four alternatives that are allowed by different permutations of architectures and norm-based or exemplar-based implementations (labelled N1, N2, E1 and E2) are shown in Figure 1.3. Each of these alternatives can accommodate the findings we reported above, but they would do so using different explanations.

N1	N2	E1	E2
Norm-based architecture implemented on face space from Figure 1b	Norm-based architecture implemented on face space from Figure 1c	Exemplar-based architecture implemented on face space from Figure 1b	Exemplar-based architecture implemented on face space from Figure 1c

Figure 1.3 Possible permutations of child face spaces and norm- and exemplar-based architectures

The competing hypotheses are as follows:

N1. The Figure 1.1b architecture and a norm-based model suggests that the distinctiveness advantage is not present because typical faces are no closer to their neighbours than distinctive faces. This model suggests that the density gradient in the child face space will be less steep than in the adult version.

N2. The Figure 1.1c architecture, together with a norm-based model, suggests that the distinctiveness advantage is not present because distinctive faces now have a neighbour which is as close as the neighbour of a typical face. This model suggests that the density gradient in the child face space can be effectively the same as in the adult version, but that all faces are now so close together that any effect of this is negated.

E1. The Figure 1.1b architecture combined with an exemplar-based model implies that the distinctiveness advantage is not present because typical faces are no closer to their neighbours than distinctive faces. This model suggests that the density gradient in the child face space will be less steep than in the adult version.

E2. The Figure 1.1c architecture and an exemplar-based model suggests that the distinctiveness advantage is not present because distinctive faces now have a neighbour which is as close as the neighbour of a typical face.

While all of the above hypotheses provide an adequate explanation for the distinctiveness effect in the recognition memory experiment paradigm, there may be ways in which distinctiveness effects can be manifested with which they have more difficulty. In all the above cases the differential processing of distinctive and typical faces is based on differences in the distance/angle between a target face and its nearest neighbour. In the young child's face space it appears that the distance between a typical face and its neighbour is little different from the distance between a distinctive face and its neighbour. There is another way in which distinctiveness effects are manifested with respect to face processing by adults, however, and this phenomenon provides a means to discriminate further between these four options.

Some years ago, Valentine and Bruce (1986a) devised a paradigm which they called the face classification task in which subjects are shown either intact or jumbled faces and are asked to make a judgement of whether or not the target stimulus is a face. Valentine and Bruce demonstrated that 'facedness' decisions could be made faster to typical rather than distinctive faces. Valentine (1991b) has explained how both the exemplar-based model and the norm-based model can permit this effect. Fortuitously, the mechanisms which Valentine outlines are quite different for norm-based and exemplar-based architectures. The exemplar-based model offers an explanation which is based on exemplar density. To classify the presented stimulus as a face it is necessary to judge how closely that stimulus resembles the central tendency of the population of all known faces. Consequently, the high exemplar density which impedes recognition of a previously encountered face can be advantageous when the task is simply to determine that a face is a face. The norm-based model predicts this same effect but via a different mechanism. Classifying a face is considered to depend on how closely the stimulus resembles the prototypical or norm face. Therefore the time needed to respond will be related to the length of the vector derived from the stimulus face, i.e. the distance between the face and the norm. Coincidentally, the length of this vector will usually be negatively correlated with exemplar density, but the effect is independent of this feature.

Given these observations we should be able to exploit this difference in order to reduce further the number of possible arrangements for describing a child's face space and indeed we were able to do just that (Johnston and Ellis, in press). We managed to show experimentally that children of the same age groups tested in our original experiment on recognition memory (5, 7, 9, 11 and 13 years) were able to classify typical faces as 'faces' more rapidly than they were able to respond to distinctive faces. Subjects of all age groups exhibited the characteristic adult advantage for classifying typical faces as faces (see Figure 1.4). There is no significant interaction between age and distinctiveness.

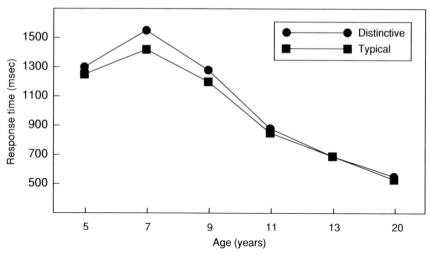

Figure 1.4 Mean time (msecs) to classify correctly typical and distinctive faces

We are thus in a position to explore how the four accounts (N1, N2, E1 and E2) which we described on page 10 are capable of accommodating two different manifestations of the distinctiveness effect in our youngest proposed face space – that of the 5-year-old subjects. In other words, which combinations of the architectures derived from Ellis (1992) and Valentine's (1991a) exemplar-based or norm-based alternatives will provide the most efficient explanations?

N1: As children of 5 years of age show the advantage for typical faces in the facedness task, but not for distinctive faces in a recognition memory task, we should prefer to explain each of these phenomena by a different mechanism. This account of the young child's face space provides just such an opportunity. We think that the density gradient in the child's face space is not as steep as in the adult version, but the relative distance from the norm of distinctive and typical faces is the same, since the child's space shares the parameters of the adult space. As a consequence of this, neighbouring faces will be generally no closer to target typical faces than they are to target distinctive faces and so there is no advantage for recognition of the latter. However, distinctive faces will usually be farther from the norm compared with typical faces and so distinctive faces will require more time to be classified as a face.

N2: This explanation accounts for the lack of a recognition advantage for distinctive faces by suggesting that the face space is compressed on to fewer dimensions (or on a restricted scale on all dimensions) and, consequently, that the distinctive faces are now as disadvantaged (in terms of closeness of neighbour) as typical faces. Unfortunately, this arrangement does not fit easily with the finding that 5 year olds do show a faster classification time for typical faces compared with distinctive ones. If the time to make a facedness decision is dependent on the distance between a representation and the norm, we should not expect the distinctive–typical difference in the 5-year-old group to be present or at least as strong as in the adult group. In the 5 year olds' face space the difference in relative distance from the norm is very much reduced. Not only is it unexpected to find this effect at all, but an examination of our data revealed that the difference between response times to typical and distinctive faces for our 5 year olds and our adults was 13 per cent and 3.5 per cent, respectively, of the mean time required for a facedness decision. Account N2 would predict that if the typical face advantage were to occur at all then this difference should lie in the opposite direction.

E1: This account relies on the dissociation of exemplar density from the distance between a target face and its nearest neighbour. As in N1, it is assumed that in the 5-year-old face space neither distinctive nor typical target faces have nearest neighbours close enough to interfere in the recognition task. The advantage for typical faces in the facedness task is explained by the fact that the distance from a face to its nearest neighbour can be independent of the exemplar density of the region in which it is situated. This relies on the assumption that the volume of the space pertinent to a recognition task is smaller than the volume of the space pertinent to a classification task. For example, a face may only suffer interference in the recognition task if its nearest neighbour is closer than x units away. The closest neighbour to typical faces in Figure 1.1b may be at 2x units and the closest neighbour to distinctive faces may also be at 2x units (or further) and so there would not be an observed advantage for distinctive faces in a recognition memory experiment. For typical faces, however, there may be many more neighbouring faces at a distance of 2x compared with the situation for distinctive faces. This means that typical faces still have an advantage in the face classification task. But this account does not cope so effectively with the facedness results. While this model allows a differential density gradient for the areas surrounding distinctive and typical faces it should not be as steep as in the adult version and certainly cannot be steeper. Once again this account suggests an absence, or at least dissipation, of the typical advantage in the facedness task which does not fit with what we found.

E2: The last solution to be considered also involves a compression of face representations owing to faces being coded on fewer dimensions or a restricted scale. However, while there are fewer faces, there are also likely to be a smaller number of dimensions and so we expect that the distribution of faces through this space will reflect the same arrangement as in an adult space (i.e. a steep density gradient with typical faces in the area of greatest exemplar density). This explains the facedness result in a parsimonious way; as in the adult space, there are simply more faces around a typical face which help in making a facedness decision. Using this explanation to account for findings in the recognition memory task needs more detailed consideration. Essentially, this is the converse of E1. Once more it is dependent on a disentanglement of the distance from a target face to its nearest neighbour and the local exemplar density of the target face. Here it is assumed that if the recognition of a face is impaired when the nearest neighbouring face is less than x units away then all faces – typical and distinctive – have neighbouring faces within that radius. This is a more persuasive account for the lack of a distinctiveness advantage in the recognition task than one based on the assumption that to a child all faces are 'distinctive'. It also suggests that for the purposes of the recognition task, the child's face space contains face representations which are all effectively typical.

We will now try to weigh up these various solutions. First we can dispense fairly rapidly with N2. This explanation cannot properly handle the data from either task. The account admits differential numbers of neighbours for distinctive and typical faces and yet there is no recognition advantage for distinctive faces. In addition it suggests the typical advantage in the facedness task should be absent or at least weakened in the youngest group and yet this is as strong as in adults.

Solution E1 suggests that in a child's face space all faces are effectively distinctive. This is not an unreasonable proposition, as we could imagine that a face which may seem very typical to an adult because s/he has already seen many similar ones could still be very distinctive to a child with a less extensive experience of faces. A consequence of this, however, should surely be that a child's accuracy in a recognition task should be as good if not better than that of an adult. The data which we collected did not suggest that this was the case. Our children were revealed as less accurate than our adult subjects (see Figure 1.2). This is also at odds with data from elsewhere that suggest children are troubled more than adults by similarities between faces (e.g. Flin, 1980; Ellis et al., in preparation). If children find faces so distinctive, why are they so liable to category-inclusive errors? Also the typicality advantage in the facedness task fits uncomfortably with this model. Assuming an exemplar density gradient which is not as steep as the one present in the adult suggests that the typicality advantage should be reduced or eliminated in the child face space but instead it appears as strong or even stronger than in the adult space.

On the other hand, the explanation offered in E2 to account for the lack of a distinctiveness effect appears more likely. If all faces are coded as representations which makes them 'typical' (as defined by target faces having a nearest neighbour close enough to impair recognition), then the poorer rates of accuracy for younger children would be expected. As an added bonus this also directly predicts the tendency to think all bald men are 'Uncle John'.

Even more evidence is available from Valentine (1991b), who considers that the representations of other-race faces in an adult face space may be compressed because 'the dimensions of the space might be inappropriate' (1991b, p.120). We are not proposing that the dimensions of the child's face space displayed in Figure 1.1c are *inappropriate*, but they may be *less* appropriate – particularly if we take into account the assumption that the adult face space employs further dimensions to facilitate storage. It is reasonable to suppose that a compression, similar to that postulated to give rise to the effect of race on face recognition, contributes to the phenomenon of all faces being typical in a recognition task for young children.

The proposed explanation of N1 is able to fit very easily with the data we describe here. This version explains the differential processing of typical and distinctive faces in the recognition memory task and the facedness task through different mechanisms. Therefore we do not need any further elaborated rationalizations for the performance of 5 year olds in the two different tasks.

Consequently we suggest that there are two viable alternatives for the nature of the child face space: N1 or E2. Either children have a face space based on the adult parameters but which is less densely populated with faces (Figure 1.1b) and is implemented as a norm-based account. Alternatively, children have a face space which is compressed because faces are coded on fewer dimensions but where there is a normal distribution of face representations (Figure 1.1c), and this is implemented as an exemplar-based account.

Given that we consider the accounts outlined in N1 and E2 to be good descriptions for our data, would it be possible to decide between them? Certainly at a general level our preference would be for an exemplar-based account. Indeed, Valentine and Endo (1992) have pointed out that an exemplar-based account is the more parsimonious since it does not require the storage and abstraction of a norm and yet can still reconcile all the empirical recognition phenomena. Nevertheless, is it possible to find stronger empirical reasons on which to base a decision?

We proposed that one route to this may lie in taking a further look at how children are able to discriminate among faces. Moving on from the findings of Ellis *et al.* that young children have more difficulty than adults in rejecting similar alternatives to a familiar face, we have tried to examine how they fare with unfamiliar faces. In order to do this it was first necessary to establish some firm baselines with adult subjects with which we would be able to compare children's performance.

In line with opinions we have already expressed, we acknowledge that

Valentine's multidimensional model is a powerful way of understanding a large amount of existing face recognition data relating to the processing of distinctive tasks. We have only referred to two ways in which a distinctiveness effect is often seen (in recognition memory tasks and with facedness decisions). However, there are other experimental paradigms where this dimension has an influence (e.g. familiar distinctive faces can be recognized as familiar faster than familiar typical faces (Valentine and Bruce, 1986b); distinctive faces are learned more easily than typical faces (Ellis *et al.*, 1988)). It is interesting to reflect, however, that we have moved to a multidimensional model for faces on the basis of experiments using faces rated along a linear scale. A scale where the labels 'typical' and 'distinctive' represent the ends of a continuum. In a usual rating exercise subjects would be shown faces and required to rate them along a scale of typicality/distinctiveness. To give a particular example, subjects could be asked to imagine they are looking for this person at a railway station and should try to imagine how easy/difficult this would be to do; the easier they think it would be to spot the face, the higher the distinctiveness rating they should give to it (from Valentine and Bruce, 1986b). Consequently, faces are attributed a single value dependent on their overall distinctiveness and two very 'different' faces could have an identical score. (This could also apply to faces which are rated as relatively typical, but of course in terms of the Valentine framework this would be less of a problem.) It is also worth a passing mention that, although what constitutes distinctiveness is hard to put into words, subjects do not find classifying faces in this way an unreasonable or ridiculous request. Moreover, there is a good degree of reliability across subjects.

In order to explore this 'curiosity', Johnston *et al.* (submitted) took a set of faces already rated for distinctiveness and asked subjects to make similarity judgements to pairs of sequentially presented faces. Our intention was to try to explore the face space using MDS techniques. Subjects were asked to make similarity judgements but they were not instructed as to what aspect or features of the faces to use. It was predicted, however, that it would be possible to determine the attributes that were considered important from the subsequent analysis. MDS also permitted an estimation of what is an appropriate number of dimensions employed to encode faces.

Ratings were collected for every possible combination of thirty-six faces (eighteen distinctive and eighteen typical), and ratings were made for each possible pair in both directions (Face A followed by Face B and vice versa).The ratings given to each possible pairing of different faces were collapsed across subjects and order of presentation to produce a set of 630 similarity ratings. The resulting matrix was submitted to the SPSS-X procedure ALSCAL (Takane *et al.*, 1976). Five analyses were performed, generating solutions in two to six dimensions. The goodness-of-fit

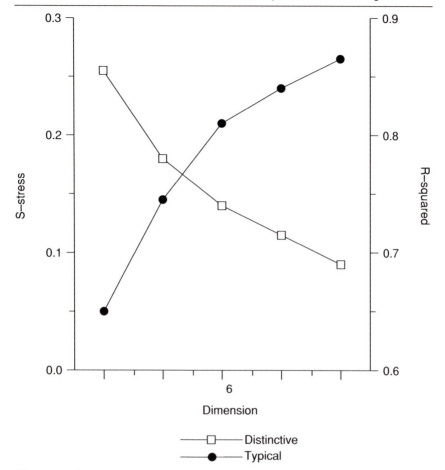

Figure 1.5 S-stress and R-square as a function of dimension of ALSCAL solution

Source: Johnston *et al.*, submitted

measures S-Stress and r^2 are shown in Figure 1.5. As can be seen from this graph, the improvement in r^2 levels off beyond dimension 4, indicating that the four-dimensional solution provides an adequate representation of the data.

Correlation coefficients were computed between the linear distinctiveness rating of each face and the distance it lay from the origin of the space for all dimensional solutions. For all five spaces there was a high positive correlation between distance from the centre of the space and the distinctiveness rating. This supports Valentine's proposal that distinctive faces will tend to be located on the periphery of the face space, while typical ones will be located more towards the centre. As an illustration of these spaces the positions of faces in the two-dimensional space are

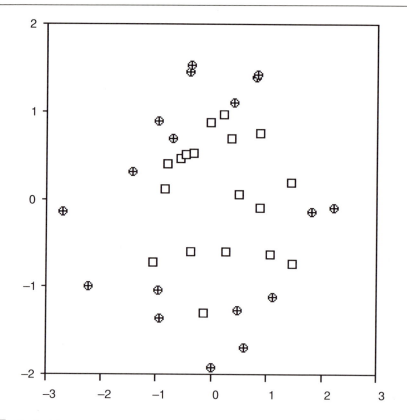

☐   Typical faces

⊕   Distinctive faces

Figure 1.6 Graph of two-dimensional plot of face space
Source: Johnston *et al.*, submitted

plotted in Figure 1.6. Our selection of this solution is dictated solely by the ease of displaying a two-dimensional figure. Numerical analyses of the higher order constructs indicate that the arrangement of typical and distinctive faces is similarly consistent with Valentine's proposals.

   The difference in spatial position between the groups of faces which had been originally designated as typical or distinctive were investigated using t-tests, and in every dimensional space it was found that the mean distance of the distinctive group of faces from the origin is greater than the mean distance of the typical group of faces. This provides neat support for the architecture of the face space which has been proposed by Valentine (1991a; 1991b).

While the above findings are clearly consistent with a multidimensional face space, they cannot directly inform us about whether that space should be thought of as norm-based or exemplar-based. Each of these alternatives could underlie the arrangement of face representations. To make use of these data in a way which can help solve this puzzle it is necessary to have an independent measure of the ease/difficulty with which faces are discriminated. This was obtained by recording response latencies to decide if pairs of sequentially presented faces were the same or different. Inter-object visual similarity has been measured by the time required to say that two objects are not identical (Podgorny and Garner, 1979). The more similarity between two items, the longer it will require to decide that they are different.

A series of experiments was conducted which at first produced single comparison latencies for all possible combinations of faces, and then produced latencies for several presentations of the same pairs. In the latter case the faces chosen were a subset of the original thirty-six faces which included the eight faces closest to the origin and the eight faces most distant from it (Johnston *et al.*, in preparation).

Taking the face spaces built up from similarity ratings it is possible to designate the distance between any pair of faces in two ways. First, we could assume that a norm-based account is appropriate and thus we would measure the distance between two faces by determining the angle between the vectors which represent them. Alternatively, we could assume that an exemplar-based account is appropriate and view the face representations as simple points in space. In the latter case the distance between faces can be computed as their straightforward linear separation. To some extent, these two solutions will be correlated with one another: faces separated by a large angle may also be separated by a large distance. However, this will not exclusively be the case. It is entirely plausible that one of these solutions will generate a better fit than the other for our reaction time data.

We have available two measures from our response latency data to determine how appropriate it is, but only one of these will have any direct bearing on the norm-based versus exemplar-based discussion. Each model posits that distinctive faces are further away from the origin of the space and located in an area of reduced exemplar density than typical faces. Whatever constitutes 'distinctiveness', it should be easier to assert that two copies of a distinctive face are identical because a distinctive face will have fewer neighbours to make this decision more confusing. In line with this we have found significant negative correlations between the distance a face lies from the origin of the face space and the time needed to decide that a pair of identical faces are the same (i.e. the farther a face is from the origin the faster subjects are able to respond on identical trials). In both of our studies this effect has proven significant.

The second measure we have access to relates directly to the issue of norm-based versus exemplar-based models. By correlating our measure of response times for each pair of different faces with the separation of that pair, based either on the angle between two vectors or the distance between two locations in space, we should be able to determine which model provides the better fit for the data. In our first experiment, where we utilized single decisions to every pair, we found very small negative correlations between the separation of pairs of faces and the time required to make a 'different' judgement. Nevertheless, these are significant and there is a better correlation between response times and separation based on linear distance between faces (i.e. the measure appropriate to an exemplar-based space than between response times and angle of separation). The exemplar-based account is at an advantage over the norm-based model for all solutions from two to six dimensions.

When we repeated the study using a subset of the original faces and collected response latencies for multiple presentations of each pair, we found the same result. The further the faces are apart on the exemplar-based solutions, the faster subjects say that the faces are different. In the latter experiment the correlation coefficients are much larger for the exemplar-based space (r reaches values above –0.4 for 120 comparison pairs – a highly significant result p < 0.001). Although it must be recognized that these correlation coefficients only account for a relatively small portion of variance in the response times, they do provide a good basis for choosing one model over the other.

To return to our original objective, trying to determine how spaces were arranged in children, we reverted to asking younger subjects to make similarity judgements to pairs of faces. In our original adult study we asked subjects to rate pairs of faces along a seven-point scale where a rating of 1 meant that the pair was of two identical faces and a rating of 7 meant that they were very different. This task was considered too hard for young subjects. Also, constraints due to limited access to subjects and the attention span of young children dictated that it would not be possible to have subjects rate every pair of faces. In order to overcome these difficulties we decided to ask subjects to rate pairs of a smaller subset of faces. Four distinctive faces and four typical faces were selected; our choice was based on the distance of these faces from the origin of the face spaces we had already constructed. In this case subjects were asked to rate pairs of faces along a three-point scale. No identical pairs of faces were shown in a further attempt to minimize confusion for younger subjects. A rating of 1 indicated that two faces were very similar and a rating of 3 meant that two faces were very different. This arrangement allowed for twenty-eight comparisons to be made in total. This study was conducted across a range of ages from 5 to adult (5, 7, 9, 11, 13 and 20 years of age).

Mean ratings of the similarity of all twenty-eight comparisons were obtained for each age group. These ratings were then correlated with the separation of these faces in the original models according to either the norm-based or exemplar-based metric. Here we found significant positive correlations for adults' judgements of dissimilarity and distance apart in an exemplar-based space r (26) = 0.72, p < 0.001. Correlations were smaller and non-significant for the ratings with the norm-based model separations (r(26) = 0.36, n.s.). If faces were far apart in terms of an exemplar-based face space they were judged as being more dissimilar. This is particularly impressive in that the original formulation was made on a seven-point scale and still holds up when made on a three-point scale by new subjects. Data collected from research in progress suggest that is true of subjects across all our age groups.

In conclusion, this suggests that the most appropriate way to understand the developing face space is as an exemplar-based model. Earlier we arrived at the conclusion that either solutions N1 or E2 were the better way to understand how the face space in young children was organized; we are now able to conclude tentatively that E2 is the preferable one of this pair. The child face space should be considered to have the architecture illustrated in Figure 1.1c (i.e. an arrangement with fewer dimensions than the adult space) with an underlying exemplar-based implementation. Of course this leaves open questions of what the 'missing' dimensions will be, whether they are implemented gradually or whether there is a sudden shift from a child space to an adult space, and indeed how they added at all, but we believe that by a judicious combination of experimental techniques it is possible to begin to tackle what hitherto seemed impossibly difficult theoretical questions concerning the way children learn to process faces. Having started we shall continue to articulate our answer.

ACKNOWLEDGEMENTS

Much of the research described here was supported by a grant from the ESRC (no. R000 23 3864) to R.A. Johnston and H.D. Ellis. Some of this work arose directly from a previous ESRC programme award (XC 5250000) to H.D. Ellis (in collaboration with V. Bruce, I. Craw, A. Ellis, D. Perrett and A. Young).

REFERENCES

Bartlett, J. C., Hurry, S. and Thorley, W. (1984) Typicality and familiarity of faces. *Memory and Cognition*, 12, 219–228.

Bateson, P.R.G. (1977) Testing an observer's ability to identify individual animals. *Animal Behaviour*, 25, 247–248.

Bruyer, R., Laterre, C., Seron, X., Feyereisen, P., Strypstein, E., Pierrard, E. and Rectem, D. (1983) A case of prosopagnosia with some preserved covert remembrance of familiar faces. *Brain and Cognition*, 2, 257–284.

Bushnell, I.W.R., Sai, F. and Mullin, J.T. (1989) Neonatal recognition of the mother's face. *British Journal of Developmental Psychology*, 7, 3–15.

Carey, S. (1981) The development of face perception, in G. Davies, H. Ellis and J. Shepherd (eds), *Perceiving and Remembering Faces*. London: Academic Press.

Carey, S. (1992) Becoming a face expert. *Philosophical Transactions of the Royal Society of London, B*, 335, 95–103.

Carey, S., Diamond, R. and Woods, B. (1980) The development of face recognition: a maturational component? *Developmental Psychology*, 16, 257–269.

Cohen, M. E. and Carr, W. J. (1975) Facial recognition and the Von Restorff effect. *Bulletin of the Psychonomic Society*, 6, 383–384.

Diamond, R. and Carey, S. (1977) Developmental changes in the representation of faces. *Journal of Experimental Child Psychology*, 23, 107–117.

Diamond, R. and Carey, S. (1986) Why faces are and are not special: an effect of expertise. *Journal of Experimental Psychology: General*, 14, 107–117.

Ellis, H.D. (1981) Theoretical aspects of face recognition, in G. Davies, H. Ellis and J. Shepherd (eds), *Perceiving and Remembering Faces*. London: Academic Press.

Ellis, H.D. (1990) Developmental trends in face recognition. *The Psychologist*, 3, 114–119.

Ellis, H.D. (1991) *The Development of Face Processing Skills*. Final report to the ESRC on Grant XC15250003.

Ellis, H.D. (1992) The development of face processing skills. *Philosophical Transactions of the Royal Society of London, B*, 335, 105–111.

Ellis, H.D., Ellis, D. M. and Hosie, J. (In preparation) Children's processing of similar and dissimilar faces.

Ellis, H.D., Shepherd, J.W., Gibling, F. and Shepherd, J. (1988) Stimulus factors in face learning, in M.M. Gruneberg, P.E. Morris and R.N. Sykes (eds), *Practical Aspects of Memory: Current Research and Issues. Vol. 1: Memory in Everyday Life*. Chichester, UK: Wiley.

Ellis, H.D., Shepherd, J.W., Shepherd, J., Flin, R.H. and Davies, G.M. (1989) Identification from a computer-driven retrieval system compared with a traditional mug-shot album search: a new tool for police investigations. *Ergonomics*, 32, 167–177.

Feinman, S. and Entwistle, D.R. (1976) Children's ability to recognize other children's faces. *Child Development*, 47, 566–580.

Flin, R.H. (1980) Age effects in children's memory for unfamilar faces. *Developmental Psychology*, 16, 373–374.

Going, M. and Read, J. D. (1974) The effect of uniqueness, sex of subject and sex of photograph on facial recognition. *Perceptual and Motor Skills*, 39, 109–110.

Goldstein, A. G. and Chance, J. E. (1964) Recognition of children's faces. *Child Development*, 35, 129–136.

Goldstein, A. G. and Chance, J. E. (1980) Memory for faces and schema theory. *Journal of Psychology*, 105, 47–59.

Goren, C.C., Sarty, M. and Wu, P.Y.K. (1975) Visual following and pattern discrimination of face-like stimuli by newborn infants. *Pediatrics*, 56, 544–549.

James, W. (1890) *Principles of Psychology*. New York: Holt.

Johnston, M. H., Dziurawiec, S., Ellis, H.D. and Morton, J. (1992) Newborns preferential tracking of face-like stimuli and its subsequent decline. *Cognition*, 40, 1–21.

Johnston, R.A. and Ellis, H.D. (in press) Age effects in the processing of typical and distinctive faces. *Quarterly Journal of Experimental Psychology*.

Johnston, R.A., Milne, A.B., Williams, C.L. and Hosie, J. (submitted) Do distinctive faces come from outer space: An investigation of the status of a multi-dimensional face space.

Johnston, R.A., Milne, A.B., Williams, C.L. and Ellis, H.D. (In preparation) Determining between two models of face space.

Keil, F.C. (1987) Conceptual development and category structure, in U. Neisser (ed.), *Concept and Conceptual Development.* New York: Cambridge University Press.

Light, L.L., Kayra-Stuart, F. and Hollander, S. (1979) Recognition memory for typical and unusual faces. *Journal of Experimental Psychology: Human Learning and Memory,* 5, 212–228.

McNeil, J.E. and Warrington, E.K. (1993) Prosopagnosia: a face-specific disorder. *Quarterly Journal of Experimental Psychology,* 46A, 1–10.

Mann, V.A., Diamond, R. and Carey, S. (1979) Development of face voice recognition: parallels with face recognition. *Journal of Experimental Child Psychology,* 27, 153–165.

Maurer, D. and Young, R. (1983) Newborns' following of natural and distorted arrangements of facial features. *Infant Behavioural Development,* 6, 127–131.

Podgorny, P. and Garner, W.R. (1979) Reaction time as a measure of inter- and intraobject visual similarity: letters of the alphabet. *Perception and Psychophysics,* 26 (1), 37–52.

Rhodes, G. (1988) Looking at faces: first order and second order features as determinants of facial appearance. *Perception,* 17, 43–63.

Rhodes, G., Brennan, S. and Carey, S. (1987) Recognition and ratings of caricatures: implications for mental representations of faces. *Cognitive Psychology,* 19, 473–497.

Shepherd, J.W., Ellis, H.D. and Davies, G.M. (1977) *Perceiving and Remembering Faces.* Home Office Report, POL/73/1675/24/1.

Shepherd, J.W., Gibling, F. and Ellis, H.D. (1991) The effects of distinctiveness, presentation time and delay on face recognition. *European Journal of Cognitive Psychology,* 3, 173–146.

Takane, Y., Young, F. and de Leeuw, J. (1976) Non metric individual differences in multidimensional scaling: an alternating least squares method with optimal scaling features. *Psychometrika,* 42, 7–67.

Valentine, T. and Bruce, V. (1986a) The effects of distinctiveness in recognizing and classifying faces. *Perception,* 15, 525–535.

Valentine, T. and Bruce, V. (1986b) Recognizing familiar faces: the role of distinctiveness and familiarity. *Canadian Journal of Psychology,* 40, 300–305.

Valentine, T. (1991a) A unified account of the effects of distinctiveness, inversion and race on face recognition. *Quarterly Journal of Experimental Psychology,* 43A, 161–204.

Valentine, T. (1991b) Representation and process in face recognition. In Watt, R. (ed.) *Vision and Visual Dysfunction. Vol. 14: Pattern Recognition in Man and Machine* (series editor J. Cronley-Dillan). London: Macmillan.

Valentine, T. and Endo, M. (1992) Towards an exemplar model of face processing: the effects of race and distinctiveness. *Quarterly Journal of Experimental Psychology,* 44A, 671–703.

Vokey, J. R. and Read, J.D. (1992) Familiarity, memorability, and the effect of typicality on the recognition of faces. *Memory and Cognition,* 20, 291–302.

Winograd, E. (1981) Elaboration and distinctiveness in memory for faces. *Journal of Experimental Psychology: Human Learning and Memory,* 7, 181–190.

Young, A.W., Hay, D. and Ellis, A.W. (1985) The faces that launched a thousand slips: everyday difficulties and errors in recognizing people. *British Journal of Psychology,* 76, 495–523.

Chapter 2

Expertise and the caricature advantage

Sarah V. Stevenage

INTRODUCTION

Take any group of faces and you will see marked similarities among them. They all share the same basic size and shape. They all share the same basic configuration of two eyes above a central nose and above a central mouth. Indeed, faces form a highly homogeneous set and we have to rely on what are often subtle differences in features and feature layout in order to tell one face from another. The perception of this distinctive facial information is thus crucial to our ability to process faces. Consequently, highly distinctive faces, in which the individuating cues are obvious, are processed with much more efficiency than typical faces in which distinguishing cues are very subtle. Distinctive faces are more easily and more confidently recognized. They are more memorable and less often confused with other faces (Light *et al.*, 1979; Goldstein and Chance, 1981; Winograd, 1981; Bartlett *et al.*, 1984; Valentine and Bruce, 1986a; Shepherd *et al.*, 1991). They have also been shown to take longer to actually classify 'as a face', compared to typical faces (Valentine and Bruce, 1986b), and Valentine suggests that this may be because they are less similar to some sort of norm or central tendency (Valentine, 1991).

Recent work has replicated each of these effects using stimuli in which distinctiveness is enhanced within a set of faces rather than across faces. This can be achieved by using caricatures, which magnify the distinctive qualities of a face relative to a norm, and by comparing the processing of these caricatures to the processing of the veridical or undistorted faces. Using such a technique, caricatures have been successfully used to demonstrate distinctiveness effects: familiar faces are more quickly recognized from caricatures compared to veridical images (Rhodes *et al.*, 1987; Benson and Perrett, 1991), and they are more slowly classified as faces compared to veridical images (Stevenage, 1992). Furthermore, in a best likeness, or goodness of likeness paradigm, it is the caricature that is selected as most representative of a familiar face, even compared to the veridical image (Benson and Perrett, 1991).

One distinctiveness effect has, however, remained difficult to elicit with caricatured and veridical stimuli. This involves the demonstration of a distinctiveness advantage, and thus a caricature advantage, when processing unfamiliar faces. The purpose of the present chapter is to examine what has gone wrong with attempts to replicate this effect. It is argued that when viewed in the broader context of expertise effects a caricature advantage for unfamiliar faces is not only expected but predicted. A closer examination of the methodologies previously used highlights weaknesses in their design. With attention to such details a caricature advantage for unfamiliar faces is evident. Furthermore, viewing the caricature advantage as an indicator of expert facial processing (see Carey, 1992) allows us to challenge the notion of the child as a novice face processor. Indeed, evidence is presented which suggests that young children are a lot more expert with faces than we might first acknowledge.

THE NOTION OF EXPERTISE

Expertise in facial processing is an issue that has long been of interest to psychologists. The face itself is a highly complex stimulus but perhaps more impressive than the face as a stimulus is our ability to process that stimulus. Not only do faces show extremely fine differences between members of a highly homogeneous set but we, as expert face processors, have the ability to respond to those differences. We can reliably tell someone's race, general age and gender. We can also reliably say whether or not a face is familiar to us, and very often we are able to fit a unique name and identity-specific information to a familiar face. Furthermore, we are sensitive to the momentary changes that signal alteration of emotion and yet we are able to recognize a person despite these changes. Indeed, considering the number of faces we know and the subtlety of differences between those faces, we make very few errors of recognition. Moreover, Bahrick *et al.* (1975) report that our ability to recognize familiar faces remains at 90 per cent or more, even when some of those faces have not been seen for fifty years!

There is no doubt that we can be regarded as expert face processors. The question then arises; what do we mean by the term 'expert'? Moreover, how does an expert differ from a novice and how does one attain expertise? These are all questions that have received much attention in the past decade and research has recently tried to uncover the qualities that set the expert apart from the novice. This has been done by trying to identify the behaviours that reliably distinguish the two. Two such criteria of expertise have been identified. The first and most widely documented of these is an effect known as the differential inversion effect.

The differential inversion effect

The differential inversion effect was first demonstrated by Yin (1969; 1970) and describes the state in which inversion of a stimulus is more detrimental to its subsequent recognition if that stimulus is a face rather than an aeroplane, a house or a running stick-man. These results have been replicated by Scapinello and Yarmey (1970) and Yarmey (1971), using unfamiliar faces, and subsequent replications have refined Yin's initial methodology by using comparison materials that were equivalent to faces on the dimensions of familiarity, complexity and psychosocial importance (Ellis, 1975; Goldstein and Chance, 1981). Across these studies the results appear quite clear: the subsequent recognition of all mono-oriented stimuli is hampered when they are presented upside-down, but facial stimuli appear to be more affected than non-facial stimuli.

These results were taken as strong support for the suggestion that faces were in some way unique, and have a specialized manner of processing and/or a specific neural site for this processing. However, more recent work carried out by Diamond and Carey (1986) suggests that the differential inversion effect is not something that is specific to faces. Rather, it is an effect that is specific to experts for any class of stimuli in which exemplars differ only in configuration. Diamond and Carey used sporting dog profiles as their stimuli. These were chosen because they form a relatively homogeneous class which can only be distinguished by the configurational, or second order relational features. That is, the exemplars within the class of sporting dogs possessed the same components as each other and differed only in the layout of these components. In this respect the task of differentiating between individual dogs was comparable to the task of differentiating between individual human faces. What emerged was that sporting dog experts were equally hampered by inversion when encoding dog profiles (22 per cent) as when encoding human faces (20 per cent). However, the dog novices were only affected by inversion when encoding the human faces (23 per cent) and showed only a 2 per cent detriment when encoding inverted dogs.

Clearly, the differential effect of inversion is not face-specific but is peculiar to experts. Furthermore, it can be demonstrated for familiar and unfamiliar faces and for non-facial stimuli. Inversion must therefore be upsetting some manner of processing shown only by experts. What could this be?

Initial explanations for the differential inversion effect which implicated the degree of stimulus familiarity (Ellis, 1975) or the overtaxing of a corrective orientation mechanism (Rock, 1973; Phillips, 1979) have given way to the suggestion that the inversion effect occurs because inversion disrupts the configurational processing of a stimulus (for a review see Valentine, 1988). Evidence consistent with this explanation is diverse. For

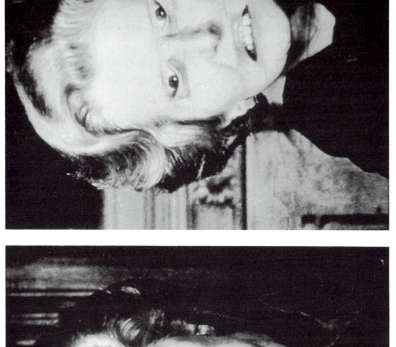

Figure 2.1 The Margaret Thatcher Illusion (reproduced with permission from Thompson, 1980). When the faces are viewed upside-down (as above) there is no perceived anomaly. However, when the page is turned and the faces are viewed the right way up, the grotesqueness of the composite face is clear

instance, Yin noted how expression – which is intrinsically configurational in nature – became very hard to extract from the inverted face. Furthermore, three experimental demonstrations exist which suggest that inversion interferes with configurational encoding. First, there is the case of the Thatcher Illusion. In an upright representation of Margaret Thatcher's face, Thompson (1980) inverted the mouth and the eyes. The resulting face looked 'grotesque' when upright, but this grotesqueness was not perceived when the whole display was inverted (see Figure 2.1). It was suggested that the grotesqueness of the upright display arose due to the perception of the incorrect featural relationships. However, when inverted, this configurational information became difficult to extract and so the grotesqueness of the display went unnoticed.

A second demonstration of the effect of inversion on configurational processing was reported by Sergent (1984). Sergent presented subjects with pairs of schematic faces that were mismatched either in internal spacing of features (configurational mismatch) or in the eyes or face contour (featural mismatch). It was found that the reaction time to perform a same–different decision was affected by inversion only when the mismatch was configurational – configurational discrepancies were noticed significantly more slowly when the faces were inverted whereas featural discrepancies were noticed equally well in both orientations.

A final demonstration of the effect of inversion on configurational processing was provided by Young *et al.* (1987). These workers constructed composite faces made by aligning the top half of one face with the bottom half of another face (see Figure 2.2). It was found that when aligned in such a way a new face resembling each of the originals seemed to emerge and it became incredibly difficult to identify the persons from either half. Conversely, if the top half of one face and the bottom half of another face were placed one above the other but were offset so as to create a 'non-composite', then the two halves did not appear to fuse to create a new face, and the constituent halves remained identifiable. The interesting point for the present discussion is the effect that inversion had on this composite fusion. The upright composite contained enough correct configurational information for a single and novel face to be perceived, thus making the constituent halves very hard to identify. However, the inverted composite did not spontaneously fuse to create a new face. Indeed, when inverted, the constituent halves of the composite (aligned) display were as easy to identify as the constituent halves of the non-composite (non-aligned) display. Inversion appears to impede the fusion of the face halves that configurational processing affords in the upright composite.

The discussion so far has centred on the differential inversion effect as an indicator of expertise. Evidence has been presented which suggests that this effect arises as a result of disruption to configurational processing. With this effect being limited to experts it is likely that it is only the

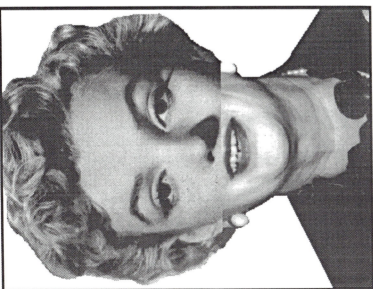

Figure 2.2 A composite and non-composite of Margaret Thatcher and Marilyn Monroe (adapted with permission from Young *et al.*, 1987). When upright, a new face seems to emerge from the composite such that the original identities become very hard to extract. However, the Gestalt formed in the upright composite appears to be removed when the image is inverted and in this situation the original identities can be extracted as easily from the composite as from the non-composite (many thanks to Tim Valentine for producing the figures)

experts who have the ability to process stimuli configurationally. This is thus one way in which the expert and the novice may differ.

The caricature advantage

The caricature advantage has recently been acknowledged as a second indicator of expertise (Carey, 1992). This describes the situation in which a stimulus is recognized more quickly from a caricatured image than from a veridical image (see Rhodes *et al.*, 1987; Benson and Perrett, 1991). It seems quite counter-intuitive to be able to recognize a distorted image better than a faithful one but Carey *et al.* (1992) recently demonstrated that the effect is shown only when the distortion is meaningful. For example, a face can be thought of as being encoded in terms of a vector within a multidimensional face space. The dimensions that define this space are those that serve to discriminate one face from another. Lateral caricaturing in which distortion is perpendicular to the norm-face vector does not produce a superior image, but caricatures in which the distortion is away from the norm and in the same direction as the norm-face vector does produce a superior image (see Figure 2.3).

This type of distortion is meaningful because it effectively identifies the distinctive information in a face, relative to a norm, and enhances that information. In this way, the caricature can be thought of as a distinctive exemplar compared to the veridical image which can be thought of as a typical exemplar. Consequently, the caricature effects reported in the literature can be usefully viewed as demonstrations of natural distinctiveness effects but with distinctiveness varied within a face set rather than across it. The superiority of naturally distinctive exemplars and distinctiveness-enhanced, or caricatured, exemplars suggests that distinctive information is important to the efficient processing of a face. Indeed, with the caricature advantage being viewed as a second indicator of expertise, the ability to make use of distinctive facial information presents itself as a second quality that differentiates the expert from the novice.

The caricature advantage is a robust finding and has been demonstrated most notably with adults and with familiar facial stimuli. Furthermore, caricature effects have been demonstrated when using artists' caricatures as well as computer-generated caricatures in line-drawn and photographic detail. Caricature studies show a remarkable consistency in the pattern of results produced. The processing of familiar faces from caricatures is clearly superior, compared to the processing of undistorted images, when the speed of recognition is measured (Rhodes *et al.*, 1987; Benson and Perrett, 1991; 1994a; 1994b). Moreover, the caricature is commonly preferred in a 'goodness of likeness' paradigm in which the subject has to indicate which, from an array of caricatured, veridical and anti-caricatured images, is most like the target (Rhodes *et al.*, 1987; Benson

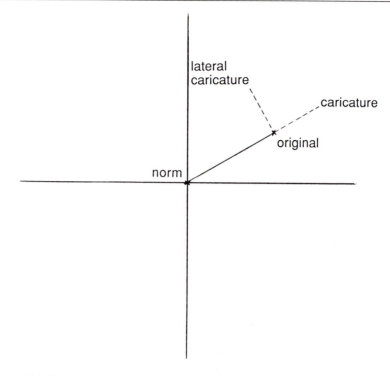

Figure 2.3 Representation of a standard caricature and a lateral caricature in vector terms

Source: Carey *et. al.,* 1992

and Perrett, 1991; 1994a; 1994b). Interestingly, as Benson and Perrett (1991) discuss, the pattern of results is typically clearer when using artists' caricatures rather than when using computer-generated caricatures. Consequently, it may be worth considering that something is lost when creating caricatures by computer. Perhaps the artists' caricature effects are not merely the result of the enhancement of the distinctiveness of an image relative to a norm. Perhaps there is some other factor at work in the creation of the artists' caricatures which the computer-generated caricatures fail to mimic. In this case, the lower significance of the caricature effects when using computer-generated images may be attributable to the fact that only one factor – distinctiveness-enhancement relative to a norm – is being varied. Further work could profitably be directed to this point in order to clarify the difference in the magnitude of the caricature effects when using artists' and computer-generated materials.

Research using caricatured and veridical images has not been confined to the examination of performance with facial stimuli. Indeed, it is interesting to note that, again, this criterion of expertise is not face-specific.

Rhodes and McLean (1990) succeeded in demonstrating a caricature advantage for a particularly homogeneous subset of birds (songbirds). More important to the present discussion, however, was the fact that this advantage was shown only by bird experts – bird novices gained no advantage from a caricatured bird image as opposed to a veridical bird image.

Here it is important to pause for a minute and review the evidence that has been presented. It has been suggested that there are two indicators of the expert processing of a stimulus – a differential inversion effect and a caricature advantage. Taking the differential inversion effect first, it is evident that this effect can be demonstrated by experts with a class of non-facial stimuli and by adults with faces of both familiar and unfamiliar people. This would imply that normal adult subjects can be considered to be expert face processors regardless of the familiarity of the face. The second indicator of expertise – the caricature advantage – has so far been reliably demonstrated for experts with non-facial stimuli (as above) and for normal adults with familiar faces. Clearly, if we are to be considered as experts with faces regardless of their familiarity, then the caricature advantage should also be elicited by unfamiliar faces. Evidence relating to this point is contradictory and so far, a reliable demonstration of a caricature advantage for unfamiliar faces has not been forthcoming. However, it is considered here that the previous attempts to demonstrate a caricature advantage for unfamiliar faces have been hampered by the use of inappropriate methodologies. In the section that follows, these methodologies are carefully reviewed with a view to highlighting their inherent weaknesses.

THE CARICATURE ADVANTAGE FOR UNFAMILIAR FACES

Several workers have tried to demonstrate a caricature advantage for unfamiliar faces. For instance, Hagen and Perkins (1983) tested the accuracy of recognition of artists' caricatures compared to undistorted images of unfamiliar faces. Their subjects were presented with a target set of faces, either as caricatured or veridical images, and they subsequently had to pick out the targets from a set of target and distracter faces. Hagen and Perkins found no caricature advantage in the accuracy of performance on this task; however, their comparison of photographic undistorted stimuli and line-drawn caricatured stimuli may have confounded their results. The use of computer-generated caricatured and veridical images has addressed the problem of ensuring an equivalent comparison. Rhodes *et al.*, (1987) presented a study assessing the effectiveness of computer-generated, line-drawn caricatures of unfamiliar faces. Their subjects were required to indicate the 'goodness of likeness' of an array of caricatured, veridical and anti-caricatured images. Unfortunately, using computer-generated stimuli and a 'goodness of likeness' paradigm, Rhodes *et al.* also failed to demonstrate a caricature advantage for unfamiliar faces.

So far, it is clear that caricatures of unfamiliar faces are not recognized with any more accuracy than photographs of the faces. Moreover, caricatures are not considered to be very representative of the unfamiliar face when compared to the undistorted image. However, Rhodes and Moody (1990) suggested that in the same way as a super-releaser can elicit a higher level of performance despite an unrealistic appearance, the caricatured image of an unfamiliar face may be recognized more quickly than the undistorted image, even though it is considered to have a lower degree of resemblance to the original. Rhodes and Moody tested this hypothesis with the materials used by Rhodes *et al.* Subjects were presented with a series of target faces, either as caricatures or as veridical images, and at a subsequent test stage the subjects were required to perform an old/new recognition task with a set of target and distracter faces. Additional to accuracy, recognition speed was recorded since it was considered to be a more sensitive measure of caricature advantage. The results that Rhodes and Moody obtained were quite mixed. On the one hand they found no caricature advantage for unfamiliar caricatures in terms of speed of recognition. However, they did find a caricature advantage for unfamiliar caricatures in terms of speed of rejection. That is, caricatured distracters were rejected more quickly than veridical distracters. A similar pattern of results has recently been demonstrated by May *et al.* (in press) using photographic quality caricatures. They too found that unfamiliar faces were not better recognized from caricatures in an old/new recognition paradigm; however, caricatured distracters were more quickly, and more accurately, rejected.

From the evidence presented so far, there seems to be no clear caricature advantage for unfamiliar faces. However, all of these studies have utilized a recognition-type task. It is argued that this sort of task may be intrinsically unfair when dealing with unfamiliar faces. After all, it is unlikely that a face that has been seen only once can be recognized in the same way as a familiar face. Consequently, the use of an old/new recognition paradigm for unfamiliar faces may bias the results against a successful performance with unfamiliar faces regardless of their degree of caricature.

If this reasoning is correct, then a change of paradigm away from one that requires the recognition of a face may elicit the expected pattern of results. The evidence to this end is certainly encouraging. For instance, Mauro and Kubovy (1992) presented subjects with very brief exposures of unfamiliar Identikit faces and their caricatures. The subjects' task was to decide, following the brief exposure of one face followed by another, whether the two faces were the same or different. Their results indicated that subjects were slower to respond 'different' when the face preceded its caricature than when the face effectively preceded its anti-caricature. Consequently, it was suggested that the unfamiliar target face was more similar to its caricature than to its anti-caricature. This result would support the suggestion that the processing of unfamiliar faces, as well as familiar faces, is sensitive to the distinctiveness (or the degree of caricature) of the face.

One further study provides the clearest evidence so far for the existence of a caricature advantage for unfamiliar faces. Stevenage (1992) has recently used a learned identification task to examine the caricature effects for unfamiliar faces. Rather than involving the recognition of a stimulus as 'old' or 'new' in a recognition paradigm, the learned identification task involves learning the names associated with a set of unfamiliar faces. This sort of paradigm is ideal for unfamiliar face studies because an explicit recognition of the face is not required. Indeed, this task requires no prior knowledge of the target face at all.

The procedure was such that one set of subjects learnt the names associated with a set of artist-caricatured faces while a second set of subjects learnt the same names for the same faces represented by veridical images (see Figure 2.4).

Each face was individually presented and the appropriate name was supplied verbally. Following this, the faces were re-presented, in a random order, to the subjects whereupon they had to volunteer a name for each face. Any errors were corrected and the procedure was repeated until the subjects could correctly name all faces on two successive presentations. The number of presentations taken to reach this criterion level of learning was recorded and it was found that subjects reached this criterion in fewer presentations when the faces were represented by caricatures as opposed to veridical images. That is, the names for a set of unfamiliar faces were learnt more quickly when those faces were presented in a caricatured fashion. Furthermore, a restricted amount of training with caricatured stimuli, compared to training with veridical stimuli, led to better transfer of learning – the subjects were better able to correctly name photographs of the faces if they had been trained with the caricatured stimuli initially. These results provide a clear illustration of the fact that the processing of unfamiliar faces is sensitive to the distinctiveness of the face, and hence the caricatured-ness of the face. Just as caricatures produced a superior performance in tasks that required the processing of familiar faces, so too it can be shown that caricatures produce a superior performance when processing unfamiliar faces. Consequently, as with the differential inversion effects described earlier, caricature effects can also be demonstrated across familiarity.

Finally, it is important to acknowledge the work of Benson and Perrett (1991; 1994b) with photographic quality caricatured and veridical images. Although this work did not use unfamiliar facial stimuli, the results from

Figure 2.4 Examples of unfamiliar caricatured and veridical facial stimuli, taken from Stevenage (1992)

these studies do have indirect bearing on the issue of a caricature advantage for unfamiliar faces. Their results are, however, somewhat contradictory. On the one hand they found that the best-likeness of a stimulus face was caricatured and that the degree of caricature advantage obtained was positively correlated with the degree of familiarity of the face (Benson and Perrett, 1991). This would indicate that the more familiar the face, the more caricatured the best-likeness. On the other hand, a subsequent study revealed quite different results. In this study the internal features of familiar faces were presented in caricatured or veridical form, and the subject was asked to perform a speeded recognition task (Benson and Perrett, 1994b). The usual caricature advantage in terms of speed of recognition was evident; however, this time a negative correlation was found between familiarity and speed-up. Contrary to their previous finding, this would indicate that the greater the familiarity with a target, the smaller the caricature advantage. This latter result would certainly lend support to the suggestion of a caricature advantage for unfamiliar stimuli. The apparent contradiction of Benson and Perrett's results may be resolved when it is remembered that neither study actually included unfamiliar stimuli. The positive correlation between familiarity and degree of caricature in the best-likeness paradigm merely showed that the more familiar the face the more caricatured the best-likeness. This does not mean that, given an unfamiliar face, the best-likeness would not also be caricatured. It may be less caricatured than the best-likeness of a familiar face, but it may still be caricatured, and that is the important point.

In summary, the present review of the literature would suggest that a caricature advantage for unfamiliar faces does exist. Previous attempts to demonstrate this were hampered by the use of an inappropriate methodology. Careful assessment of the methodologies used suggests that a caricature advantage can only be demonstrated reliably when the task does not demand the explicit recognition of the unfamiliar face (see Table 2.1 for a summary).

With this point resolved it is clear that two indicators of expertise exist – the differential inversion effect and the caricature advantage. Moreover, both the effects can be elicited by experts when presented with exemplars of a non-facial stimulus class and by adults when presented with familiar and unfamiliar faces. This last point would imply that by the criteria used to define Diamond and Carey's dog experts (differential inversion effect, 1986) and Rhodes and McLean's bird experts (caricature advantage, 1990), we, as adults, should be considered experts with faces regardless of their familiarity.

WHAT OF CHILDREN AS FACE PROCESSORS?

With the consideration that adults are expert at the processing of facial stimuli regardless of familiarity, it is pertinent to ask what can be expected of children as face processors? Do they perform at the level of a novice, as we might expect, or are they capable of more expert processing? According to the expertise criteria discussed so far, if children perform at the level of a novice when processing faces then they should neither show a differential inversion effect nor a caricature advantage for facial stimuli. The next section examines the evidence regarding this point.

The available evidence certainly seems to challenge the notion of the young child as a face novice. Indeed, infants of only 15 months preferentially fixate on facial stimuli as opposed to scrambled features (Haaf and Bell, 1967) and this preference can even be demonstrated at just 9 minutes old if the stimuli are moving (Goren *et al.*, 1975). Carey (1992) notes that after only a few days the infant has formed representations sufficient for distinguishing the mother's face from a stranger's (Bushnell *et al.*, 1989; Walton and Bower, 1991). Furthermore, by 7 months, the infant can encode new faces with minimal exposure such that s/he can discriminate these from distracters in an old/new recognition task (Fagan, 1979).

Using the two indicators of expertise discussed above, the available evidence is also encouraging. Controlled experiments show that children as young as 6 years (Carey, 1981; Young and Bion, 1981; Flin, 1983) and even infants (Watson, 1966; Fagan, 1979) show a detrimental effect of inversion on face processing. The effect increases with age such that adults show a more marked disruption due to inversion (Carey, 1981; Flin, 1983),

Table 2.1 Methodologies used to assess the caricature advantage for unfamiliar faces

	Stimuli	Task	Result
Against			
Hagen and Perkins (1983)	Unfamiliar artists' stimuli	Old/new accuracy	No c-adv
Rhodes *et al.* (1987)	Unfamiliar computer-generated stimuli	Best-likeness	No c-adv
Mixed			
Rhodes and Moody (1990)	Unfamiliar computer-generated stimuli	Old/new speed	Hits: no c-adv Rejects: c-adv
May *et al.* (in press)	Unfamiliar photographic quality caricatures	Old/new speed	Hits: no c-adv Rejects: c-adv
For			
Mauro and Kubovy (1992)	Unfamiliar Identikit stimuli	Same/different speed	c-adv
Stevenage (1992)	Unfamiliar artists' stimuli	Learned identification	c-adv

but the important thing to note is that very young children are affected. This merely demonstrates that very young children possess enough sensitivity to the configuration of a face such that inversion has a negative effect. In order to demonstrate a differential inversion effect it is necessary to show that the child is more disrupted when recognizing inverted faces than when recognizing other inverted stimuli. Evidence in support of this point has not so far been forthcoming. For instance, Carey and Diamond (1977) report that 6 and 8 year olds (relative to 10 year olds) do not show a differential effect of inversion when recognizing faces as opposed to when recognizing houses. Unfortunately, Carey and Diamond used faces that were unfamiliar to the children. As will be seen later, the use of unfamiliar facial stimuli when testing children can result in the child being unable to perform at the level of expertise that they are capable of. Consequently, their results should be accepted with caution until the comparable study has been carried out using familiar faces. Carey *et al.* (1980) later repeated this experiment, again using unfamiliar facial stimuli and houses. However, they do not report the effect of inversion on the recognition of houses.

In addition to the child's sensitivity to inversion, children also reflect an adult (expert) pattern of performance with upright and inverted composites (Carey and Diamond, 1992). Six year olds, 10 year olds and adults all performed in the manner described by Young *et al.* (1987): the faces making up the upright composite were named much more slowly and with less accuracy when the top and bottom halves were aligned than when not aligned. However, when inverted, there were no differences across the aligned and non-aligned images.

The young child appears to have enough expertise with faces *per se* to suggest an 'expert' pattern of performance when faces are inverted. The remaining effect that must be attended to in order to confirm their level of face expertise is the young child's performance with caricatured faces. Very little work has been attempted with children and the caricature advantage; however, Ellis (1992) recently reported data to suggest that in a perceptual paradigm children chose a caricatured image as the best-likeness of each of two familiar figures. This suggests that, as adults (face experts) and Rhodes and McLean's bird experts, the children were sensitive enough to the distinctiveness of the faces to respond preferentially to the distinctiveness-enhanced (caricatured) images.

Evidence to the contrary does, however, exist. Johnston and Ellis (1993) describe two sets of experiments which assess the child's recognition of typical and distinctive faces. When the task demanded a recognition of a target as old or new, children of 5–13 years did not show the effect of distinctiveness shown by adult subjects. However, when the task was changed to a face classification task (i.e. distinguishing intact faces from jumbled faces) the results suggested that children did show an effect of distinctiveness from 7 years old. Consequently, the use of an old/new recognition task did not elicit the true extent of the child's capabilities, but the use of a face classification task suggests that children, as adults, are expert enough with faces to respond to facial distinctiveness.

One further study provides support for this conclusion. Stevenage (1992) has previously used a learned identification paradigm to address the question of a caricature advantage for unfamiliar faces. This paradigm was considered appropriate for unfamiliar faces because it did not demand previous exposure to the stimulus face and consequently did not bias the results against the demonstration of an effect for unfamiliar stimuli. The learned identification paradigm was considered appropriate for use with young children for exactly the same reasons. No experience or knowledge of the stimulus face was required, and consequently the demands of the task were not biased against the successful performance of the child relative to the adult. The learned identification paradigm involved the child learning fictitious names for a number of unfamiliar faces that were presented as veridical or artist-caricatured images. However, several modifications to the adult's learning procedure were employed in order to make the child's task as short, active and interesting as possible. The stimulus set was reduced from twelve faces to ten. Moreover, the child was required to pair faces with bodies according to the Christian names that were printed on each of the T-shirts that the bodies wore. This procedure meant that the child did not have to remember which name had been allocated to a face, for the allocations were visible as paired heads and bodies. With this procedure the question of whether a young child could show a caricature advantage for unfamiliar faces was examined.

Using this methodology, twenty children of 6 years, 7 years and 8 years were tested, with equal numbers of girls and boys in each age group. One limitation of this method is that the children have to have a sufficient degree of reading ability in order to be able to perform effectively. With this in mind, two children had to be removed from the sample and replaced, because their standard of reading was too poor. The children effectively followed the same method as described for adults with unfamiliar faces (above). With all of the bodies laid out in front of the child, each face was handed to the child with the instruction, 'This is X, can you find their body and put them together?' Once all of the faces had been paired with all of the bodies, the child was encouraged to remember the name for each face. Then, all the heads were removed and shuffled and the positions of all the bodies were altered to ensure that the child was pairing each face with the correct name rather than with a discrete location. The child was then given each face one at a time and encouraged to find the right body. Any errors were corrected and the procedure was repeated until the child could correctly pair the right faces with the right named bodies without any help. It emerged that the children reached this criterion of learning more quickly when they were learning the names for caricatured images rather than the names for veridical images. Furthermore, the superior pattern of learning for caricatured faces was not affected by the age of the child (see Figure 2.5). Children at every age tested showed superior learning from the caricatured stimuli.

The results of this study clearly demonstrate the existence of a caricature advantage for children as young as 6 years when learning the names of unfamiliar faces. Taken together with the literature illustrating a sensitivity to the inversion of faces for young children, it can be concluded that by the standards used to define dog experts (inversion effect – Diamond and Carey, 1986) and bird experts (caricature advantage – Rhodes and McLean, 1990) children as well as adults may have to be considered face experts.

One point that arises from this study concerns the lower age limit to be defined as face experts. The existing design revealed that children as

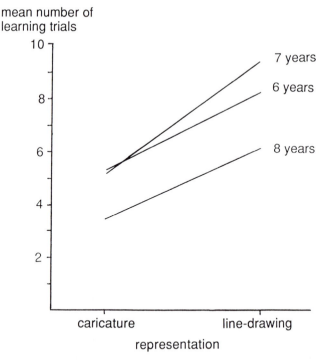

Figure 2.5 Graphical representation of the performance of 6–8 year olds when learning the names for unfamiliar faces

Source: Stevenage (1992)

young as 6 years could be regarded as face experts. Children younger than this could not be tested because of the need for a sufficient degree of reading ability when pairing the heads and the bodies. However, the task could easily be adapted so that faces could be paired with some non-linguistic identifier, perhaps coloured cards, so as to reduce the task demands. This would make it possible to test children younger than 6 years in order to discover the lower age boundary for the attainment of facial expertise.

IMPLICATIONS OF CHILDHOOD EXPERTISE

So far, we have identified two criteria of expertise – the differential inversion effect and the caricature advantage. It emerges that, according to these criteria, children as young as 6 years seem to perform in a manner equivalent to adults when presented with faces. That is, they should be considered as face experts.

This conclusion raises some serious questions. Previous research has consistently highlighted the inferior performance of children aged less than 10 years relative to adults (see Carey, 1992 for a review), so how can this fact be equated with their apparent expertise? More specifically, the two criteria of expertise suggest that the ability to utilize the configurational and the distinctive aspects of a face set the expert apart from the novice. However, the ability to process configurational information (at least) has previously been denied to young children. Consequently, how can the properties of expertise and of youth be reconciled? The following section takes a second look at the literature that assesses the performance of children relative to adults. When attention is focused on methodologies that make allowances for the child's lower mental speed and capacity in relation to the adults, then a more favourable view of the child as a face processor emerges. What follows is certainly not intended as an exhaustive review of the child's face processing capacities. Only the evidence that is pertinent to the issue of the child's expertise is included.

If young children are to be included as face experts then the ability to process distinctive and configurational information must be granted to them. Little is known regarding the child's sensitivity to distinctiveness, although Johnston and Ellis (1993) suggest that the conditions under which young children show a sensitivity to the distinctiveness of a face may be restricted. Evidence concerning the child as a configurational processor is also quite mixed. Early work showed that young children aged less than 10 years were significantly affected when recognizing faces if paraphernalia were added or removed (Carey and Diamond, 1977). This was taken in support of the suggestion that children younger than 10 years were primarily piecemeal processors, involving attention to discrete features rather than feature relationships. Such a manner of processing rendered the young child more vulnerable to paraphernalia-to-fool situations than the older child or adult who could also process configurational information. More recent work by Carey (1981) has, however, taken a less extreme stance. Children were not fooled by addition or removal of paraphernalia when the target faces were familiar. Moreover, children as young as 3 years were successful in such a paraphernalia-to-fool paradigm when the set size was reduced to one. These results can be taken as indirect evidence in support of the suggestion that young children can process configuration aspects of a face. This is not to say that such a manner of processing is preferred by the child; however, the important thing to note is that configurational processing is available to the child.

THE CARICATURE ADVANTAGE AS A RELIABLE INDICATOR OF EXPERTISE

An interesting suggestion to emerge from the present discussion is that as an indicator of expertise, the caricature advantage appears to be more robust than the differential inversion effect. The latter effect is quite difficult to elicit when using young subjects. The methodology must be carefully controlled so as to avoid floor and ceiling effects, and the use of a small target set maximizes the chance that the young child will be able to perform at a level indicative of their expertise. The caricature advantage however, does not suffer from the need for such highly controlled conditions. Indeed, the effect can be elicited across a perceptual and a learning paradigm and with both familiar and unfamiliar facial stimuli. The caricature advantage should thus be regarded as a more reliable and robust indicator of expertise than the differential inversion effect.

CONCLUSIONS

Throughout the course of this chapter, the caricature advantage has been re-examined in the context of the issue of expertise. It was considered that, on the basis of studies using both dog experts, bird experts and adults as face experts, two indicators of expertise existed. The first was a differential effect of inversion. This was thought to arise due to the disruptive influence of inversion on the extraction of configurational information from a stimulus. Given that only experts with a stimulus class were affected, it was suggested that only experts possessed this ability to use the configurational information. The second indicator of expertise was a caricature advantage. This effect was thought to arise due to the enhancement of the valuable distinctiveness of the stimuli by the caricaturing process. Again, the fact that only experts with a stimulus class showed this effect suggested that only experts had the ability to utilize this distinctive information. The identification of these two criteria of expertise thereby helps to define the differences between the processing of experts and novices.

Two lines of thought followed from viewing the caricature advantage as an indicator of expertise. First, the differential inversion effect could be elicited by adults using faces, regardless of their familiarity, and yet the caricature advantage had only been reliably demonstrated for familiar faces. This contradiction prompted a reassessment of the studies attempting to demonstrate a caricature advantage for unfamiliar faces. It was considered that an inappropriate methodology had prevented the reliable demonstration of the caricature advantage. With this point attended to, the caricature advantage emerged as expected.

Second, the identification of two indicators of expertise prompted an examination of the performance of novices as well as experts. It was expected that children would represent a group of novices with facial stimuli. However, contrary to expectation children as young as 6 years performed at an expert level according to these criteria. A reassessment of the capabilities of the child as a face processor suggested that while they may not be as expert as adults, they seem to possess sufficient ability to process faces in an expert manner.

FURTHER REMARKS

Consideration of the chapter so far would suggest that the dimension of expertise may no longer be very useful at differentiating the performance of groups of subjects; even the youngest testable subjects appear to perform at an expert level. Consequently, it is suggested that, rather than relying on expertise to distinguish performance across subjects, it may be more valuable to use expertise to distinguish performance between faces. This can be done by directing one's enquiry to groups of faces with which the subjects may have different amounts of expertise.

One clear example of this is with own-race and other-race faces. It is generally accepted that we have greater expertise with own-race faces than with other-race faces. Indeed, faces of one's own race are identified much more efficiently and accurately than faces of another race (Elliott *et al.*, 1973; Luce, 1974; see also Valentine, Chiroro and Dixon, Chapter 4, this volume). Interestingly, whereas we appear to be expert enough to meet the expertise criteria regardless of familiarity, the same may not be true across race. Evidence suggests that while the inversion effect and the caricature advantage can be demonstrated for own-race faces, other-race faces may not be as affected by inversion as own-race faces (Rhodes *et al.*, 1989). Unfortunately, contradictory evidence from uni-cultural designs exists (Valentine and Bruce, 1986a; Valentine, 1991) and the issue remains unclear. The complementary study exploring the existence of a caricature advantage for other-race faces is still to be tackled. However, again, the available evidence for a distinctiveness effect for other-race faces seems mixed. Distinctiveness effects do emerge for other-race faces (Valentine and Endo, 1992) but it may be that this is only demonstrated when the subject has had a relatively high degree of contact with other-race faces (Chiroro, personal communication). This implies that although we may be considered as experts of own-race faces *per se*, even from a very early age, our expertise of other-race faces requires a considerably greater degree of exposure to those faces. The illustration of an inversion effect and a caricature advantage with other-race faces by a high-contact group of subjects but not by a low-contact group of subjects would support this conclusion. In such a case, the skills identified as differentiating experts and novices may be important in explaining the other-race effect.

ACKNOWLEDGEMENTS

My thanks go to Dr Amina Memon and Dr Tim Valentine for endless helpful comments and to Patrick Chiroro for his suggestions regarding caricature effects for other-race faces. I would also like to thank Mr Roger Crow for drawing the caricatures used in the learned identification tasks, and St Sidwell's Primary School, Exeter, and Banister First School, Southampton, for their assistance with the child studies.

REFERENCES

Bahrick, H.P., Bahrick, O.O. and Wittlenger, R.P. (1975) Fifty years of memory for names and faces: a cross-sectional approach. *Journal of Experimental Psychology: General,* 104, 54–75.
Bartlett, J.C., Hurry, S. and Thorley, W. (1984) Typicality and familiarity of faces. *Memory and Cognition,* 4, 373–379.
Benson, P.J. and Perrett, D.I. (1991) Perception and recognition of photographic quality caricatures: implications for the recognition of natural images. *European Journal of Cognitive Psychology,* 3, 105–135.
Benson, P.J. and Perrett, D.I. (1994a) Visual processing of facial distinctiveness. *Perception,* 23, 75–93.
Benson, P.J. and Perrett, D.I. (1994b) Recognition of famous face photographic quality caricatures from their internal facial features. Unpublished manuscript.
Bushnell, I.W.R., Sai, F. and Mullin, J.T. (1989) Neonatal recognition of the mother's face. *British Journal of Developmental Psychology,* 7, 3–15.
Carey, S. (1981) The development of face recognition, in G.M. Davies, H.D. Ellis and J.W. Shepherd (eds), *Perceiving and Remembering Faces.* London: Academic Press.
Carey, S. (1992) Becoming a face expert. *Philosophical Transactions of the Royal Society, London,* 335, 95–103.

Carey, S. and Diamond, R. (1977) From piecemeal to configurational representation of faces. *Science*, 195, 312–314.

Carey, S. and Diamond, R. (1992) Do young children rely less on configural information when processing faces than do adults? (in press.)

Carey, S., Diamond, R. and Woods, B. (1980) Development of face recognition – a maturational component? *Developmental Psychology*, 16, 257–269.

Carey, S., Rhodes, G., Diamond, R. and Hamilton, J. (1992) Comparing the recognizability of caricatures, anticaricatures and lateral caricatures. (In press.)

Chiroro, P. (1994) Personal communication.

Diamond, R. and Carey, S. (1986) Why faces are, and are not special: an effect of expertise. *Journal of Experimental Psychology – General*, 115, 107–117.

Elliott, E.S., Wills, E.J. and Goldstein, A.G. (1973) The effects of discrimination training on the recognition of white and Oriental faces. *Bulletin of the Psychonomic Society*, 2, 71–73.

Ellis, H.D. (1975) Recognizing faces. *British Journal of Psychology*, 66, 409–426.

Ellis, H.D. (1992) The development of face processing skills. *Philosophical Transactions of the Royal Society of London, B*, 335, 113–119.

Fagan, J.F. (1979) The origins of facial pattern recognition, in M.H. Bornstein and W. Kessen (eds), *Psychological Development from Infancy: Image to Intention*. Hillsdale, NJ: Erlbaum.

Flin, R.H. (1983) *The development of face recognition*. PhD. thesis, Aberdeen University.

Goldstein, A.G. and Chance, J.E. (1981) Laboratory studies of face recognition, in G.M. Davies, H.D. Ellis and J.W. Shepherd (eds), *Perceiving and Remembering Faces*. London: Academic Press.

Goren, C.C., Sarty, M. and Wu, P.Y.K. (1975) Visual following and pattern discrimination of face-like stimuli by new born infants. *Pediatrics*, 56, 544–549.

Haaf, R.A. and Bell, R.Q. (1967) A facial dimension in visual discrimination by human infants. *Child Development*, 38, 893–899.

Hagen, M. A. and Perkins, D. (1983) A refutation of the hypothesis of the superfidelity of caricatures relative to photographs. *Perception*, 12, 55–61.

Johnston, R.A. and Ellis, H.D. (1993) Exemplar-based vs. norm-based models of development of face recognition. Paper presented at the International Conference on Face Processing, Cardiff, 21–23 September.

Light, L.L., Kayra-Stuart, F. and Hollander, S. (1979) Recognition memory for typical and unusual faces. *Journal of Experimental Psychology: Human Learning and Memory*, 5, 212–228.

Luce, T.S. (1974) The role of experience in inter-racial recognition. *Personality and Social Psychology Bulletin*, 1, 39–41.

Mauro, R. and Kubovy, M. (1992) Caricature and face recognition. *Memory and Cognition*, 20, 433–440.

May, K.A., Perrett, D.I., McLeod, C. and Estachy, C. (submitted) The effects of caricaturing on recognition of unfamiliar faces.

Phillips, R.J. (1979) Some exploratory experiments on memory for photographs of faces. *Acta Psychologica*, 43, 39–56.

Rhodes, G. and McLean, I.G. (1990) Distinctiveness and expertise effects with homogeneous stimuli: towards a model of configural coding. *Perception*, 19, 773–794.

Rhodes, G. and Moody, J. (1990) Memory representation of unfamiliar faces: coding of distinctive information. *New Zealand Journal of Psychology*, 19, 70–78.

Rhodes, G. Brennan, S. and Carey, S. (1987) Identification and ratings of caricatures: implications for mental representations of faces. *Cognitive Psychology*, 19, 473–497.

Rhodes, G., Brake, S., Taylor, K. and Tan, S. (1989) Expertise and configural coding in face recognition. *British Journal of Psychology*, 80, 313–331.

Rock, I. (1973) *Orientation and Form*. New York: Academic Press.

Scapinello, K. and Yarmey, D. (1970) The role of familiarity and orientation in immediate and delayed recognition of pictorial stimuli. *Psychonomic Science*, 21, 29–33.

Sergent, J. (1984) An investigation into component and configurational processes underlying face recognition. *British Journal of Psychology*, 75, 221–242.

Shepherd, J.W., Gibling, F. and Ellis, H.D. (1991) The effects of distinctiveness, presentation time and delay on face recognition. *European Journal of Cognitive Psychology: Special Issue, Face Recognition*, 3, 137–145.

Stevenage, S.V. (1992) *The Perception of Caricature*. Unpublished Ph.D. Thesis, University of Exeter, Devon.

Thompson, P. (1980) Margaret Thatcher – a new illusion. *Perception*, 9, 483–484.

Valentine, T. (1988) Upside down faces: a review of the effect of inversion upon face recognition. *British Journal of Psychology*, 79, 471–491.

Valentine, T. (1991) A unified account of the effects of distinctiveness, inversion, and race in face recognition. *Quarterly Journal of Experimental Psychology*, 43A, 161–204.

Valentine, T. and Bruce, V. (1986a) The effect of race, inversion and encoding activity on face recognition. *Acta Psychologica*, 61, 259–273.

Valentine, T. and Bruce, V. (1986b) The effects of distinctiveness in recognizing and classifying faces. *Perception*, 15, 525–535.

Valentine, T. and Endo, M. (1992) Towards an exemplar model of face processing: the effects of race and distinctiveness. *Quarterly Journal of Experimental Psychology*, 44A, 671–703.

Walton, G.E. and Bower, T.G.R. (1991) Newborn preference of familiar faces. Paper presented at SRCD, Seattle.

Watson, J.S. (1966) Perception of object orientation in infants. *Merrill-Palmer Quarterly*, 12, 73–94.

Winograd, E. (1981) Elaboration and distinctiveness in memory for faces. *Journal of Experimental Psychology: Human Learning and Memory*, 7, 181–190.

Yarmey, A.D. (1971) Recognition memory for familiar 'public' faces: effects of orientation and delay. *Psychonomic Science*, 26, 286–288.

Yin, R.K. (1969) Looking at upside down faces. *Journal of Experimental Psychology*, 81, 141–145.

Yin, R.K. (1970) Face recognition: a dissociable ability? *Neuropsychologia*, 23, 395–402.

Young, A.W. and Bion, P.J. (1981) Accuracy of naming laterally presented known faces by children and adults. *Cortex*, 17, 97–106.

Young, A.W., Hellawell, D. and Hay, D.C. (1987) Configurational information in face perception. *Perception*, 16, 747–759.

Chapter 3

Face recognition and configural coding

Gillian Rhodes

Borrowing from Gertrude Stein, Martha Farah (1992) recently asked, 'Is an object an object an object?' This is an important question for those of us interested in face recognition, because it forces us to consider just what we are studying. Are we studying an important, but idiosyncratic, recognition system? Or are we studying the operation of some more general purpose system?

The idea that faces might be special has considerable initial plausibility. After all, evolution has given neonates a special interest in faces (for a review see Johnston and Morton, 1991), and there are neural areas dedicated to face recognition. When these areas are damaged the result is prosopagnosia, a remarkably specific inability to recognize faces (for reviews see de Renzi, 1986; Damasio *et al.*, 1990; Farah, 1990). Moreover, face recognition is surely valuable enough to drive selection pressure for a special recognition system were one needed, given that it allows us to avoid immediate danger (is the person an enemy?) as well as to exploit the benefits of complex social organization. Finally, a special system may well be needed because of the unusual homogeneity of faces. All faces share a configuration, having the same basic parts in the same basic arrangement, and this homogeneity poses a difficult computational problem for the visual system.

All of this notwithstanding, the current consensus is that face recognition is not computationally special (e.g. Diamond and Carey, 1986; Davidoff, 1986; Ellis and Young, 1989; Levine, 1989; Morton and Johnson, 1989; Farah, 1992; Rhodes, 1995a). No evidence has been found for a processing system that deals exclusively with faces. I will present the details later, but the bottom line seems to be that the computations used to recognize faces are also used to recognize at least some other classes of stimuli that present a similar computational problem.

So face recognition is not special. However, the computations used to recognize faces are not part of a general purpose recognition system either, at least not the kind used to recognize objects at the basic level (recognizing a dog versus a table versus an umbrella – Rosch *et al.*, 1976). Basic level recognition relies on a perceptual decomposition of the object into its parts and their spatial arrangement (e.g. Marr, 1982; Hoffman and Richards, 1984; Biederman, 1987; Corballis, 1991). The resulting part-based representation is ideal for basic level recognition because at that level objects differ primarily in the parts that they have (Tversky and Hemenway, 1984). But a part-based analysis will not work for recognizing homogeneous objects such as faces that have the same basic component parts in the same basic arrangement. It can tell us that we are looking at a face, but not whose face it is.

Nor are the computations that are used to recognize faces used across the board for within-category discriminations, as some researchers have proposed (e.g. Damasio *et al.*, 1982). The idea that they might be came from the observation that prosopagnosics often have difficulty recognizing members of other classes, such as animals, buildings, cars, chairs, foods, flowers, houses, monuments and/or personal effects (Pallis, 1955; Bornstein, 1963; Cole and Perez-Cruet, 1964; de Renzi and Spinnler, 1966; Lhermitte *et al.*, 1972; Newcombe, 1979; Damasio *et al.*, 1982; Marciani *et al.*, 1991). However, these associated problems are much less consistent than would be expected if prosopagnosics had a general problem making within-category discriminations (Ellis, 1989). Furthermore, there is at least one prosopagnosic who has no such difficulties (de Renzi, 1986). He could identify his own wallet, razor, glasses, necktie and handwriting when each was shown together with six to ten similar items. He could also sort foreign from local coins and could identify a Siamese cat from various breeds of cat.

A critic might worry that these discriminations are easier than face recognition, but other results resist this criticism. In one case a prosopagnosic could distinguish new pairs of glasses from previously seen pairs just as well as normal subjects, even though normal subjects found this task *more* difficult than an analogous face recognition test (Farah, 1994). Yet another prosopagnosic became proficient at recognizing sheep faces, which normal subjects found extremely difficult (McNeil and Warrington, 1993). Therefore, faces do not seem to be recognized by a general system for within-category discriminations that is knocked out in prosopagnosia.

Rather, as I will argue below, faces appear to be recognized using computations that are specialized for representing the variations of a shared configuration that individuate the members of a homogeneous class. My aim in this chapter is to consider the nature of the computations used by this 'configural system' and its domain of operation. I will focus here, as I have done in my research, on investigations of how inversion and caricaturing affect recognition.

INVERSION EFFECTS AND RELATIONAL FEATURES

About twenty-five years ago, Yin (1969; 1970) discovered that inversion disrupts the recognition of faces much more than discriminations within other categories of mono-oriented objects. Recent reviews place the drop in accuracy at around 20–30 per cent for faces compared with 0–10 per cent for other stimuli (Diamond and Carey, 1986; Valentine, 1988; Rhodes *et al.*, 1993; Carey and Diamond, 1994). Yin believed that faces are unusually vulnerable to inversion because their special quality of expressiveness is lost in inverted faces. However, more recent results show that the disproportionate inversion effect is neither unique to faces nor due to the loss of expression.

Diamond and Carey (1986) found equally large inversion decrements for recognizing faces and side views of dogs (for some subjects see below). Therefore the large inversion decrement is not unique to faces and it is not due to loss of expression (for further discussion see Valentine, 1988). Moreover, there was no disproportionate inversion decrement for complex stimuli like landscapes that do not share a configuration, suggesting that the large inversion decrement is a feature of homogeneous objects.

Diamond and Carey (1986) proposed that inversion selectively disrupts the processing of relational features in stimuli that share a configuration, and hence that such features are crucial for recognizing homogeneous objects. They refer to these perturbations within a shared configuration as *second order relational features*, to distinguish them from the relatively unconstrained *first order relational features* in stimuli like landscapes that don't share a configuration. Because most of the present discussion concerns homogeneous objects, which do not vary on first-order relational features, I will use the simpler term, relational features, to refer to second-order *relational features*. Examples of relational features in a face would be the spacing of internal features and ratios of distances between parts of the face. Diamond and Carey (1986) suggest that the coding of isolated features, such as the visibility of teeth or the presence/absence of facial hair, glasses, wrinkles, etc., is much less disrupted by inversion than the coding of relational features,[1] so that recognition based largely on isolated features will be much less vulnerable to inversion than recognition based on relational features.

We recently tested Diamond and Carey's proposal by examining whether relational features are indeed more difficult to encode in inverted faces than are isolated features (Rhodes *et al.*, 1993). First we showed our subjects a set of study faces. Then each study face was paired with a distracter face that differed from it on a single feature and subjects had to select the study face. Figure 3.1 shows the kind of features that were changed. For some faces an isolated feature was changed (F1 – glasses or a moustache were added or removed; F2 – the eyes or mouth were

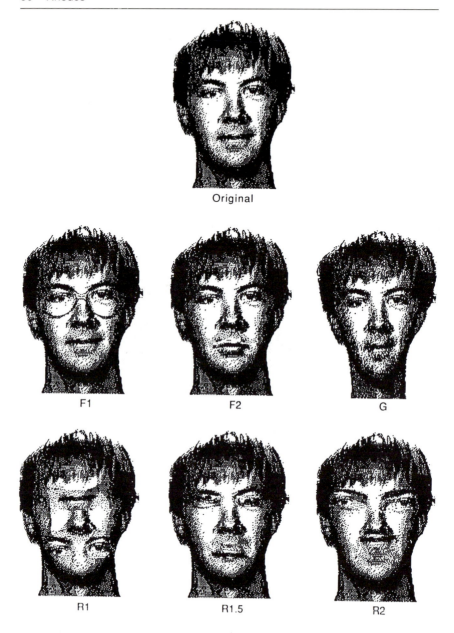

Original

F1   F2   G

R1   R1.5   R2

Figure 3.1 An original face plus examples of the six different types of change. F1 (glasses added) and F2 (mouth changed) are isolated feature changes, G is a global change (trapezoid stretch), R1 is a first-order relational change to the face configuration, and R1.5 (eyes and mouth inverted in face) and R2 (internal feature spacing changed) are (second-order) relational changes

Source: By permission of Rhodes *et al.* (1993)

switched with those from another face) and for others a relational feature was changed (R1.5 – the eyes and mouth were inverted relative to the rest of the face; R2 – the spacing of internal features was changed). We also examined the effect of inversion on two other types of change, a global change (G) and a first-order relational change (R1), but these are not relevant to testing Diamond and Carey's proposal (first-order relational changes are not expected to show large inversion decrements).

The salience of each type of change was adjusted so as to be equally noticeable when the faces were upright. But what about when the pairs were viewed upside-down? Would the relational feature changes (R1.5 and R2) be more difficult to detect than the isolated feature changes (F1 and F2), as Diamond and Carey had predicted? Our results showed that

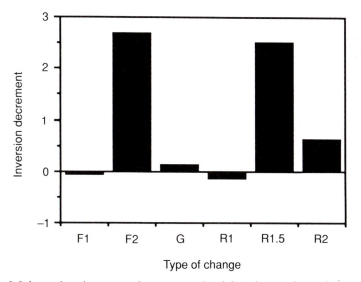

Figure 3.2 Inversion decrement in accuracy (upright – inverted; maximum difference obtainable = 10) as a function of type of change. Figure 3.1 gives an example of each type of change

Source: By permission of Rhodes *et al.* (1993)

they were more difficult to detect than one of the isolated feature changes (see Figure 3.2). But inversion had its biggest effect when we swapped the eyes or mouth with those from another face, a swap that we had classified as an isolated feature change!

However, Diamond and Carey might argue that changing the eyes or mouth also changes all the relational features into which these component features enter and that it may not even be possible to process the components as isolated features (see Tanaka and Farah, 1993 for a similar view). Thus it is really the resulting relational changes that are responsible for the large inversion effect.[2] To test this idea we presented the

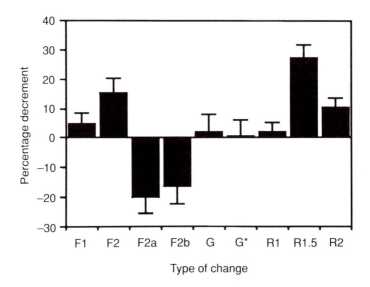

Figure 3.3 Percentage inversion decrement in accuracy, [(U-I)/U] x 100 per cent, as a function of type of change in follow-up experiment. F2a and F2b were eyes or mouths presented alone (out of the face context). G* was an additional global change. All other changes were the same as in figures 3.1 and 3.2

Source: By permission of Rhodes *et al.* (1993)

component features, eyes or mouth, alone (i.e. not in a face). If the large inversion decrement for changing these components is really due to relational feature changes, then it should be greatly reduced when they are presented alone. As Figure 3.3 shows, this is precisely what happened. (The isolated eyes and mouths were actually recognized better inverted than upright, but inverted study sets were smaller than upright study sets, to avoid floor and ceiling effects, so only the relative sizes of the inversion decrements are meaningful.) As before, relational changes (R1.5, R2 and now F2!) were generally larger than isolated feature changes (F1).

Further support for Diamond and Carey's claim that the disproportionate inversion effect reflects reliance on relational features comes from work by James Bartlett and Jean Searcy (Bartlett and Searcy, 1993; Bartlett, 1994). They found that faces made to look grotesque by changing the spatial relations between parts no longer looked grotesque when inverted, whereas faces whose grotesqueness was due to isolated feature changes (e.g. fangs added, teeth painted out, eyes reddened) continued to look grotesque when inverted. These results confirm that inversion disrupts the coding of relational features more than isolated features (see Rhodes *et al.*, 1993 for a review of other less direct evidence).

Interestingly, these subtle relational features cannot be used whenever they are present. Expertise with the class seems to be needed, presumably so that subjects can learn which variations distinguish the individuals in that particular homogeneous class. The large inversion decrement for dog recognition found by Diamond and Carey (1986) was confined to dog experts (US kennel club judges) and the inversion decrement for face recognition seems to grow with expertise. As expertise with unfamiliar faces increases throughout childhood, so too does the inversion decrement (for reviews see Carey, 1992; Carey and Diamond, 1994). Even inverted faces can yield their relational features after massive amounts of practise (Takane and Sergent, 1983). In contrast, without expertise, even simple dot patterns that vary about a shared prototype do not seem to allow relational feature coding (Tanaka and Farah, 1991).

The idea that expertise is needed to code relational features suggests an intriguing explanation for the difficulty people experience with other-race faces (for a recent review of race effects in face recognition see Bothwell *et al.*, 1989). Perhaps lack of expertise with these faces means that relational features cannot be used effectively and that people must rely largely on isolated feature cues. This speculation leads to the counterintuitive prediction that inversion should be *less* disruptive to recognizing other-race faces than own-race faces. My students and I tested this hypothesis, using Caucasian subjects from New Zealand and Chinese subjects from Singapore, and found that inversion did indeed have a larger effect on recognition of own- than other-race faces (Rhodes *et al.*, 1989) (see Figure 3.4). However, this result has not been consistently found. Valentine and Bruce (1986) carried out a study with white subjects viewing white and black faces and found a larger inversion decrement in A' (a measure of sensitivity) for the other-race faces. Another study, with both black and white subjects, found no difference in the effect of inversion on recognition (per cent correct in an old/new recognition task) of own- and other-race faces (Buckhout and Regan, 1988). Perhaps a direct comparison of people's sensitivity to changes in relational features in own- and other-race faces would resolve this issue.

The picture that emerges so far is of a configural system that codes the subtle relational features that distinguish homogeneous objects and that is fundamentally different from the part-based system used for basic level recognition. I will refer to this idea as the *relational features hypothesis*. Faces are a prime example of a homogeneous class for which this configural system is used, but the system can be used whenever people have expertise with a homogeneous class of objects. Its hallmark is an unusual vulnerability to inversion.

The relational features hypothesis predicts that prosopagnosics should have difficulty, not just with faces, but with any homogeneous objects with which they are expert. Of course for many people faces may be the only

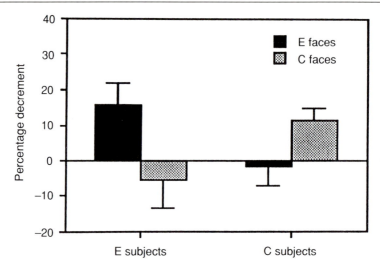

Figure 3.4 Percentage inversion decrement in accuracy as a function of race of face and race of subject (E = European, C = Chinese)
Source: By permission of Rhodes (1994)

homogeneous class for which they are really expert – hence the remarkable selectivity of the deficit for faces in many prosopagnosics. However, if a prosopagnosic has expertise with another homogeneous class, then performance on that class should also be impaired. There is some support for this prediction from cases where ornithologists and farmers have become prosopagnosic and have lost the ability to recognize species of birds (Bornstein, 1963) and their individual animals (Bornstein *et al.*, 1969; Assal *et al.*, 1984), respectively. Another prosopagnosic lost the ability to recognize racehorses (Newcombe, 1979) and others have trouble with classes such as animals and animal faces (relying on isolated feature cues, such as the beard for a goat and whiskers for a cat, e.g. Pallis, 1955), which are relatively homogeneous and with which people typically have some expertise (for a review see Farah, 1990).

However, not all the data fit so well. First, consider the prosopagnosic LH, described by Farah (1994), who was unimpaired at recognizing different pairs of glasses. If prosopagnosics suffer damage to a configural system that codes relational features, then surely LH should have been poor at this task. After all, glasses are a pretty homogeneous class for which relational features would be needed (assuming that obvious isolated feature cues such as colour, texture, flamboyant wings and so on were reasonably infrequent). LH's normal performance seems problematic, until one realizes that normal performance was itself very poor. Apparently no-one had much expertise with glasses and so there is no reason to think that relational features could be used effectively by anyone. This conjecture could be tested by looking at the size of the inversion decrement for recognizing glasses, which should be small.

Two other cases might be problematic, but the evidence is anecdotal and it is difficult to know how seriously they should be taken. One is a farmer who recovered from prosopagnosia but still could not recognize his cows (Assal *et al.*, 1984) and the other is a farmer who became prosopagnosic but could still recognize his cows and dogs (Bruyer *et al.*, 1983). Even if these deficits are as described, they may not be at odds with the relational feature hypothesis. For example, if cows were harder than faces for the first patient (who remained mildly prosopagnosic), then differential difficulty could explain his selective improvement. Also, the second farmer's animals varied in colour and markings which could have provided isolated feature cues for recognition.

McNeil and Warrington's (1993) case presents the clearest problem. Their prosopagnosic took up farming after his illness and became an expert at recognizing sheep. But how is this possible if he had lost the ability to use relational features? One possibility is that expertise can be acquired in other ways and that he learned to recognize sheep using other kinds of cues. For example, some, although apparently not all, of the sheep had markings that could serve as isolated feature cues. This admittedly *post hoc* and not overwhelmingly plausible possibility could be tested by examining the effect of inversion on his ability to recognize the sheep. A small inversion decrement would suggest the use of isolated features, whereas a large inversion decrement would suggest the use of relational features. The latter result would clearly embarrass the relational feature hypothesis.

More detailed examination of prosopagnosics could provide valuable tests of the relational features hypothesis. It predicts that prosopagnosics should be impaired on all homogeneous classes with which they are expert and that no remaining areas of competence should exploit relational features.

Farah offers another hypothesis about the nature of the configural system, namely that which is specialized for *holistic coding*. By holistic coding she means that parts are not explicitly represented at all or are extremely complex (e.g. Farah, 1991; Tanaka and Farah, 1993). At its sharpest, the distinction between holistic and relational feature coding concerns whether or not a face is parsed into separate elements. The most extreme version of holistic coding would be that there is no parsing and that faces are stored as unanalysed wholes or templates. In contrast, with relational feature coding a face would be parsed into features, although many would be complex, relational features. More recently, Farah has offered a formulation of holistic coding that is virtually indistinguishable from relational feature coding, namely that relations between parts are more important than the parts themselves (Farah *et al.*, 1994). What both notions capture is the intuition that we need a special system for coding the subtle variations in a shared configuration that individuate homogeneous objects.

In this section I have argued that one tool in the armoury of the configural system is its ability to code subtle relational features. In the next section I will consider a quite different tool, namely the ability of the configural system to code variations in a shared configuration as deviations from a *norm* or average for the class.[3]

CARICATURE EFFECTS AND NORM-BASED CODING

In contrast with the vulnerability of faces to inversion, caricaturing does not disrupt the recognition of faces (Rhodes *et al.*, 1987; Benson and Perrett, 1991; Mauro and Kubovy, 1992; Rhodes and Tremewan, 1994; Carey *et al.*, 1995) or other homogeneous objects (e.g. Rhodes and McLean, 1990; for a review see Rhodes, 1995b). On the contrary, caricatures, which exaggerate distinctive information, are at least as recognizable as undistorted images, and both are more recognizable than anti-caricatures, which reduce distinctive information. Sometimes caricatures even function as 'super-portraits', with the paradoxical quality of being more recognizable than undistorted images (Rhodes *et al.*, 1987; Rhodes and McLean, 1990; Rhodes and Tremewan, 1994). In fact the best way to signal category membership is often to display exaggerated, rather than typical or average characteristics of the category, a phenomenon referred to as 'peak shift' in the discrimination learning literature (for reviews see Purtle, 1973; Thomas *et al.*, 1991) and 'supernormality' in ethology (Tinbergen, 1951; Baerends, 1982) and behavioural ecology (e.g. Staddon, 1975; ten Cate and Bateson, 1988). Preferences for caricature-like extremes may even underlie the evolution of extreme sexual ornaments and displays used by some animals to attract mates (for recent reviews see Cronin, 1991; Rhodes, 1995b).

My colleagues and I have interpreted the effectiveness of caricatures as evidence that faces (and possibly other homogeneous objects) are coded as deviations from a spatial norm or average (Rhodes *et al.*, 1987; Rhodes and McLean, 1990; Rhodes and Tremewan, 1994; Carey *et al.*, 1995). To see why a norm-based coding hypothesis is appealing, consider how the caricatures are made. Using a computerized caricature generator created by Susan Brennan (1982; 1985), a photograph of the 'victim' is digitized and fixed landmark points (e.g. the tip of the nose or the peak of the eyebrow) are located. These are marked using a mouse and then the program 'joins the dots' to produce a simple line-drawing image of the face (see Figure 3.5). Next, the program compares the target face with a norm or average face. The norm can be generated by averaging a set of faces or simply by taking a highly typical face, and different norms can be used for structurally distinct classes of face such as males and females.

Once the corresponding points on the face and norm have been found, the program exaggerates all the differences between the pairs of points by an amount specified by the user, say 50 per cent. Anti-caricatures are created by moving the points on the victim's face closer to the corresponding points on the norm. These basic drawings can then be enhanced by filling in the hair, eyebrows and irises, and adding glasses, facial hair, jewellery or idiosyncratic facial lines. Figure 3.6 shows a set of enhanced caricatures and anti-caricatures for Rowan Atkinson.

Under the caricature transformation all the points that describe a face move systematically with respect to the norm, so that one can think of the norm as a frame of reference in which caricature transformations are systematic and simple. In any other co-ordinate system, such as the x-y co-ordinates of the picture plane or the x-y-z co-ordinates of 3-D space, all the points on the face move haphazardly. If, as seems reasonable, caricatures are effective because they exaggerate the very features we use to recognize faces (and anti-caricatures are ineffective because they reduce them), then those features appear to be norm-deviation features. By a norm-deviation feature I mean some explicit description of how a face deviates from the norm value for that feature. An example would be how much a feature differs from its norm value or mean $(X - M)$. This simple subtractive measure was the one used by peak shift theorists. A more sophisticated norm-deviation feature would be a z-score, which expresses the value of the feature in terms of how many standard deviations it is above or below its mean value $[(X - M)/S]$. This kind of representation makes the relative distinctiveness of facial features immediately apparent. It requires knowledge about how each feature varies in the population, but people almost certainly have such knowledge about facial features. If we think of faces as mentally represented in a face space, whose dimensions correspond to facial features (see Valentine, 1991 for a fuller discussion), then both sorts of norm-deviation feature could be represented as vectors from the origin (norm) to the value of the face on each dimension.

Despite the appeal of norm-based coding, the peak shift literature shows that it is not the only mechanism that can produce a caricature advantage (for reviews see Thomas *et al.*, 1991; Thomas, 1993; Rhodes, 1995b). Caricature effects can also emerge simply as distinctiveness effects in a system where stimuli are coded in terms of their values on a dimension or set of dimensions (so-called absolute coding). A caricature advantage (shift in peak responding) results because the more extreme stimulus is less confusable with the other stimuli from which it must be discriminated. In the discrimination learning studies, this idea is formalized in terms of excitation and inhibition gradients that surround a rewarded and unrewarded stimulus, respectively. A more extreme version of the rewarded stimulus has less excitation than the rewarded stimulus, but this

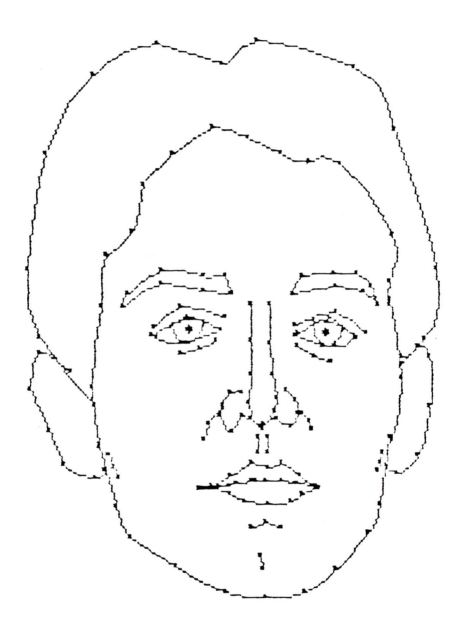

Figure 3.5 The points and lines used to depict a face. The face is represented by 169 points (darker dots) that are joined automatically to form thirty-seven line segments. Any of the lines can be made invisible

Source: By permission of Rhodes *et al.* (1987)

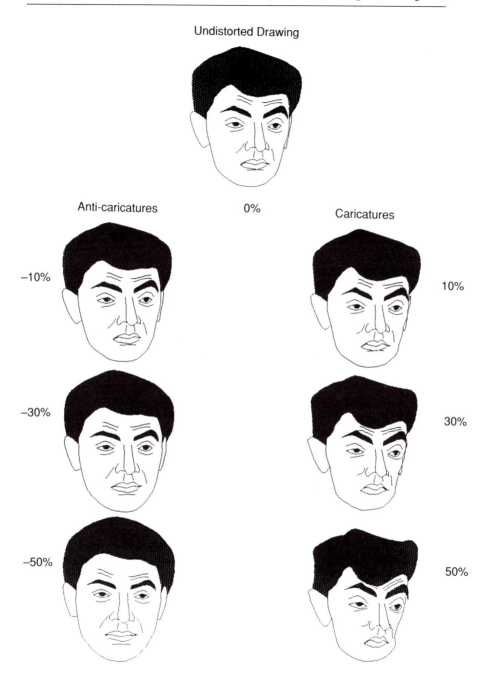

Figure 3.6 A set of enhanced caricatures and anti-caricatures of Rowan Atkinson
Source: By permission of Rhodes (1994)

reduction is offset by an even larger reduction in inhibition – hence the shift in peak response.

The peak shift literature deals primarily with discriminations between stimuli that differ on a single dimension (e.g. wavelength or intensity), but it is not hard to see how a similar account could apply to multidimensional stimuli like faces. Faces would be coded as values on some set of relevant dimensions and caricatures would be effective simply because of their greater distinctiveness. The more distinctive caricatures will activate fewer distractors than their undistorted counterparts (just as atypical or distinctive faces activate fewer distractors in memory than more typical faces, making it easier to pick out the target activation from a background of distracter activation and so recognize the face (e.g. Going and Read, 1974; Cohen and Carr, 1975; Light et al., 1979; Winograd, 1981; Bartlett et al., 1984; Valentine, 1991)). Of course, the caricatures will also activate the *targets* less strongly than the undistorted images, but this reduction in target 'excitation' could well be offset by the reduction in distracter 'inhibition'. Anti-caricatures would be especially ineffective because they both fail to match the target and are non-distinctive (thus activating many distractors). On this view faces would simply be stored as points in a multidimensional face space and norm-deviation feature vectors (or the resultant vector for the face) would have no special psychological significance (for further discussion see Valentine, 1991; Rhodes, 1995b).

However, some recent results suggest that distinctiveness effects alone cannot account for caricature effects found in face recognition (Carey et al., 1995; briefly described in Carey, 1992). If they could, then only an image's proximity to the target and its distinctiveness (i.e. density of distracters) should determine its recognizability. Whether or not it lies on the norm-deviation vector would be irrelevant. To test this prediction Carey et al. created a new type of distortion, a *lateral* caricature, in which the points on a face are moved orthogonally to the norm-deviation direction, rather than away from the norm as in a caricature, or towards the norm as in an anti-caricature (see Figure 3.7). Laterals, caricatures and anti-caricatures can be created that are all equidistant metrically from the undistorted face (see Figure 3.8), but that differ in their distinctiveness, with caricatures most distinctive, anti-caricatures least distinctive and laterals in between. Therefore, if caricature effects are solely distinctiveness effects, and don't depend on *how* an image deviates from the norm, then the laterals should be easier to recognize than the equally distorted but less distinctive anti-caricatures. Of course, the caricatures should be easiest of all because they are the most distinctive. As predicted, the laterals were almost impossible to recognize and were significantly worse than the anti-caricatures. Caricatures and undistorted images were recognized equally well and both better than anti-caricatures. These results suggest that caricature effects in face recognition

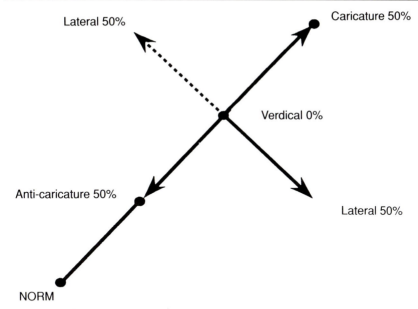

Lateral 50%

Caricature 50%

Verdical 0%

Anti-caricature 50%

Lateral 50%

NORM

Figure 3.7 Diagram of how a point on a face (veridical 0 per cent) moves in a caricature, anti-caricature and lateral caricature. The corresponding point on the norm (NORM) is found (e.g. the tip of the nose on the two faces would be corresponding points) and the point on the face is moved relative to that norm point. In a 50 per cent caricature the point on the face is moved 50 per cent further away from the corresponding point on the norm, in the direction of the vector joining the two points. In a 50 per cent anti-caricature the point is moved 50 per cent back along that vector towards the corresponding point on the norm. In the lateral caricature the point is moved orthogonally to the vector in one of the two possible directions shown. The choice of direction for the lateral move was constrained to reflect the bilateral symmetry of the face. All the points on the left side of the face moved the same way (either left or right, with respect to the norm-deviation direction) as did all points on the right side of the face. This resulted in four laterals for each face. The most face-like one was used in the recognition test

Source: By permission of Rhodes (1994)

cannot be explained *solely* as distinctiveness effects in an 'exemplar' model.[4] Rather, the way that a face deviates from a norm appears to provide crucial information for recognition.

There is actually surprisingly little evidence that distinctiveness plays much of a role in caricature effects at all. If caricatures are effective because of their greater distinctiveness, i.e. because they activate fewer distracters than the undistorted image, then one might expect caricaturing to be more helpful for less distinctive stimuli. After all, stimuli that are highly distinctive to begin with would have few neighbours with which to be confused in the first place. Therefore, caricaturing should be more helpful for recognition of typical than distinctive stimuli and more extreme

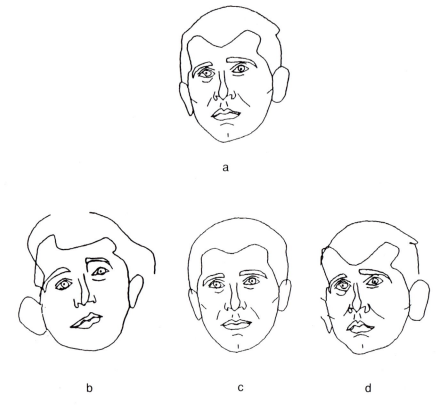

a

b   c   d

Figure 3.8 Images of Oliver North used by Carey *et al.* (1994): a) undistorted 0 per cent; b) 50 per cent lateral caricature; c) –50 per cent anti-caricature; d) 50 per cent caricature

Source: By permission of Rhodes (1994)

caricatures should be preferred for typical than distinctive stimuli. Both results have been found (Rhodes and McLean, 1990 for recognition; Benson and Perrett, 1994 for preferences). However, other studies have either found no relationship (e.g. Rhodes *et al.*, 1987 for recognition; Rhodes *et al.*, 1995 for preferences) or the opposite pattern (Rhodes *et al.*, 1995 for preferences).

None of these studies directly manipulated distinctiveness, so that failure to find the expected relationship could simply be a restricted range problem. However, we recently manipulated facial distinctiveness and still failed to find an influence of initial distinctiveness on the effectiveness of caricatures for recognition (Rhodes *et al.*, unpublished data). We divided a set of faces (spanning a wide range of distinctiveness) into low and high distinctive groups based on a median split. Subjects learned names for photographs of these faces and then identified enhanced line-drawing images at various levels of distortion (–45 per cent, –30 per cent, –15 per cent, 0 per cent, 15 per cent, 30 per cent, 45 per cent). Despite a recognition advantage for the more distinctive faces and for caricatures and undistorted images over anti-caricatures, distinctiveness did not interact with caricature level. Even when we increased the difference between low and high distinctiveness, by taking faces in the bottom and top quartiles or by using anti-caricatures and caricatures respectively as the training faces, distinctiveness still had no impact on the effectiveness of caricatures. These are surprising results if caricature effects are simply distinctiveness effects.

However, they are not definitive. The problem is that it is hard to be confident about how distinctiveness should influence the power of caricatures without knowing exactly how faces are distributed in face space. We can be pretty sure that density decreases with distance from the norm, but that's about all. Nor do we know how much a given per cent caricature distortion shifts a face, relative to distracters, at different distinctiveness levels. A typical face will not change as much as a more distinctive face when it is exaggerated by a given amount, say 50 per cent. Therefore, although there is plenty of scope to make a typical face more recognizable by caricaturing it, how can we be sure that the small change will be enough to move it into a region of lower density and make the caricature effective? Perhaps modelling studies, in which the distributions are known could help sort all this out.

There is, however, one intriguing result that side-steps all these uncertainties. In a pilot study, Hadyn Ellis found that caricatures were effective for young children (6–8 year olds) who showed no recognition advantage for distinctive over typical faces (Ellis, 1992). If this result holds up it would strongly suggest that caricature effects are not simply distinctiveness effects.

Setting aside the apparent autonomy of caricature effects from distinctiveness effects, the laterals result suggests that some kind of norm-based coding model must be considered as a serious alternative to an exemplar account of face recognition. Rather than being stored simply as points in a multidimensional face space, perhaps faces are stored as norm-deviation vectors in that space. This model would account for the importance of direction in the space, i.e. *how* a face deviates from the norm.

The question of how widely norm-based coding is used is an important topic for future investigation. The peak shift literature shows that it is not a special system for face recognition. Nor does it appear to be restricted to stimuli for which relational features can be coded, because inversion disrupts relational feature coding but leaves caricature effects intact (Rhodes and Tremewan, 1994). In three experiments, using both famous and personally known faces, and both plain and enhanced line-drawings, Tremewan and I found no influence of orientation on the effectiveness of caricatures. There was a large inversion decrement, consistent with the use of relational features irrespective of caricature level, but the effectiveness of caricatures was the same for inverted as for upright faces, with caricatures recognized as accurately as undistorted images and both better than anti-caricatures.[5] Susan Carey and I are currently investigating the possibility that norm-based coding may be a very general method of coding shape. Our strategy is to take the pattern C≥V>A>L (caricatures at least as good as veridicals, both better than anti-caricatures, and anti-caricatures better than laterals) as evidence of norm-based coding and to investigate the conditions under which it occurs.

CONCLUDING REMARKS

Along with many others (e.g. Diamond and Carey, 1986; Farah, 1992), I have argued that the computations used to recognize faces and other objects that share a configuration are different from the part-based analysis used to recognize objects at the basic level. Studies of caricature effects suggest that the 'configural system' uses a norm against which to measure the distinctive features of homogeneous objects and studies of inversion effects suggest that at least some of these features are relational features which we need expertise to use. We do not yet know how the configural and part-based systems work together (e.g. are they sequential or parallel?), but we do know that the division of labour does not depend simply on either the object (e.g. faces) or the task (e.g. within-category discriminations), but on the computational problem that their combination presents to the visual system.

ACKNOWLEDGEMENTS

My research has been supported by grants from the New Zealand Social Sciences Research Fund, the New Zealand Foundation for Research, Science and Technology and the New Zealand Lotteries Board. I thank Ian McLean and Tim Valentine for comments on an earlier draft of this chapter.

NOTES

1 Of course, all the features are still present in the inverted images in an objective sense, but something about the unfamiliar orientation seems to make relational features particularly difficult to encode. Perhaps the mismatch between the intrinsic and retinal/gravitational tops of inverted, but normally mono-oriented objects (Rock, 1974), is especially disruptive to coding subtle relational features, which already require reference to more than one part of the face. Diamond and Carey's (1986) results suggest that (first order) relational features in objects like landscapes that do not share a configuration are not especially

disrupted by inversion. These features are much less subtle than the relational features that distinguish homogeneous objects. Indeed, the former may simply encode an ordering of components (e.g. tree left of lake, lake left of mountain) just like the spatial arrangements of parts in a basic level object (e.g. handle on top of cylinder) and may be coded by the part-based system.

2 This example illustrates the inherent ambiguity of the isolated–relational feature distinction (e.g. Haig, 1984; Sergent, 1984; Bruce, 1988; Rhodes *et al.*, 1993). By altering a relatively isolated feature component (e.g. eyes and mouth) one also changes the spatial relations with the rest of the face. Similarly, by changing a clearly relational property, such as the internal spacing of component features, one also produces changes that may be coded as isolated features (e.g. the gap between the eyes, or the upper lip length). This does not invalidate the isolated–relational hypothesis, but it can make it difficult to test.

3 Carey and Diamond (1994) see norm-based coding as an intrinsic part of their (second-order) relational coding hypothesis. However, the two ideas are logically distinct - after all, it is possible to code relational features in homogeneous stimuli without any reference to a norm – and I will treat them as separate proposals. I will also present evidence that they are in fact distinct forms of coding.

4 Of course, exemplars are coded in the norm-deviation model too. However, the term 'exemplar model' is widely used to contrast with models in which a norm, average or prototype plays a role and I use it in that spirit.

5 Caricature level and orientation never interacted in these experiments, but one set of faces (out of several sets used) consistently produced a caricature advantage that was always restricted to upright faces. Expertise and relational feature coding may therefore be needed before caricatures can be super-portraits.

REFERENCES

Assal, G., Favre, C. and Anderes, J. P. (1984) Non-reconnaissance d'animaux familiers chez un paysan: Zooagnosie ou prosopagnosie pour les animaux. *Revue Neurologique*, 140, 580–584.

Baerends, G. P. (1982) Supernormality. *Behaviour*, 82, 358–363.

Bartlett, J. C. (1994) Inversion and configuration of faces. In J. Bartlett (Chair), *Face Recognition by Computers and People*. Symposium at the meeting of the American Academy for the Advancement of Science, San Francisco, February.

Bartlett, J. C. and Searcy, J. (1993) Inversion and configuration of faces. *Cognitive Psychology*, 25, 281–316.

Bartlett, J. C., Hurry, S. and Thorley, W. (1984) Typicality and familiarity of faces. *Memory and Cognition*, 12, 219–228.

Benson, P. J. and Perrett, D. I. (1991) Perception and recognition of photographic quality facial caricatures: implications for the recognition of natural images. *European Journal of Cognitive Psychology*, 3, 105–135.

Benson, P. J. and Perrett, D. I. (1994) Visual processing of facial distinctiveness. *Perception*, 23, 75–93.

Biederman, I. (1987) Recognition-by-components: a theory of human image understanding. *Psychological Review*, 94, 115–147.

Bornstein, B. (1963) Prosopagnosia, in L. Halpern (ed.), *Problems of Dynamic Neurology*. Jerusalem: Hassadah Medical Organisation.

Bornstein, B., Stroka, H. and Munitz, H. (1969) Prosopagnosia with animal face agnosia. *Cortex*, 5, 164–169.

Bothwell, R. K., Brigham, J. C. and Malpass, R. S. (1989) Cross-racial identification. *Personality and Social Psychology Bulletin*, 15, 19–25.

Brennan, S. E. (1982) *Caricature Generator*. Unpublished MA thesis. Cambridge, MA: MIT.

Brennan, S. E. (1985) The caricature generator. *Leonardo*, 18, 170–178.

Bruce, V. (1988) *Recognising Faces*. Hove and London: Erlbaum.

Bruyer, R., Laterre, C., Seron, X., Feyereisen, P., Strypstein, E., Pierrard, E. and Rectem, D. (1983) A case of prosopagnosia with some preserved covert remembrance of familiar faces. *Brain and Cognition*, 2, 257–284.

Buckhout, R. and Regan, S. (1988) Explorations in research on the other-race effect in face recognition, in M. M. Gruneberg, P. E. Morris and R. N. Sykes (eds), *Practical Aspects of Memory: Current Research and Issues, Vol 1, Memory in Everyday Life*. Chichester: John Wiley and Sons.

Carey, S. (1992) Becoming a face expert, in V. Bruce, A. Cowey, A. W. Ellis and D. I. Perrett (eds), *Processing the Facial Image*. Oxford: Clarendon Press.

Carey, S. and Diamond, R. (1994) Are faces perceived as configurations more by adults than by children? *Visual Cognition*, 253–274.

Carey, S., Rhodes, G., Diamond, R. and Hamilton, J. (1995) *Norm-based Coding of Faces: Evidence from Studies of Caricatures*. In preparation.

Cohen, M. E. and Carr, W. J. (1975) Facial recognition and the von Restorff effect. *Bulletin of the Psychonomic Society*, 6, 383–384.

Cole, M. and Perez-Cruet, J. (1964) Prosopagnosia. *Neuropsychologia*, 2, 237–246.

Corballis, M. C. (1991) *The Lopsided Ape: The Evolution of the Generative Mind*. New York: Oxford University Press.

Cronin, H. (1991) *The Ant and the Peacock: Altruism and Sexual Selection from Darwin to Today*. Cambridge University Press: Cambridge.

Damasio, A. R., Damasio, H. and Van Hoesen, G. W. (1982) Prosopagnosia: anatomical basis and behavioural mechanisms. *Neurology*, 32, 331–341.

Damasio, A. R., Tranel, D. and Damasio, H. (1990) Face agnosia and the neural substrates of memory. *Annual Review of Neuroscience*, 13, 89–109.

Davidoff, J. B. (1986) The specificity of face perception: evidence from psychological investigations, in R. Bruyer (ed.), *The Neuropsychology of Facial Perception and Facial Expression*. Hillsdale, NJ: Erlbaum.

de Renzi, E. (1986) Current issues in prosopagnosia, in H. D. Ellis, M. A. Jeeves, F. Newcombe and A. Young (eds), *Aspects of Face Processing*. Dordrecht, NL: Martinus Nijhoff.

de Renzi, E. and Spinnler, H. (1966) Visual recognition in patients with unilateral cerebral disease. *Journal of Nervous and Mental Disease*, 142, 513–525.

Diamond, R. and Carey, S. (1986) Why faces are and are not special: an effect of expertise. *Journal of Experimental Psychology: General*, 115, 107–117.

Ellis, H. (1989) Past and recent studies of prosopagnosia, in J. R. Crawford and D. M. Parker (eds), *Developments in Clinical and Experimental Neuropsychology*. New York: Plenum Press.

Ellis, H. (1992) The development of face processing skills, in V. Bruce, A. Cowey, A. W. Ellis and D. I. Perrett (eds), *Processing the Facial Image*. Oxford: Clarendon Press.

Ellis, H. D. and Young, A. W. (1989) Are faces special?, in A. W. Young and H. D. Ellis (eds.), *Handbook of Research on Face Processing*. Amsterdam, NL: North-Holland.

Farah, M. (1990) *Visual Agnosia: Disorders of Object Recognition and What They Tell us About Normal Vision*. Cambridge, MA: MIT Press.

Farah, M. J. (1991) Patterns of co-occurrence among the associative agnosias: implications for visual object representation. *Cognitive Neuropsychology*, 8, 1–19.

Farah, M. J. (1992) Is an object an object an object? Cognitive and neuro-psychological investigations of domain specificity in visual object recognition. *Current*

Directions in Psychological Science, 1, 164–169.

Farah, M. J. (1994) Specialization within visual object recognition: clues from prosopagnosia and alexia, in M. J. Farah and G. Ratcliff (eds), *The Neuropsychology of High Level Vision: Collected Tutorial Essays*. Hillsdale, NJ: Erlbaum.

Farah, M. J., Tanaka, J. W. and Drain, H. M. (1995) What causes the face inversion effect? *Journal of Experimental Psychology: Human Perception and Performance*. In press.

Going, M. and Read, J. D. (1974) Effects of uniqueness, sex of subject and sex of photograph on facial recognition. *Perceptual and Motor Skills*, 39, 109–110.

Grusser, O.-J. and Landis, T. (1991) *Visual Agnosias*. London: Macmillan Press.

Haig, N. D. (1984) The effect of feature displacement on face recognition. *Perception*, 13, 505–512.

Hoffman, D. D. and Richards, W. A. (1984) Parts of recognition, in S. Pinker (ed.), *Visual Cognition*. Cambridge, MA: MIT Press.

Johnston, M. H. and Morton, J. (1991) *Biology and Cognitive Development: The Case of Face Recognition*. Oxford, UK and Cambridge, USA: Blackwell.

Levine, S. C. (1989) The question of faces: special is in the brain of the beholder, in A. W. Young and H. D. Ellis (eds.), *Handbook of Research on Face Processing*. Amsterdam, NL: North-Holland.

Lhermitte, J., Chain, F., Escourolle, R., Ducarne, B. and Pillon, B. (1972) Etude anatomo-clinique d'un cas de prosopagnosie. *Revue Neurologique*, 126, 329–346.

Light, L. L., Kayra-Stuart, F. and Hollander, S. (1979) Recognition memory for typical and unusual faces. *Journal of Experimental Psychology: Human Learning and Memory*, 5, 212–228.

McCarthy, R. A. and Warrington, E. K. (1986) Visual associative agnosia: a clinico-anatomical study of a single case. *Journal of Neurology, Neurosurgery and Psychiatry*, 49, 1233–1240.

McNeil, J. E. and Warrington, E. K. (1993) Prosopagnosia: a face-specific disorder. *Quarterly Journal of Experimental Psychology*, 46A, 1–10.

Marciani, M. G., Carlesimo, G. A., Maschio, M. C. E., Sabbadini, M., Stefani, N. and Caltagirone, C. (1991) Comparison of neuropsychological, MRI and computerized EEG findings in a case of prosopagnosia. *International Journal of Neuroscience*, 60, 27–32.

Marr, D. (1982) *Vision*. San Francisco: Freeman.

Mauro, R. and Kubovy, M. (1992) Caricature and face recognition. *Memory and Cognition*, 20, 433–440.

Morton, J. and Johnson, M. (1989) Four ways for faces to be special, in A. W. Young and H. D. Ellis (eds.), *Handbook of Research on Face Processing*. Amsterdam, NL: North-Holland.

Newcombe, F. (1979) The processing of visual information in prosopagnosia and acquired dyslexia: functional versus physiological interpretation, in D. J. Oborne, M. M. Gruneberg and J. R. Eiser (eds.), *Research in Psychology and Medicine*, Vol. 1. London: Academic Press.

Pallis, C. A. (1955) Impaired identification of faces and places with agnosia for colors. *Journal of Neurology, Neurosurgery and Psychiatry*, 18, 218–224.

Purtle, R. B. (1973) Peak shift: a review. *Psychological Bulletin*, 80, 408–421.

Rhodes, G. (1994) Secrets of the face. *New Zealand Journal of Psychology*, 23, 3–17.

Rhodes, G. (1995a) The modularity of face recognition, in A. Kent, J. G. Williams and C. M. Hall (eds.), *Encyclopedia of Computer Science and Technology*. New York: Marcel Dekker Inc. In press.

Rhodes, G. (1995b) *Superportraits: Caricatures and Recognition*. Hove and

London: Erlbaum. Forthcoming.

Rhodes, G. and McLean, I. G. (1990) Distinctiveness and expertise effects with homogeneous stimuli: towards a model of configural coding. *Perception*, 19, 773–794.

Rhodes, G. and Tremewan, T. (1994) Understanding face recognition: Caricature effects, inversion and the homogeneity problem. *Visual Cognition*, 275–311.

Rhodes, G., Brake, S. and Atkinson, A. (1993) What's lost in inverted faces? *Cognition*, 47, 25–57.

Rhodes, G., Brennan, S. and Carey, S. (1987) Identification and ratings of caricatures: implications for mental representations of faces. *Cognitive Psychology*, 19, 473–497.

Rhodes, G., Carey, S., Diamond, R. and Tremewan, T. (1995) Are caricature effects simply distinctiveness effects? In preparation.

Rhodes, G., Tan, S., Brake, S. and Taylor, K. (1989) Expertise and configural coding in face recognition. *British Journal of Psychology*, 80, 313–331.

Rock, I. (1974) The perception of disoriented figures. *Scientific American*, 230, 78–85.

Rosch, E., Mervis, C. B., Gray, W. D., Johnson, D. M. and Boyes-Braem, P. (1976) Basic objects in natural categories. *Cognitive Psychology*, 8, 382–439.

Sergent, J. (1984) An investigation into component and configural processes underlying face perception. *British Journal of Psychology*, 75, 221–242.

Staddon, J. E. R. (1975) A note on the evolutionary significance of 'supernormal' stimuli. *American Naturalist,* 109, 541–545.

Takane, Y. and Sergent, J. (1983) Multidimensional models for reaction times and same-different judgments. *Psychometrika*, 48, 393–423.

Tanaka, J. W. and Farah, M. J. (1991) Second-order relational properties and the inversion effect: testing a theory of face perception. *Perception and Psychophysics*, 50, 367–372.

Tanaka, J. W. and Farah, M. J. (1993) Parts and wholes in face recognition. *Quarterly Journal of Experimental Psychology*, 46A, 225–245.

ten Cate, C. and Bateson, P. (1988) Sexual selection: the evolution of conspicuous characteristics in birds by means of imprinting. *Evolution*, 42, 1355–1358.

Thomas, D. R. (1993) A model for adaptation-level effects on stimulus generalization. *Psychological Review*, 100, 658–673.

Thomas, D. R., Mood, K., Morrison, S. and Wiertelak, E. (1991) Peak shift revisited: a test of alternative interpretations. *Journal of Experimental Psychology: Animal Behavior Processes*, 17, 130–140.

Tinbergen, N. (1951) *The Study of Instinct*. New York: Oxford University Press.

Tversky, B. T. and Hemenway, K. (1984) Objects, parts and categories. *Journal of Experimental Psychology*: General, 113, 169–193.

Valentine, T. (1988) Upside-down faces: a review of the effect of inversion upon face recognition. *British Journal of Psychology*, 79, 471–491.

Valentine, T. (1991) A unified account of the effects of distinctiveness, inversion and race in face recognition. *Quarterly Journal of Experimental Psychology*, 43A, 161–204.

Valentine, T. and Bruce, V. (1986) The effect of race, inversion and encoding activity upon face recognition. *Acta Psychologica*, 61, 259–273.

Winograd, E. (1981) Elaboration and distinctiveness in memory for faces. *Journal of Experimental Psychology: Human Learning and Memory*, 7, 181–190.

Yin, R. K. (1969) Looking at upside-down faces. *Journal of Experimental Psychology*, 81, 141–145.

Yin, R. K. (1970) Face recognition: a dissociable ability? *Neuropsychologia*, 8, 395–402.

Chapter 4

An account of the own-race bias and the contact hypothesis based on a 'face space' model of face recognition

Tim Valentine, Patrick Chiroro and Ruth Dixon

INTRODUCTION

It is necessary to start with a note on our use of the term 'race'. Throughout this chapter we use the term 'race' in a sociological sense to refer to the various racial groups with which people identify themselves (e.g. black, white). As distinctions among human 'races' cannot be made on the basis of defining genetic characteristics, the definition of 'race' is dependent upon social, cultural and political factors (Reber, 1985).

Our aim in this chapter is to apply a 'face space' model of the representation of faces to an analysis of the effect of race on face recognition. A number of experiments which have been guided by this theoretical framework will be reviewed. We argue that the ability to recognize faces requires a process of perceptual learning during which an observer learns which aspects of faces provide optimal information to distinguish individual faces within a population. This experience enables observers to encode the distinctive information in individual faces. Difficulties in recognition of faces of a race different from that of the observer arise when the observer has insufficient experience of the relevant population of faces. We propose that the effects of distinctiveness and race may be closely related: both arise from knowledge (or lack of knowledge) of the structure of the population of faces. Two experiments are discussed which provide evidence that appropriate experience of faces of another race will enhance the ability to recognize faces of that race. It should be stressed that in this chapter we will not be concerned with cross-racial eyewitness identification or any forensic applications of the effect of race on face recognition.

WHAT IS THE 'OWN-RACE BIAS'?

We use the term 'own-race bias' to refer to the finding that, in an experiment which requires subjects to recognize previously unfamiliar faces which have been presented in an earlier list (target faces) when mixed with faces not previously seen (distracter faces), subjects tend to be more accurate at recognizing faces of their own race than they are at recognizing faces of a different race. Typically such experiments should include two subject groups of different races, each of which are required to recognize faces of both the same two races. An own-race bias is said to occur if the results show an interaction between the effects of race of subject and race of face, such that subjects are relatively more accurate in their recognition of own-race faces than in their recognition of other-race faces. Ideally, the interaction should be a symmetrical crossover, but it can often be imposed on a main effect in which one race of face is more easily recognized (averaged across all subjects) than the other.

WHAT EVIDENCE IS THERE OF AN 'OWN-RACE BIAS'?

Bothwell *et al.* (1989) carried out a meta-analysis of fourteen samples of data (from eleven publications) in which an appropriate test of the own-race bias has been reported. The criterion for inclusion was that recognition accuracy of both black and white faces had been tested for groups of black and white subjects. Superior recognition accuracy of own-race faces compared with other-race faces was found in 79 per cent of the samples, measured by use of d' (a signal detection measure of sensitivity).[1] Across all samples the effect size was approximately 0.7, accounting for approximately 10 per cent of the variance of the data from both black and white subjects. Although the effect sizes were statistically equivalent for both black and white subjects, the 95 per cent confidence interval included zero for black subjects but not for white subjects.

The own-race bias was one of many effects examined by Shapiro and Penrod (1986) in a meta-analysis of a broad range of face recognition experiments. Performance of same-race versus cross-race recognition in seventeen experimental conditions was examined. The sample did not exclude studies in which subjects of only one race had been tested. An effect size of 0.53 was found for the effect of race on the proportion of correctly identified target faces (hits), accounting for 6.5 per cent of the variance (using the formula given by Cohen (1977, p. 23)). An effect size of 0.44 (accounting for 4.6 per cent of the variance) was obtained for false positives. The results are broadly similar to those reported by Bothwell *et al.* (1989). As cross-race recognition produced fewer hits *and* more false positives than same-race recognition, it is not surprising that a larger effect size is found on the d' measure of sensitivity than on hits and false positives alone, as both effects are combined into a single measure of sensitivity in d'. The meta-analysis conducted by Bothwell *et al.* should be considered a more reliable assessment of the own-race bias, as they took the precaution of only including studies which had tested own and other-race recognition in subjects of both races and restricted the comparison to black and white subjects.

Two studies conducted in our own laboratory have both shown a significant own-race bias: Valentine and Endo (1992) compared recognition of white British and Japanese faces by white British and Japanese students. Chiroro and Valentine (in press) compared recognition of black Zimbabwean faces and white British faces by white British, white Zimbabwean and black Zimbabwean high school students. In a recent paper Ng and Lindsay (1994) reported two experiments in which recognition of white and 'oriental' faces by white Canadian and 'oriental' subjects was investigated. A significant own-race bias was found for both races in both experiments, accounting for an average of approximately 11 per cent of the variance across both experiments.

The available data suggest that an own-race bias is reliably observed in the majority of studies. The estimates of the effect size obtained from the meta-analyses are in the range of a 'medium' effect size (Cohen, 1977). However, Lindsay and Wells (1983) argued that the available evidence of an own-race bias was inconsistent and suggested that the modest size of the effect made it of little practical importance. It should be noted that Lindsay and Wells were discussing the own-race bias in the context of eyewitness identification. The issue that they addressed was whether psychologists are justified in advising a jury that, if a witness's identification was of a suspect of a race different from their own, the jury can infer that it would be a less reliable identification than it would have been had the suspect and witness been of the same race. Obviously the relatively moderate effect size and individual differences in face identification performance are very pertinent to this issue. However, for purposes of the theoretical issues with which we are concerned here, the data clearly show that there is an own-race bias which any theoretical model of face processing must be able to explain. Indeed, Ng and Lindsay (1994) conclude from their own experiments 'that the cross-race effect was strongly supported'.

We have defined the own-race bias as an effect observed in recognition memory experiments. There is some evidence that the own-race bias may be restricted to tasks which require a memory component. Shepherd and Deregowski (1981) found that subjects were capable of using appropriate cues to distinguish triads of faces presented simultaneously. Shepherd (1981) suggests that when other-race faces are presented one at a time in a recognition memory experiment, subjects resort to encoding them in terms of familiar but inappropriate cues. Therefore, it appears that the own-race bias may be a consequence of the manner in which faces are remembered rather than an effect of face perception *per se*.

WHY DOES THE OWN-RACE BIAS OCCUR?

Our review of the literature on the possible factors that give rise to the own-race bias is necessarily brief; for further information the reader is referred to reviews by Yarmey (1979); Brigham and Malpass (1985); and Ng and Lindsay (1994). We consider the evidence relating to four hypotheses identified by Brigham and Malpass (1985). First, faces of one race may be inherently more difficult to recognize than faces of another race. This hypothesis could not account for comparable levels of the own-race bias observed among black and white subjects (Bothwell *et al.*, 1989). If, say, Caucasian faces are more variable, subjects of another race should recognize them more accurately than non-Caucasian own-race faces. Therefore, inherent difficulty alone cannot account for the data, but it is interesting to note that in both of the studies conducted in our own laboratory we have found the own-race bias superimposed upon a main effect of race of face in which, averaged across all subjects, white faces were better recognized than Japanese or black African faces (Valentine and Endo, 1992; Chiroro and Valentine, in preparation). Anthropometric studies have not found any evidence of differences in cranial heterogeneity of faces across different races (Goldstein, 1979a; 1979b). However, these studies did not consider variability in hair length, texture and colour. Hairstyles were visible in the stimuli used in our studies and may account for the advantage for white faces.

Second, it has been suggested that racial prejudice might account for the own-race bias in face recognition. According to this hypothesis, racially prejudiced attitudes lead to poorer recognition of other-race faces. Evidence consistent with this hypothesis has been reported by Seeleman (1940) and Galper (1973). Galper found that white subjects enrolled on a black studies course recognized black and white faces with equal accuracy but white students not taking the course showed the own-race bias using the same tests of face recognition. Galper interpreted the result in terms of the 'allegiance and interest' of white students enrolled on a black studies course, but it is possible that racial attitudes and experience of other-race faces are confounded in this study. Lavrakas *et al.* (1976), Brigham and Barkowitz (1978), and Carroo (1987) did not find a significant relationship between inter-racial attitudes and subjects' recognition accuracy of other-race faces.

A third hypothesis proposed by Chance and Goldstein (1981) suggests that superficial orienting to other-race faces at encoding may cause poorer recognition of faces of that race. However, Devine and Malpass (1985) found a similar magnitude of the own-race bias in face recognition under both superficial and inferential encoding instructions.

The fourth hypothesis suggests that the own-race bias in face recognition might be the result of limited contact with multiple exemplars of other-race faces. Past research on this hypothesis has produced an inconsistent pattern of results. For example, a study by Cross *et al.* (1971) found that white adolescents from segregated neighbourhoods showed a greater own-race bias in face recognition than did white adolescents from integrated neighbourhoods, but this study did not find a similar difference among black adolescents. Feinman and Entwisle (1976) found some evidence among children attending an integrated school that the own-race bias was greater among children living in segregated neighbourhoods than it was among children living in integrated neighbourhoods. Thus a reduction in the own-race bias appears to be associated with integration of the neighbourhood of residence rather than the racial mix of the school attended. Further evidence of a relationship between cross-racial contact and the own-race bias in face recognition was reported by Brigham *et al.* (1982), who found a significant correlation between white convenience store clerks' self-reported degree of cross-racial experience and their recognition of black customers.

Lavrakas *et al.* (1976) reported a relationship between whites' contact with blacks and recognition accuracy for black faces whereby attendance at an integrated elementary or secondary school was negatively related to recognition accuracy for black faces, but the number of black friends reported was positively related to recognition accuracy. Malpass and Kravitz (1969), Luce (1974), and Brigham and Barkowitz (1978) did not find a significant relationship between self-reported degree of cross-racial contact and recognition of other-race faces, although Malpass and Kravitz did describe their test of the relationship as 'weak'.

The relationship between cross-racial contact and the own-race bias does not appear to be a simple one. At best, the available data can be described as inconsistent. Inadequate cross-racial controls might account for these inconsistencies. Brigham (1986) suggested that 'measures of contact and experience which more accurately assess the quality and depth of contact, as well as its frequency, may help us identify the relationship between experience and a cross-race effect if indeed one exists' (p.175). A major problem that is often encountered in 'neighbourhood' studies of the own-race bias is that it is often difficult to control for demand characteristics. For example, the desire to present oneself as non-racist may significantly influence subjects' ratings of their own degree of cross-racial interaction. A further problem is that living in an integrated neighbourhood does not necessarily result in more cross-racial interaction. Mobility between neighbourhoods, the influence of television and the nature and context of employment are all factors that affect an individual's degree of cross-racial experience. In order to avoid these problems and investigate the contact hypothesis more directly, it is essential to find and test groups of subjects whose degree of cross-racial experience can be more objectively specified. Owing to the multiracial nature of most contemporary societies, such groups are difficult to find.

Ng and Lindsay (1994) found no evidence to support the contact hypothesis in two experiments. The test of the contact hypothesis in Experiment 1 relied upon self-report of cross-racial contact and so is susceptible to some of the problems discussed above. In order to avoid this problem, a second experiment tested own and other-race face recognition by 'oriental' and white subjects in Singapore and Canada. There are, however, difficulties in interpreting this experiment. A factorial design with unequal numbers of subjects in some cells was used (n's range from 6 to 46). The data are subjected to a split-plot analysis of variance with repeated measures on two factors (race of face and sex of face). The d' scores reported indicate that performance in some conditions was extremely good and many subjects must have performed close to ceiling.[2] The ceiling effect in some conditions is likely to have produced data which violate the assumption of homogeneity of variance. In fact, ANOVA including repeated measures makes the stronger assumption of sphericity of the data. It is often said that ANOVA is robust to violations of the assumed distribution of the data. However, ANOVA is not robust if the distribution of the data is not similar in all cells and there are unequal numbers of subjects in the cells of the design (e.g. Howell, 1992, p. 308). Therefore, there are good reasons to doubt the reliability of the analysis of variance reported by Ng and Lindsay (1994). It can be concluded that Ng and Lindsay have not carried out an adequate test of the contact hypothesis in either of their experiments.

In summary, there is no overwhelming evidence in support of any of the four hypotheses considered. There is some evidence to support the contact hypothesis but much of it is inconsistent. There are difficulties in interpreting many of the studies, as the manipulation of inter-racial contact has often been rather indirect. Lindsay and Wells (1983) point out that research on the own-race bias has not been based on a clear theoretical understanding of the effect. Similarly, it can be said that there is no clear theoretical basis for the mechanism by which contact is hypothesized to improve recognition of other-race faces. We argue below that a multidimensional 'face space' model of face processing can provide a theoretical framework for understanding both the own-race bias and the contact hypothesis.

THE MULTIDIMENSIONAL SPACE (MDS) FRAMEWORK OF FACE ENCODING

The main assumption of the MDS framework is that a location in the space provides an appropriate metaphor for the representation of a face in memory (Valentine, 1991a; 1991b). The dimensions of the space represent the physiognomic features that are used to encode and remember faces. It is assumed that for any given population of faces, the number of dimensions is large enough to represent any aspect of a face that could serve to discriminate between faces. The origin of the multi-dimensional space is defined as the central tendency of values on all dimensions of the population of faces encoded in the space. That is, an average of all faces would be located at the origin of the space. Typical faces are assumed to be relatively similar to the average (and to each other) and will therefore be located close to the origin of the space. Distinctive faces are assumed to differ from the average value on at least one dimension and therefore will be located distant from the origin. (See Johnston and Ellis (Chapter 1, this volume) for evidence from multi-dimensional scaling that distinctive faces are located further from the central tendency of a set of faces than are typical faces.) It is assumed that the density of faces along all dimensions will be normally distributed around the origin. Thus there will be many typical faces (which by definition are commonly encountered) located near to the origin. The density of points representing individual faces decreases as the distance from the origin increases. Figure 4.1 shows a two-dimensional representation of faces encoded in a multidimensional space. It is assumed that an individual's lifetime experience with faces will contribute to the distribution of faces within the multidimensional space. The dimensions of the space are assumed, through a process of perceptual learning, to be scaled to give optimal recognition performance for the population of faces which has been experienced. Two specific models within this framework were identified by Valentine (1991a): the norm-based coding model and the purely exemplar-based model (see also Johnston and Ellis, Chapter 1, this volume). However, in this chapter we shall restrict our discussion to the purely exemplar-based model in which the similarity between two faces is a monotonic function of the distance between them. (The metric of the space is unknown as the dimensions are also unidentified. For the present discussion it can be assumed to be Euclidean but see Craw (Chapter 9, this volume) for discussion of this point.)

It is assumed that face recognition involves a process of encoding a stimulus face as a location in the multidimensional space and determining whether this location matches that of a known face. The error associated with encoding a face will depend upon the encoding conditions (e.g. viewing time, inversion, etc.). The matching process will be affected by the magnitude of the encoding error and the proximity of neighbouring faces. These factors will affect the probability that a novel face will match the location of a known face and give rise to a false positive response and the probability that a known face will either match the location of a previously encountered face which is not sufficiently familiar to be recalled (e.g. somebody seen in the street) or not match any face in the space and will give rise to a 'miss'. In both cases increased encoding errors (i.e. poor viewing conditions) and close neighbours (i.e. high density of exemplars in the relevant region of the space) will increase the probability of erroneous responses and is also assumed to increase reaction time of correct responses.

This framework has been used to account for the effects of distinctiveness and inversion on recognition and classification of familiar and unfamiliar faces (Valentine, 1991a; Johnston and Ellis, Chapter 1, this volume). The account of the effect of distinctiveness is relevant to our discussion. According to the framework, typical faces are clustered relatively close together near to the origin of the space and are therefore located in a region of high exemplar density. When a typical stimulus face is encoded, previous experience with many similar faces (i.e. high exemplar density in the region of the stimulus face) makes it difficult to judge whether the stimulus matches any particular encoded face, as there will be many neighbours close to the 'target' face. Distinctive faces are thought to suffer less from interference effects in memory because they are encoded further away from the central tendency in regions of the space with low exemplar density (see Figure 4.1). Thus, recognition of typical faces is often associated with higher false positive rates, lower hit rates and longer response latencies compared with recognition of distinctive faces.

A MULTIDIMENSIONAL SPACE FRAMEWORK ACCOUNT OF THE OWN-RACE BIAS

If faces of two different races are represented within a multidimensional face space, the central tendency of faces of the different races will be at different locations in the space. That is, the average values of some dimensions will differ between the populations of faces. It is just such differences between races and similarity within races that enable the race of a face to be judged. If a person's experience of faces during their lifetime has been predominantly with faces of only one race (own-race faces), the dimensions of their multidimensional face space will be those that are optimal for distinguishing own-race faces. However, these dimensions will not necessarily be optimal for distinguishing faces of another race. There is evidence which suggests that faces from different races are encoded on the basis of different dimensions or physiognomic properties. Ellis *et al.* (1975) found that different facial features are used to describe black and white faces. Shepherd and Deregowski (1981) found that when three faces of the same race are presented simultaneously, the facial features used to judge similarity among black faces differed from the facial features used to judge similarity among white faces. Lack of exposure to multiple exemplars of other-race faces will make a population of other-race faces

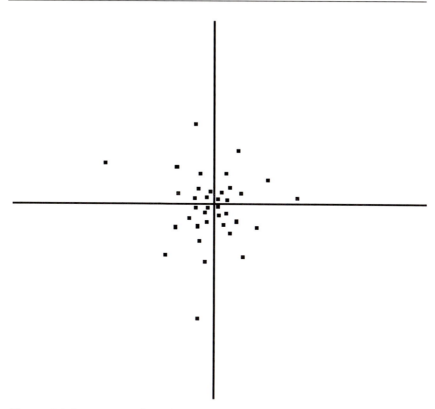

Figure 4.1 A representation of the distribution of distinctive and typical faces encoded in the face space. The central tendency of own-race faces is located at the origin. Typical faces will be located close to the origin; more distinctive faces are located in the outlying, less densely populated regions of the space. Only two dimensions are shown for the purposes of illustration

Source: Adapted with permission from Valentine and Endo, 1992

encoded in the multidimensional space more densely clustered in the space compared with own-race faces, because the dimensions which capture important variation amongst other-race faces may not be used (or only lightly weighted) in recognition of own-race faces. A face space in which own and other-race faces are encoded is illustrated in Figure 4.2.

This framework suggests that the exemplar density of encoded faces can account for the own-race bias in the same way as it accounts for the effects of distinctiveness on face processing. As the dimensions of the space are optimized only for encoding own-race faces, other-race faces will be more densely clustered than own-race faces. Therefore, the higher exemplar density of other-race faces will make recognition more error-prone in the same way that recognition of typical faces is more error-prone than recognition of distinctive faces.

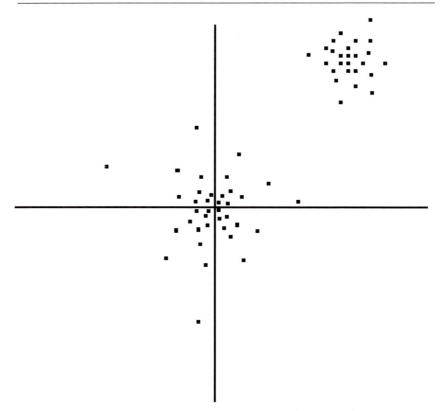

Figure 4.2 A representation of own-race and other-race faces encoded in the face space. It is assumed that the two races differ in their central tendency on the dimensions shown. The central tendency of own-race faces is located at the origin of the space. The other-race faces are more densely clustered than the own-race faces because it is assumed that the dimensions of the space are not optimal to recognize other-race faces. Again, two dimensions are shown for the purposes of illustration only

Source: Adapted with permission from Valentine and Endo, 1992

In conclusion, the multidimensional framework can provide a theoretical basis for the own-race bias; it suggests that the effect is due to exemplar density in the face space which also gives rise to the effects of distinctiveness on face recognition. This analysis also suggests that the own-race bias should be restricted to tasks involving a *memory* component, in line with Shepherd's (1981) suggestion, because the MDS framework relates specifically to the mental representation of faces in memory. The framework also suggests that the effects of race and distinctiveness are closely related phenomena. However, previous studies of the own-race bias have failed to control or manipulate distinctiveness. Therefore, a feature of the studies reported by Valentine and Endo (1992) and

Chiroro and Valentine (in press) was to investigate the effects of race and distinctiveness within the same experiment.

A MULTIDIMENSIONAL SPACE FRAMEWORK ACCOUNT OF THE CONTACT HYPOTHESIS

A key aspect of the MDS framework of face encoding is that the effect of distinctiveness and the own-race bias is a product of *learning*. In effect the MDS framework suggests a mechanism by which contact with the relevant population of faces may facilitate face recognition. The effect of distinctiveness in recognition memory for faces can only be defined in relation to a specific population of faces which the subject has experienced. It is experience with the population of faces that gives rise to the expertise necessary to exploit distinctive information in recognizing faces (see Rhodes, Chapter 3, and Stevenage, Chapter 2, this volume). The expertise to make use of distinctive information leads to experts' high level of performance in face recognition. If people are less adept in their recognition of other-race faces because they have insufficient experience to be able to enhance their recognition abilities by knowledge of the structure of the relevant population of faces, subjects should show less of an effect of facial distinctiveness on their ability to recognize other-race faces than on own-race recognition. This prediction motivated a study by Valentine and Endo (1992) of recognition of Japanese and white British faces by Japanese and white British college students.

EXPERIMENTAL INVESTIGATION OF THE EFFECT OF DISTINCTIVENESS, THE OWN-RACE BIAS AND THE CONTACT HYPOTHESIS

Valentine and Endo (1992) examined the effects of distinctiveness and race in a number of face processing tasks including recognition memory for previously unfamiliar faces. Sets of Japanese and white British faces were divided into groups of 'distinctive' and 'typical' faces on the basis of subjective ratings made by subjects of the same race as the faces rated. Although these ratings were obtained for a factorial design for which only own-race ratings were used to select the stimulus sets, the opportunity was taken to examine the correlation between distinctiveness ratings made by own and other-race subjects by obtaining ratings for all stimuli from subjects of both races. The correlation coefficients between the ratings made by subjects of the two races were 0.82 for the white British faces and 0.65 for the Japanese faces, indicating broad agreement on which faces were distinctive across race.

In the recognition memory experiment, subjects saw eight white British and eight Japanese faces. They were then required to identify the sixteen faces previously seen from a list of thirty-two faces in which the sixteen 'target' faces were mixed at random with sixteen 'distracter' faces. All target faces displayed a different facial expression during the test phase from that shown in the initial list (changed from smiling to neutral or vice versa). All of the results discussed below refer to the dependent measure A', which is a non-parametric measure of sensitivity based on signal detection theory.[3] An own-race bias in recognition accuracy was observed, although the interaction between race of subject and race of face was superimposed on an overall advantage for recognition of the white British faces (see Figure 4.3). Distinctive faces were recognized more accurately than typical faces, but the advantage for recognition of distinctive faces was consistent across race of face and race of subject (see Figure 4.4). Thus, although subjects were relatively less accurate in their recognition of other-race faces than in recognition of own-race faces, the effect of distinctiveness on recognition of own and other-race faces was equivalent.

The prediction that the effect of distinctiveness on recognition accuracy of other-race faces should be reduced or absent had not been supported. The highly significant correlations between own-race and other-race ratings of distinctiveness of faces suggests that there are many aspects of

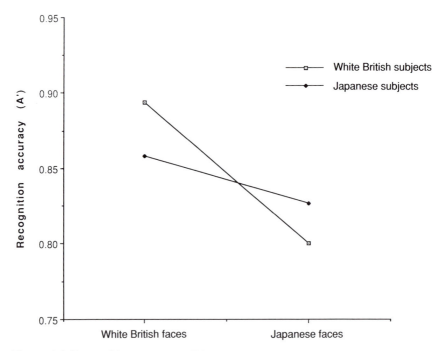

Figure 4.3 Recognition accuracy (A') plotted as a function of race of face and race of subject

Source: Adapted with permission from Valentine and Endo, 1992

a face that will determine distinctiveness of a face regardless of its race (e.g. face shape). Furthermore, as our subject populations (college students in Japan and Britain) have wide access to the media (e.g. television, films), it is possible that they have had sufficient exposure to the relevant other race to have acquired a sufficient degree of expertise to be sensitive to distinctiveness in the other-race population. However, their exposure to the other race was not sufficient to eliminate an own-race bias in recognition accuracy. Therefore, the data impose an important constraint on any model of face processing: it must be possible to show an equivalent effect of distinctiveness in recognition of own and other-race faces and to show an own-race bias in recognition accuracy *simultaneously*.

Valentine and Endo pointed out that the purely exemplar-based model (but not the norm-based coding model) identified by Valentine (1991a) could account for the data they reported. The advantage for recognition of distinctive faces over typical faces assumes that the *relative* exemplar

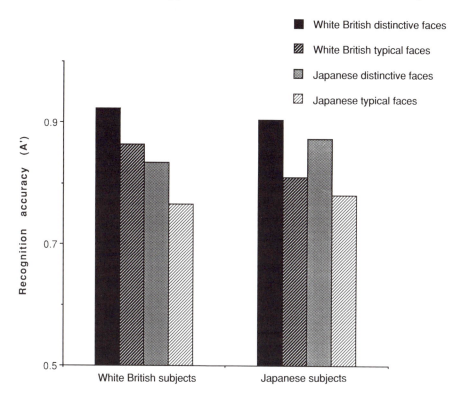

Figure 4.4 Recognition accuracy (A') plotted as a function of race of face, race of subject and distinctiveness of the stimulus faces

Source: Adapted with permission from Valentine and Endo, 1992

density around distinctive faces is lower than the exemplar density surrounding typical faces of the same race. The own-race bias is explained in terms of the *relative* exemplar density between own-race and other-race faces. Therefore, it is plausible to have a situation in which other-race faces are more densely clustered than own-race faces (because the selection and scaling of dimensions is optimized for the own-race), but the *difference* in exemplar density around typical and distinctive other-race faces is as great as the *difference* in exemplar density around typical and distinctive own-race faces.

Even though the purely exemplar-based model of the MDS framework can account for an effect of distinctiveness on recognition of other-race faces in the presence of an own-race bias, the issue remains of why an effect of distinctiveness for other-race faces that was equivalent to that found for own-race faces was observed? Is it because the subjects did have *some* experience of other-race faces? Or is it the case that even if the subjects had little or no experience of faces of the relevant race, an equivalent effect of distinctiveness would be observed? This issue was addressed in a study of face recognition by black and white high school students from Zimbabwe and Britain conducted by Patrick Chiroro as part of his doctoral research.

Chiroro and Valentine (in press) tested four groups of subjects for their recognition of distinctive and typical, own-race and other-race faces. Subjects were either black Africans or whites, and in each racial group half of the subjects were deemed to have a high degree of contact with both black and white faces [high contact (HC) subjects] and the other half of the subjects in each racial group had little or no exposure to faces of the opposite race [low contact (LC) subjects]. High contact black and white subjects (mean age = 16.3 years) were drawn from a multiracial school located in an integrated neighbourhood in Harare, Zimbabwe. Low contact black subjects (mean age = 16.2 years) were drawn from a high school located in a remote rural village in southern Zimbabwe where except for the white priest, the students were unlikely to have seen many other white people. Low contact white subjects (mean age = 16.4 years) were obtained from a college located in a small village in north-east England. Altogether, sixty-eight subjects participated in the study: seventeen in each group. All the subjects were male. We shall restrict our discussion of the results obtained using A' as the dependent variable.

The results showed a significant interaction between race of subject and race of face. Black subjects recognized black faces more accurately than they recognized white faces, and white subjects recognized white faces more accurately than they recognized black faces. Thus, a significant own-race bias was observed for *both* races of subjects. (See Figure 4.5.)

Evidence for the contact hypothesis of the own-race bias in face recognition was strong among black subjects. High contact black subjects were significantly more accurate in their recognition of white faces than were low contact black subjects. However, high contact black subjects showed an unexpectedly lower level of recognition accuracy on black faces than did the low contact black subjects. This result suggests that perhaps learning to recognize faces of another race proficiently incurs a 'cost' on the accuracy of own-race recognition. Contrary to the contact hypothesis, the white subjects showed no effect of contact on the own-race bias.

The effect of distinctiveness was confined to recognition of own-race faces for the low contact black subjects, but the high contact black subjects showed a significant effect of distinctiveness on recognition of faces of both races. The equivalent effect was also found for white subjects; the low contact subjects showed an effect of distinctiveness on recognition of white faces only, but the high contact white subjects showed a significant effect of distinctiveness on recognition of faces of both races.

Valentine and Endo had predicted that the effect of distinctiveness would be found in recognition of own-race faces but no effect of distinctiveness would be observed in other-race recognition. However, they failed to find any evidence for the prediction in a comparison of recognition of white British and Japanese faces. Chiroro and Valentine *did* observe the predicted lack of an effect of distinctiveness in recognition of other-race faces; however, it was restricted to subjects with a low degree of contact with the other race. High contact subjects showed a consistent effect of distinctiveness across race. The results reported by Chiroro and Valentine can be considered to be consistent with the results of Valentine and Endo's study if it is assumed that the subjects in the latter study had sufficient experience of other-race faces to be more similar to Chiroro and Valentine's high contact subject groups than their low contact groups. Comparisons between experiments are difficult, but it is likely that the college student subjects in Valentine and Endo's study had more experience of other-race faces than Chiroro and Valentine's low contact groups but less experience than their high contact groups.

It should be noted that Chiroro and Valentine found that, overall, white faces were better remembered than were black faces. Valentine and Endo (1992) also found a significant advantage for recognition of white faces in their study involving recognition of white and Japanese faces by white and Japanese subjects. This may be evidence that black faces and Japanese faces are inherently more difficult to recognize than white faces. However, such a conclusion cannot be justified on the basis of the results obtained by Chiroro and Valentine. The main effect of race could be attributable to the fact that the high contact black subjects recognized white faces as accurately as black faces but the high contact white subjects showed no benefit of contact and exhibited an own-race bias which was similar in magnitude to that of the low contact white subjects. In the case of Valentine and Endo's study, the main effect of race could be explicable

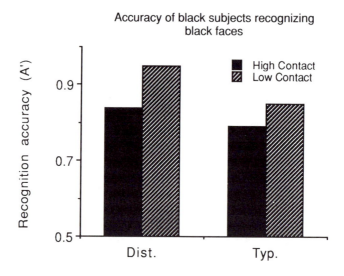

Accuracy of black subjects recognizing
black faces

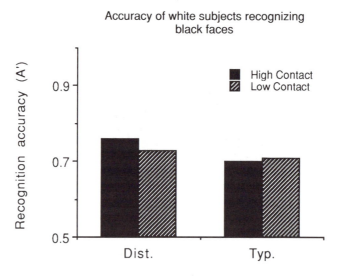

Accuracy of white subjects recognizing
black faces

Figure 4.5 Recognition accuracy (A') plotted as a function of race of subject, extent of contact with the other race, race of face and facial distinctiveness

Source: Chiroro and Valentine, in press

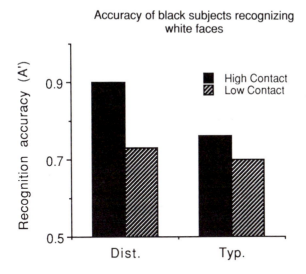

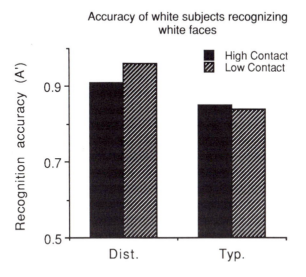

in terms of a bias in the sample of faces selected which do not truly reflect the variability of the populations (i.e. the sample of white faces might have been more distinctive than is average in the population), or the possibility that the Japanese subjects were more familiar with white faces than the white British subjects were with Japanese faces (perhaps due to the influence of the media).

The results obtained by Chiroro and Valentine clearly support the existence of an own-race bias in face recognition. They also support the contact hypothesis of the own-race bias in face recognition to the extent that the black subjects who had everyday experience in recognizing white faces showed a far superior recognition accuracy of other-race faces compared with black subjects who had very little exposure to white faces. However, white subjects did not show the same benefit of contact on their ability to recognize other-race faces. The immediate assumption might be to consider the differences in the groups of 'low contact' black and white subjects. The low contact black subjects will have had very little exposure to white faces either personally or through the media. Of course, this situation is not true of the 'low contact' white subjects from north-east England. However, examination of the data shown in Figure 4.5 reveals that the low contact black and white subjects showed very similar levels of recognition accuracy of other-race faces. It is the high contact white subjects who appear to show little, if any, benefit of contact on their ability to recognize black faces.

This asymmetry in the benefit of contact on recognition of other-race faces is all the more striking because both groups of 'high contact' subjects were students at the same school in Harare. It strongly suggests that sheer exposure to other-race faces alone is not sufficient to result in the perceptual learning required to proficiently recognize other-race faces. The experience of black and white students in the same school might be very different. For example, the majority of the staff in the school are white. Therefore, black schoolchildren would need to recognize other-race faces to deal with people in authority. It may be less important for white schoolchildren to learn to recognize other-race faces, particularly if they tend to associate with peers of the same race. These comments are necessarily *post hoc* and largely based on conjecture. However, these results emphasize Brigham's (1986) suggestion that the exact nature of contact between races and its effect on the own-race bias is worthy of more detailed investigation.

One further aspect of the results obtained by Chiroro and Valentine was somewhat unexpected and is worthy of comment. The reduction in the own-race bias demonstrated by high contact black subjects on recognition of white faces appears to have been achieved at a cost of reduced recognition accuracy for own-race (black) faces, in comparison to the level of performance of the low contact black subjects (i.e. low contact black subjects showed more accurate own-race face recognition than did the high contact black subjects). Although this effect was not predicted, with hindsight it can be appreciated that an implementation of the multi-dimensional space framework in terms of a connectionist model using distributed representations might be expected to show a degradation of own-race recognition from interference from learning other-race faces (see O'Toole *et al.*, 1991; Valentine and Ferrara, 1991; O'Toole *et al.*, 1994; O'Toole *et al.*, Chapter 8, this volume). If, after having learnt faces of the own race, a large number of faces from a different population are encoded within the same network, the statistical structure of the faces stored in the network would be different. The changing statistical structure repre-sented within a network might benefit recognition of the 'minority' race of faces encountered, but be less optimal for encoding faces of the 'majority' race than the state of the network prior to experience with other-race faces.

A PROSPECTIVE STUDY OF THE CONTACT HYPOTHESIS

Chiroro and Valentine's results raise two important questions: first, what are the essential features of cross-racial contact that are necessary to facil-itate recognition of other-race faces? And second, does the acquisition of expertise in other-race face recognition necessarily incur a 'cost' on the performance of own-race recognition?

The research reviewed above suggests that the quality of contact is potentially extremely important (e.g. Brigham and Malpass, 1985; Chiroro and Valentine, in press). From a theoretical point of view, the multidi-mensional space framework can be used to specify two minimum aspects of contact that would be necessary to learn the statistical structure of a new population of faces. First, it is necessary that the individual must *need* to recognize individuals of the other race from their face. Contact that does not require other-race faces to be remembered would not necessitate an attunement of the dimensions of the face space to the population of other-race faces. Second, the contact must require the individual to recognize a sufficient number of other-race faces to *enable* the statistical structure of the population of other-race faces in the face space to be abstracted and to *require* that the structure is abstracted in order to be able to recognize the necessary individuals. (As an extreme example, the necessity to recognize one black person in an otherwise exclusively white group will clearly not enhance recogni-tion of other-race faces by a white observer.)

Most tests of the contact hypothesis have involved comparison between two groups of subjects assumed to differ in their cross-racial experience. Many studies have relied upon comparisons drawn from 'integrated' versus 'segregated' areas (see the discussion above). Chiroro and Valentine were able to use an extremely powerful manipulation of cross-racial contact for black subjects, but the *quality* of the cross-racial experience of the groups of white subjects is less clear. It is extremely difficult to assess cross-racial experience retrospectively for individual subjects in any objective manner. Indeed, such assessment is not usually even attempted, or self-rating methods used. A second disadvantage of between-groups designs is that the subject groups may differ on factors other than cross-racial experience (e.g. educational level, social class, etc.). Even if the subject groups are matched on a number of chosen variables, the design rests on the assumption that the experience of other-race faces is the critical variable rather than some other extraneous variable. A within-subjects design in which the own-race bias in face recognition is evaluated before and after a period during which recognition of other-race faces has been required would provide a better controlled study. A within-subjects design is essential to clearly demonstrate any 'cost' of learning to recognize other-race faces on the ability to recognize own-race faces. Although the high contact black subjects in Chiroro and Valentine's study recognized own-race faces less accurately than the low contact black subjects, we do not know whether the high contact subject group would have performed as well as the low contact group if they had not learnt to recognize other-race faces. However unlikely it may seem, it is possible that the results may simply reflect between-group differences in own-race face recognition.

Ruth Dixon recently undertook an undergraduate project at the University of Durham in which she carried out a prospective study of the contact hypothesis. The subjects in her project were white people (students, teachers and a nurse) who were involved in a voluntary teaching project in Ghana or Tanzania for eight weeks during the summer vacation. They participated in a face recognition task involving white British and black African faces before leaving Britain and again (using different faces) shortly before leaving Africa. The performance of these subjects (the 'African' group) was compared with a control group of students who participated in the same tests of face recognition but who stayed in Britain during the eight-week interval between the first and second tests. This 'prospective' study of the contact hypothesis has a number of advantages. First, all of the subjects will share similar experience of other-race faces between the two tests. As subjects were teaching black African children during this period, they were exposed to a large number of other-race faces with the need to be able to recognize their students. Second, data 'before' and 'after' exposure to other-race faces were collected, so it was possible to make within-subjects comparisons when testing for an improvement in other-race face recognition and any associated impairment to 'own-race' recognition.

In both tests subjects were shown twenty-four faces in an initial list (twelve black African faces and twelve white British faces). Three hours later subjects had to identify the faces seen in the first list from a list of forty-eight faces (twenty-four black, twenty-four white). Target faces were shown with a different expression from that seen earlier (changed from smiling to unsmiling or vice versa). The sets of targets and distracters in the two test lists were matched on distinctiveness ratings obtained from other subjects. Photographs of different target and distracter faces were used in the first and second tests (before and after the teaching project or eight-week interval). The assignment of photographs to Test 1 or Test 2 was counterbalanced within the African and control groups. Usable data were collected from fifteen subjects in the African group and fourteen control subjects. The second (post-exposure) test was conducted by using photographs in a ring-bound book for all subjects. The original intention had been to carry out the first test by testing all of the African group on one single occasion, presenting the faces using a slide projector. However, seven subjects did not attend the meeting during which the group test was carried out, and subsequently were tested individually using a ring-bound book. In order to control for any effect of the mode of the initial test, seven subjects in the control group were tested using photographs for the initial test and seven were tested using slides. The dependent variable was recognition accuracy. The following discussion of the results is based on analysis of A' scores.

The results showed clear support for the contact hypothesis. There was a general trend for recognition in Test 2 to be more accurate than in Test 1, but this effect was much more marked for the African group (see Figure 4.6). The subjects who spent eight weeks teaching in Africa showed enhanced recognition of black African faces compared with the control group. Thus, in this situation eight weeks' experience of teaching provided sufficient quality and quantity of contact to eliminate the own-race bias on face recognition. There was a trend in the direction of a reduction in recognition accuracy of own-race faces for the African group, but this effect was not statistically significant. This result suggests that an improvement in the ability to recognize other-race faces is not always accompanied by an equivalent decrement in the ability to recognize own-race faces.

There are a number of differences between Ruth Dixon's project and the Chiroro and Valentine study. The low contact black Africans in Chiroro and Valentine's study had virtually no experience at all of white faces. Although Ruth Dixon excluded subjects who had previously visited Africa for more than three weeks or who had at least weekly contact with more than five people of another race, the subjects in her study will have had some experience of black African faces through the media and everyday life. It is possible that a cost on accuracy of own-race face

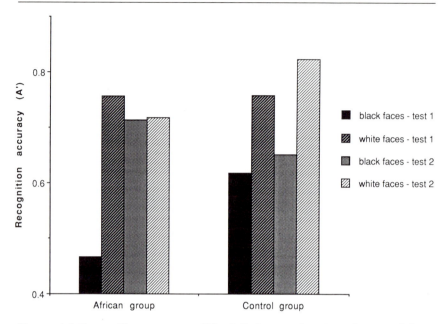

Figure 4.6 Recognition accuracy (A') plotted as a function of race of face, experimental group and test. (Test 1 was prior to, and Test 2 was following, experience of black faces for the African group)

Source: Dixon, 1994

recognition is only observed in comparison with subjects who have had experience exclusively restricted to own-race faces. Perhaps exposure to some other-race faces throughout the life span makes the representation of the statistical structure of faces more stable when a large number of other-race faces are subsequently experienced.

There are some limitations to this study imposed by the constraints of an undergraduate project which means these results should be regarded as preliminary. One unusual aspect of the data is that in the initial test the 'African' group showed a very marked own-race bias and in fact did not recognize black African faces above chance. However, the data are sufficiently encouraging to suggest that 'prospective' studies could provide a powerful method for further investigation of the own-race bias. An issue of some practical significance is the long-lasting effect of eight weeks' experience of other-race faces on the own-race bias. We intend to attempt to replicate and extend these results in future work at the University of Durham.

SUMMARY AND CONCLUSIONS

The multidimensional space framework provides a plausible theoretical basis for understanding both the own-race bias and the contact hypothesis.

It suggests that the effect of distinctiveness and the own-race bias both reflect the influence of the statistical structure of the sample of faces that have been experienced. This led to the prediction that the effect of distinctiveness should be attenuated in recognition of other-race faces. There was no support for this prediction in a study of face recognition by Japanese and British students. However, the prediction was supported in a group of black and white 16-year-old subjects who had little contact with members of the other race. The relationship between the own-race bias and the effect of distinctiveness is not straightforward. Subjects can still show an own-race bias even though they show an effect of distinctiveness which is equivalent to the effect observed in own-race subjects. Therefore, the decline in the own-race bias that occurs as an observer becomes more proficient in recognizing faces of another race does not occur *only* because they become better able to use the distinctive information available in distinctive other-race faces, although this may be a component of the process of perceptual learning that occurs early in the process with a relatively small degree of contact (cf. Valentine and Endo, 1992). Subsequently, with greater contact any reduction in the own-race bias must affect recognition of both typical and distinctive other-race faces: this process might reflect a decrease in the perceived similarity between other-race faces. In the MDS framework this would be equivalent to 'stretching' the scale of the dimensions which serve to discriminate other-race faces but not own-race faces. Learning to recognize faces of another race might involve two stages: first, identifying the dimensions which are most useful in recognizing other-race faces. Once this stage is completed an effect of distinctiveness equivalent to that observed for own-race faces emerges. Second, the 'weight' or attention paid to these dimensions gradually increases. When this second process is complete, recognition accuracy of own and other-race faces would be equivalent.

Good evidence for the contact hypothesis emerged from a comparison between black Zimbabwean subject groups with either virtually no experience or a very high degree of experience in recognition of white faces. However, no evidence for the contact hypothesis was obtained from the white subjects in this study. This may reflect a difference in the quality of contact for white and black subjects in the same school in Harare. Further support for the contact hypothesis also emerged from a prospective study of white subjects who visited Africa for eight weeks.

An issue which emerged from these studies is whether learning to recognize other-race faces incurs a 'cost' in the ability to recognize own-race faces. Evidence for just such an effect was found in the comparison between black subjects who have had very little contact of other-race faces and the black subjects who have had very extensive experience in recognizing people of the other race. No evidence of the 'cost' effect was observed for white subjects who spent eight weeks in Africa, even though their own-race bias in face recognition was eliminated. It is possible that any decrease in the recognition accuracy of own-race faces is only observed either a) when the experience of other-race faces has been over an extensive period of time; or b) when performance of the 'high contact' group is compared with subjects who have virtually no contact with the other race. At present it is impossible to conclude from the data available whether learning to recognize faces of another race has any effect on own-race face recognition and if so, under what conditions it occurs. Further research is required to resolve this issue. Prospective studies of other-race face recognition are likely to provide the most powerful methodology to explore this issue and other aspects of the contact hypothesis.

Finally, it should be noted that the theoretical framework in which we have considered the effect of race on face recognition is essentially a theory of perceptual learning. The hypothetical face space we discuss here has much in common with the autoassociative memory model described by O'Toole *et al.* (Chapter 8, this volume) and the coding system described by Craw (Chapter 9, this volume), although these authors make much more detailed assumptions, with some important differences, about the dimensions and similarity metric of the space.

ACKNOWLEDGEMENT

We thank Charles Heywood for comments on an earlier draft of this chapter.

NOTES

1 d' (d prime) is a measure of sensitivity based on signal detection theory. In this context, d' is a measure of the ability of a subject to distinguish previously presented faces (targets) from 'new' distracter faces. The value of d' is independent of any bias of the subject to make one response rather than the other (old vs. new). A d' of 0 reflects chance performance.

2 A d' score of 4.00 was the highest group mean reported by Ng and Lindsay (1994). As an approximate guide, a mean probability of 0.96 of correctly identifying target faces and a mean probability of 0.01 of making a false positive to a distracter face would yield a d' of 4.07. Probabilities of 0.99 and 0.04 respectively would yield the same value of d'.

3 A' is a measure of sensitivity analogous to d' but the statistic does not require an assumption that the underlying distributions are normally distributed. The upper limit of A' is 1. A level of performance equivalent to chance would yield an A' score of 0.5.

REFERENCES

Bothwell, R.K., Brigham, J.C. and Malpass, R.S. (1989) Cross-racial identification of faces. *Personality and Social Psychology Bulletin*, 15, 19–25.

Brigham, J.C. (1986) The influence of race on face recognition, in H.D. Ellis, M.A. Jeeves, F. Newcombe and A. Young (eds), *Aspects of Face Processing*. Dordrecht: Martinus Nijhoff.

Brigham, J.C. and Barkowitz, P. (1978) Do they look alike? The effect of race, sex, experience and attitudes on the ability to recognize faces. *Journal of Applied Social Psychology*, 8, 306–318.

Brigham, J.C. and Malpass, R.S. (1985) The role of experience and contact in the recognition of own- and other-race faces. *Journal of Social Issues*, 14, 139–155.

Brigham, J.C., Maass, A., Snyder, L.D. and Spaulding, K. (1982) Accuracy of eyewitness identification in a field setting. *Journal of Personality and Social Psychology*, 42, 673–681.

Carroo, A. (1987) Recognition of faces as a function of race, attitudes, and reported cross-racial friendships. *Perceptual and Motor Skills*, 64, 319–325.

Chance, J. E. and Goldstein, A. G. (1981) Depth of processing in response to own- and other-race faces. *Personality and Social Psychology Bulletin*, 7, 475–480.

Chiroro, P. and Valentine, T. (in press) An investigation of the contact hypothesis of the own-race bias in face recognition. *Quarterly Journal of Experimental Psychology*.

Cohen, J. (1977) *Statistical Power Analysis for the Behavoral Sciences* (revised edn). New York: Academic Press.

Cross, J. F., Cross, J. and Daly, J. (1971) Sex, race, age and beauty as factors in recognition of faces. *Perception and Psychophysics*, 10, 393–396.

Devine, P. G. and Malpass, R. S. (1985) Orienting strategies in differential face recognition. *Personality and Social Psychology Bulletin*, 11, 33–40.

Dixon, R.H. (1994) *A Prospective Investigation of the Contact Hypothesis as an Explanation of the Own-race Bias in Face Recognition*. Unpublished undergraduate dissertation, Department of Psychology, University of Durham.

Ellis, H. D., Deregowski, J. B. and Shepherd, J. W. (1975) Descriptions of white and black faces by white and black subjects. *International Journal of Psychology*, 10, 119–123.

Feinman, S. and Entwisle, D.R. (1976) Children's ability to recognize other children's faces. *Child Development*, 47, 506–510.

Galper, R. E. (1973) 'Functional race membership' and recognition of faces. *Perceptual and Motor Skills*, 37, 455–462.

Goldstein, A. G. (1979a) Race-related variation of facial features: anthropometric data I. *Bulletin of the Psychonomic Society*, 13, 187–190.

Goldstein, A. G. (1979b) Facial feature variation: anthropometric data II. *Bulletin of the Psychonomic Society*, 13, 191–193.

Howell, D. C. (1992) *Statistical Methods for Psychology* (third edn). Boston: PWS-Kent Publishing.

Lavrakas, P. J., Buri, J. R. and Mayzner, M. S. (1976) A perspective on the recognition of other-race faces. *Perception and Psychophysics*, 20, 475–481.

Lindsay, R.C.L. and Wells, G.L. (1983) What do we really know about cross-race eyewitness testimony?, in S.M.A. Lloyd-Bostock and B.R. Clifford (eds), *Evaluating Eyewitness Evidence: Recent Psychological Research and New Perspectives*. Chichester, Sussex: John Wiley.

Luce, T. S. (1974) The role of experience in inter-racial recognition. *Personality and Social Bulletin*, 1, 39–41.

Malpass, R. S. and Kravitz, J. (1969) Recognition of faces of own and other race. *Journal of Personality and Social Psychology*, 13, 330–334.

Ng, W-J. and Lindsay, R. C. L. (1994) Cross-race facial recognition: failure of the contact hypothesis. *Journal of Cross-cultural Psychology*, 25, 217–232.

O'Toole, A. J., Deffenbacher, K.A., Abdi, H. and Bartlett, J. C. (1991) Simulating the 'other-race' effect as a problem in perceptual learning. *Connection Science: Journal of Neural Computing, Artificial Intelligence and Cognitive Research*, 3, 163–178.

O'Toole, A.J., Deffenbacher, K.A., Valentin, D. and Abdi, H. (1994) Structural aspects of face recognition and the other-race effect. *Memory and Cognition*, 22, 208–224.

Reber, A. S. (1985) *The Penguin Dictionary of Psychology.* Harmondsworth: Penguin

Seeleman, V. (1940) The influence of attitude upon the remembering of pictorial material. *Archives of Psychology*, 36, 258.

Shapiro, P. N. and Penrod, S. (1986) Meta-analysis of facial identification studies. *Psychological Bulletin*, 100, 139–156.

Shepherd, J. W. (1981) Social factors in face recognition, in G. M. Davies, H. D. Ellis and J. W. Shepherd (eds), *Perceiving and Remembering Faces.* London: Academic Press.

Shepherd, J.W. and Deregowski, J.B. (1981) Races and faces – A comparison of the responses of Africans and Europeans to faces of the same and different races. *British Journal of Social Psychology*, 20, 125–133.

Valentine, T. (1991a) A unified account of the effects of distinctiveness, inversion and race in face recognition. *Quarterly Journal of Experimental Psychology*, 43A, 161–204.

Valentine, T. (1991b) Representation and process in face recognition, in R. Watt (ed.), *Pattern Recognition by Man and Machine. Vision and Visual Dysfunction, Vol. 14* (series editor J. Cronley-Dillon). Basingstoke: Macmillan.

Valentine, T. and Endo, M. (1992) Towards an exemplar model of face processing: the effects of race and distinctiveness. *Quarterly Journal of Experimental Psychology*, 44A, 671–703.

Valentine, T. and Ferrara, A. (1991) Typicality in categorisation, recognition and identification: evidence from face recognition. *British Journal of Psychology*, 82, 87–102.

Yarmey, A.D. (1979) *The Psychology of Eyewitness Testimony.* New York: Free Press.

Chapter 5

Distinctiveness and memory for unfamiliar faces

Judith A. Hosie and Alan B. Milne

The concept of distinctiveness pervades almost every area of research on memory and has been invoked as a potential explanation for a diverse range of memory phenomena (for a review, see Schmidt, 1991). Although the operational definition of distinctiveness is not the same in different areas of research, the concept is frequently introduced to account for why stimuli which are unusual, bizarre or atypical in appearance are more memorable than stimuli which are common, normal or average in appearance.

Face recognition is one area in which there is an apparently strong link between stimulus distinctiveness and memory. A consistent empirical finding is that unfamiliar faces which are judged as distinctive or unusual in appearance are recognized more accurately than faces which are judged as typical or average in appearance (e.g. Going and Read, 1974; Cohen and Carr, 1975; Light *et al.*, 1979; Shepherd *et al.*, 1991; Valentine, 1991). Distinctiveness not only affects episodic recognition of unfamiliar faces; it also influences our ability to identify faces which are familiar to us. For example, distinctiveness facilitates speed of recognition to personally familiar faces (Valentine and Bruce, 1986a) and to famous faces (Valentine and Bruce, 1986b).

The effect of distinctiveness on recognition provides evidence that faces are processed in terms of their deviation from a prototypic or average representation and that distinctive faces deviate more from this prototypical representation than do typical faces. Valentine and Bruce (1986b) proposed that if the effect of distinctiveness on the latency to recognize familiar faces arises from the use of a facial prototype, then typical faces should be classified as faces more quickly than distinctive faces, since the former are closer in proximity to the prototype than the latter. This was confirmed in a task requiring subjects to distinguish intact faces (faces in which the features were normally positioned) from jumbled faces (faces in which the features had been arbitrarily arranged). Intact typical faces were classified as faces more quickly than intact distinctive faces.

Research on facial caricatures has provided an independent body of evidence for the role of a prototypical representation in face processing. Rhodes *et al.* (1987) examined recognition of line-drawn familiar faces in which distinctiveness was varied using a computerized caricature generator. The program produces veridical drawings of faces by joining the co-ordinates of 169 key points on an individual face by a set of lines. A facial norm is computed by averaging the position of the key points across several faces. Caricatures are created by exaggerating distinctive aspects of each face relative to the appropriate norm face; anti-caricatures are produced by de-emphasizing distinctive aspects to a metrically equivalent degree. Rhodes *et al.* found that caricatures of familiar faces were identified more rapidly and accurately than anti-caricatures and more rapidly, but not more accurately, than the veridical representations of faces. They proposed that these results are consistent with the existence of a facial norm against which distinctive (identifying) information is encoded. A caricature advantage for familiar faces has also been observed for photographic quality images (Benson and Perrett, 1991).

One interesting feature of the recognition advantage for caricatures is that it may be related to the degree of familiarity with the caricatured face. Rhodes *et al.* (1987) failed to find a caricature advantage for goodness of likeness judgements to unfamiliar faces, and for old/new judgements in a recognition test for unfamiliar faces (Rhodes and Moody, 1990). (However, see Stevenage (Chapter 2, this volume), who found a recognition advantage for artists' caricatures of unfamiliar faces compared to veridical line drawings.) This is contrary to studies examining speed of familiarity judgements to familiar and unfamiliar faces. For example, Valentine and Bruce (1986a) found that although the distinctiveness and familiarity of familiar faces were negatively correlated with decision time (shorter latencies were found for faces high in distinctiveness and familiarity), they were not correlated with one another.

It is clear from an examination of the literature that in the area of face processing, distinctiveness is not merely used in a descriptive sense but as an explanatory concept for understanding the way in which faces are encoded and represented in memory. This chapter will concentrate on the relationship between distinctiveness and episodic memory for unfamiliar faces. First, the results of empirical work on distinctiveness and recognition will be reviewed and this will be followed by a discussion of some of the explanations and models proposed to account for the results of these studies. Finally, the importance of the experimental context to understanding the nature of the relationship between distinctiveness and face recognition will be addressed, including the effect of stimulus context and experimental design on memory for typical and distinctive faces.

THE EFFECT OF DISTINCTIVENESS ON MEMORY FOR UNFAMILIAR FACES

Distinctive faces are not only recognized more accurately than typical faces but are less likely to be erroneously identified as having been seen before (e.g. Going and Read, 1974; Cohen and Carr, 1975; Light et al., 1979; Shepherd et al., 1991; Valentine, 1991). Also, distinctive faces are found to yield a higher correlation between self-rated confidence and recognition accuracy than non-distinctive faces (Brigham, 1990).

Although attempts have been made to obtain objective measurements from faces to ascertain what makes a face distinctive or typical in appearance (e.g. Bruce et al., 1994), the terms typical and distinctive are commonly used in a subjective sense. That is, subjects are normally required to rate faces for distinctiveness on a Likert-type scale (e.g. Valentine, 1991), or rank order a set of faces in terms of their distinctiveness (Cohen and Carr, 1975). A less common method was used by Ellis et al. (1988) and Shepherd et al. (1991), who obtained an index of memorability for faces based on the proportion of subjects correctly recognizing them and then sorted the most and least memorable faces into nine categories running from 'least distinctive' to 'most distinctive'. Both studies found almost perfect agreement between memorableness and distinctiveness. All of these methods have been used to derive a set of typical and distinctive faces which are employed as target and distracter stimuli for tests of recognition memory.

This is not to suggest, however, that there is a commonly applied definition of distinctiveness. Indeed, some researchers have preferred to adopt the converse term 'typicality' (e.g. Light et al., 1979; Vokey and Read, 1988; 1992). Also, a variety of terms have been used to anchor typicality and distinctiveness rating scales, such as typical versus atypical, typical versus unusual and non-distinctive versus distinctive. Although the use of so many different descriptors is not desirable, it seems likely that the terms typicality and distinctiveness refer to the same psychological variable: regardless of the terminology adopted, most studies in which this variable has been manipulated have produced superior recognition of distinctive, unusual or atypical faces compared to that for typical or non-distinctive faces.

One of the most striking characteristics of the distinctiveness effect is that it is highly robust and appears to operate independently of other experimental manipulations. For example, the effect has been demonstrated at exposure durations as short as one second (Shepherd et al., 1991) to as long as fifteen seconds (Light et al., 1979) and over a variety of test intervals ranging from immediate testing (e.g. Light et al., 1979; Shepherd et al., 1991) to delayed testing of three and twenty-four hours (Light et al., 1979) and four weeks (Shepherd et al., 1991).

One possible exception to this rule, however, is the effect of orienting task or encoding activity on memory for typical and distinctive faces. Light *et al.* (1979) suggested that if unusual faces undergo more lengthy or elaborative processing than typical faces then a reduction in the distinctiveness effect should be observed under conditions that do not require detailed facial analysis. They manipulated encoding activity by requiring subjects to judge faces with respect to either likeableness or gaze direction and observed a reduction in the distinctiveness effect in the latter task. However, the interaction fell below conventional levels of significance (Light *et al.*, 1979, Experiment 3). In a follow-up experiment, the difference between typical and unusual faces was greater under intentional learning conditions than under two incidental learning conditions. Although this finding was consistent with an elaborative processing hypothesis, interpretation of the data was made difficult due to the poor recognition of typical faces in the intentional learning task. Nevertheless, these are interesting results which have not been followed up by research in this area.

One puzzling aspect of the distinctiveness effect is that despite its robustness, it does not manifest itself consistently across the various indices of recognition performance. Although the effect is frequently found for overall measures of recognition sensitivity based on signal detection theory (e.g. A' or d'), this occurs as a result of two different underlying patterns of performance. Some researchers have reported a distinctiveness effect for responses to target items, demonstrating a higher hit rate to distinctive faces compared to typical faces (e.g. Bartlett *et al.*, 1984 (Experiment 1); Shepherd *et al.*, 1991; Valentine, 1991 (Experiment 2)). Other studies have demonstrated an effect for false alarms to distracter items, reporting a lower false alarm rate to distinctive faces compared to typical faces (Light *et al.*, 1979 (experiments 2, 3 and 4); Valentine, 1991 (Experiment 2)). A number of models and explanations have been proposed to account for these observations. These will now be examined.

EXPLANATIONS AND MODELS OF THE EFFECT OF DISTINCTIVENESS ON MEMORY FOR UNFAMILIAR FACES

One of the first studies which drew attention to the relationship between facial appearance and different measures of memorability was conducted by Cross *et al.* (1971). They examined the effects of beauty, age, race and sex on face memory and observed that within each of these categories faces differed in terms of their memorability. They found that when faces were ordered in an array from most memorable to least memorable, their colleagues could accurately identify the high and low ends of the array in terms of hit and false alarm frequency and suggested that the well-remembered faces were less ordinary looking while the more misidentified faces were more ordinary looking. Cross *et al.* suggested an explanation of this effect in terms of an interference theory in which typical faces are more easily confused with previously seen faces.

Bartlett *et al.* (1984) proposed that context-free familiarity could account for the difference in recognition accuracy between typical and distinctive faces (that is, the feeling of familiarity that arises from experience of many similar exemplars of the same category). They found that the initial familiarity for new faces was greater for those rated as typical than for those rated distinctive. However, prefamiliarization to typical and distinctive faces led to a greater increment in familiarity to distinctive faces, so that in a recognition task, in which distracter faces had been seen before, the advantage in false alarm rate to distinctive faces was reduced compared to a test in which the distracters were new faces.

Other researchers have suggested that the difference in evoked familiarity between typical and distinctive faces must itself arise from the similarity structure of faces and that typical faces are more similar to previously encountered faces (and to one another) than distinctive faces. A recent model of distinctiveness and recognition which is based on the concept of interstimulus similarity has been proposed by Valentine (1991). This model uses a spatial metaphor for understanding the mental representation of faces. Faces are represented as points (in an exemplar-based representation) or vectors (in a norm-based representation) in a multi-dimensional 'face space'. The dimensions of this space represent the parameters by which faces are encoded.

In the norm-based model faces are encoded at locations which are normally distributed about a prototypical representation. This representation is located at the origin of the face space and faces are represented by vectors from the origin to the appropriate location. According to this model the density of faces decreases with increasing distance from the norm so that typical faces located close to the origin will lie in densely clustered regions of the face space, whereas distinctive faces which are less common and which deviate more from the prototype will be located in less dense regions of the space. Recognition is assumed to be determined by the density of points (faces) located in the face space. The high exemplar density around the origin produces poor discrimination and probable misidentification in the case of typical faces; the relatively lower exemplar density towards the periphery results in more rapid and accurate identification of distinctive faces.

Valentine (1991) has proposed that although a norm-based model provides a good account of the existing data, an exemplar-based model may provide a more parsimonious explanation. The most important distinction between the two models is that in the norm-based model the similarity between two faces is a function of the similarity between two vectors (e.g. dot products) but in the exemplar model, similarity is a function of the distance separating any two points. Thus, in the exemplar model, the position of a norm plays no role. However, both models assume that faces are normally distributed and that exemplar density accounts for the differential recognition of typical and distinctive faces. Recent work by Johnston *et al.* (submitted) has provided some empirical support for Valentine's model. They asked subjects to rate all possible pairings of a set of typical and distinctive faces for similarity and submitted the resulting data to a multidimensional scaling analysis (MDS). They found that faces independently rated as typical were significantly closer to the origin of a six-dimensional MDS solution than were the distinctive faces.

Other researchers, however, have suggested that the superior recognition of distinctive faces cannot be accounted for solely in terms of interstimulus similarity. For example, Light *et al.* (1979) also suggested that typical faces evoke a stronger feeling of familiarity than distinctive faces because they resemble a prototype face or many other similar faces in memory. As a result, typical faces are more likely to be misidentified than distinctive faces. Furthermore, they demonstrated that the structural basis of this effect was interstimulus similarity: typical faces were rated as looking more similar to one another than were distinctive faces. However, they also proposed that distinctive faces may be more uniquely encoded than typical faces resulting in a superior specific memory component. Thus, according to this model, false alarms to typical faces are a product of schematic memory (or knowledge of category structure), whereas performance for distinctive faces is due to the specific memory component formed for such faces at the time of encoding.

Vokey and Read (1988) also suggested that more than one component of rated typicality may mediate recognition. They asked subjects to rate a set of male and female faces for typicality (subjects were asked to indicate which faces were unusual), familiarity (a familiar face was described as one that might be confused with 'one that you know') and recognition (subjects were required to judge if a face had appeared previously in the sequence of slides). They found that familiarity did not predict the false alarm rate to faces, despite its reliable correlation with typicality and despite the fact that typicality itself was related to false alarms. They argued that two types of familiarity may exist: *context-free* familiarity (the type of familiarity on which subjects based their ratings) and *specific* familiarity (which mediates episodic judgements of familiarity in most face recognition tasks).

This distinction was supported by later work in which a principal components analysis of subjects' ratings of faces for typicality, familiarity, attractiveness, memorability and likeableness was conducted (Vokey and Read, 1992). Two orthogonal components were extracted, one consisting of the ratings of familiarity, attractiveness and likeability and reflecting context-free familiarity, and the other consisting of the memorability rating. They proposed that the effect of typicality on recognition is essentially a result of both of these components functioning in opposition, so that increased typicality is associated with increased general familiarity and decreased memorability. Atypical faces are discriminated better in tests of recognition than typical faces because their lower level of general familiarity results in fewer false positive responses and their higher level of memorability results in increased hits. This was confirmed in a recognition study in which both components were found to contribute equally to face discrimination. Furthermore, separate analyses of the hits and false alarms as a function of these components showed that general familiarity contributed to the production of false alarms, whereas memorability had an effect on both hit and false alarm rates. Indeed, the major impact of memorability on recognition was not on hits but on false alarms.

According to Vokey and Read, memorability itself comprises two elements. The first relates to distinctiveness of encoding (a similar proposal to that of Light *et al.*) and contributes to the superior hit rate to distinctive faces. The second component, relating to retrievability, contributes to the lower false alarm rate associated with distinctive faces. Vokey and Read proposed that retrievability is related to the process of *negative* recognition (i.e. the failure of retrieval for what should be an easily retrieved item (an atypical face) is strong evidence that the item should not be accepted as a target).

More recently, Bruce *et al.* (1994) provided confirmation of these results. Using a large database of male and female faces, they obtained subjective ratings of facial distinctiveness, objective facial measurements and ratings of memorability for faces when they appeared as targets and distracters in a face recognition task. On the basis of the physical measurements obtained, a deviation score was calculated for each face (based on the sum of the modulus of z-scores, or the sum of the squared z-scores) providing a measure of distance of each face from the average. They found that provided faces were rated with the hair concealed, a reasonably high correlation was observed between subjective ratings of distinctiveness and physical deviation from the average. This supports the contention that distinctiveness and deviation from the average are closely related. As expected, rated distinctiveness was positively correlated with how well a face was remembered as a target and negatively correlated with how familiar it appeared when acting as a distracter. However, a correlation was not observed between the two ratings of memorability, indicating that faces which were easy to remember when they were familiar were not the same ones that were easy to reject when they were unfamiliar. The absence of a negative correlation provides some support for the theory that typicality comprises two separate components which exert independent effects on recognition accuracy.

These results show that the relationship between distinctiveness and recognition performance is complex. The elevated hit rate to distinctive faces may result from episodic factors such as distinctiveness of encoding (e.g. Light *et al.*, 1979; Valentine and Ferrara, 1991; Vokey and Read, 1992), whereas the low false alarm rate to distinctive faces may result from both episodic factors, such as retrievability, and semantic factors, such as context-free or general familiarity (e.g. Vokey and Read, 1992).

It is fair to suggest that relatively little is known about the way in which distinctiveness of encoding and retrieval exert their influence on recognition memory. There is undoubtedly evidence that distinctive faces enjoy an encoding advantage in comparison to typical faces. For example, Ellis *et al.* (1988) presented subjects with an initial set of target faces followed by fifteen test sequences during which subjects were required to identify the original targets from a set of randomly mixed distracter faces. The results showed that faces which ranked high on memorability and distinctiveness were identified as being familiar more accurately and rapidly than those faces which ranked low on both dimensions. Furthermore, this advantage was maintained across trials, indicating a processing advantage for distinctive faces regardless of their level of familiarity. To date however, attempts to isolate the basis of this encoding advantage have not been successful.

Evidence for elaborative or deeper processing of distinctive faces compared to typical faces is inconclusive (Light *et al.*, 1979). Nevertheless, it is still generally assumed that an encoding advantage of some sort may exist, perhaps involving more extensive processing of distinctive faces. Such a hypothesis is consistent with the work of Winograd (1981), who proposed that memory for faces is an increasing function of the number of features encoded and that the probability of encoding a distinctive feature is correlated with the number of features extracted from a face. Winograd suggested that the improvement in recognition accuracy observed for faces judged in terms of personality attributes is due to a greater sampling of features which in turn increases the probability of encoding a distinctive feature. Light *et al.* (1979) and Shepherd *et al.* (1991), however, reasoned that if the superior recognition of distinctive faces is due to them being encoded on distinctive features then reducing the inspection time should diminish this superiority by reducing the opportunity to identify and encode a distinctive feature. However, reducing inspection time to two seconds in the Light *et al.* study and to one second in the Shepherd *et al.* study failed to produce the desired effect.

Of course, such work is based on the assumption that encoding distinctive information requires processing time. A study conducted in our own laboratory, however, suggests that whatever is distinctive about an atypical face can be picked up and encoded very rapidly. In this study we examined ratings of facial distinctiveness made at different exposure durations (for the shortest exposure durations, additional conditions were included in which a visual patterned mask followed the offset of each face): 60 ms., 60 ms. plus mask, 100 ms., 100 ms. plus mask, 500 ms., 500 ms. plus mask, 1000 ms. and 8000 ms.. Within each of the exposure durations, twelve subjects rated sixty male faces on a seven-point scale, ranging from 1 (typical) to 7 (distinctive). The ratings obtained from the timed exposure conditions were compared with the ratings obtained from an untimed inspection task. The data showed that mean distinctiveness ratings for all of the timed exposure durations, including the shortest duration, were highly correlated with those obtained from the untimed inspection period (see Table 5.1). This would appear to indicate that distinctiveness judgements obtained from faces shown for a very brief period of time (one which allows only one eye fixation) are comparable with those obtained when subjects are allowed to scan each face freely.

Table 5.1 Correlations between distinctiveness ratings obtained from untimed viewing task, with distinctiveness ratings obtained for fixed viewing times of 60ms., 100ms., 500ms., 1000ms. and 8000ms. (N=60)

viewing time (ms)								
8000	1000	1000 +mask	500	500 +mask	100	100 +mask	60	60 +mask
0.80	0.69	0.71	0.71	0.69	0.59	0.52	0.51	0.52

THE EFFECT OF EXPERIMENTAL CONTEXT ON MEMORY FOR TYPICAL AND DISTINCTIVE FACES

All of the explanations and models of distinctiveness discussed in the previous section are based on the results of laboratory studies of memory for unfamiliar faces. Yet the contribution of experimental context to the effect, such as the structure of the stimulus list and experimental design, has not been examined in these studies. Clearly, one of the reasons for this is the implicit assumption that the distinctiveness effect reflects the similarity structure of the representation of faces in memory and is independent of experimental manipulations (e.g. Valentine, 1991). However, Vokey and Read (1992) have demonstrated that one of the factors influencing the effect of typicality on recognition is memorability which comprises two components, distinctiveness of encoding and retrievability, and it is possible that these are sensitive to experimental context variables.

A distinction which may help contribute to our understanding of the relationship between distinctiveness and recognition relates to the way in which distinctiveness is defined or understood. A face may be distinctive relative to one's previous experience of faces (which we will term 'absolute' distinctiveness), and/or a face may be distinctive relative to the context in which it is shown or in relation to other faces included in the same stimulus pool ('relative' distinctiveness). Whether this distinction is important or valid is an empirical question. However, it is clear that it is not one which is explicitly made in studies of face recognition memory. Although there is an implicit assumption that distinctiveness is judged relative to faces in the stimulus set, the instructions given to subjects often encourage a more 'absolute' form of judgement. For example, subjects are instructed to rate each face for 'how easy it would be to spot in a crowd' (e.g. Valentine, 1991), or they are asked to 'try to think how similar each face is to the typical high school male senior' (Light *et al.*, 1979). Thus, the way in which ratings are obtained often confound 'absolute' and 'relative' distinctiveness. More important, however, is the relative influence of these two descriptions of distinctiveness on recognition memory.

The distinction between 'relative' and 'absolute' distinctiveness is not a new one and has been alluded to in studies of face memory and distinctiveness for some time. For example, Cohen and Carr (1975) found that distinctive faces were recognized more accurately than typical faces in a study in which distinctiveness was defined relative to other faces in the experimental set. They likened the distinctiveness effect for faces to the von Restorff effect (von Restorff, 1933). To obtain the von Restorff effect, a single item is either made perceptually distinctive in relation to other items in the set (e.g. a single red-coloured word within a list of black-coloured words) or conceptually distinctive compared to other items (e.g. the name of a fruit included in a list of names of vegetables or a nonsense syllable among meaningful words). Another technique involves the manipulation of the structural organization of items within a list so that memory for massed versus isolated items can be tested. Isolation is produced by embedding an item of one type within a series of items of another type and a massed item is one which is preceded by items from the same element type. The von Restorff effect was largely studied in relation to recall of words, letters and digits and, although it is empirically indisputable, an adequate theoretical explanation of the effect has not been found (Wallace, 1965).

Interestingly, with reference to the foregoing discussion Schmidt (1991), in a recent review of distinctiveness and memory, distinguished between *primary* and *secondary* distinctiveness. The first term describes the distinctiveness of an item relative to the context in which it appears. Under Schmidt's definition, an item may be conceptually or perceptually distinctive relative to other items in a set. (Note the similarity of this definition to the von Restorff effect.) Secondary distinctiveness describes the distinctiveness of a stimulus relative to information stored in long-term memory, and according to this definition, a distinctive item is a peripheral or atypical exemplar of a natural category. Schmidt categorized memory for unusual faces as a secondary distinctiveness phenomenon. Given the evidence for the contribution of episodic memory to typicality effects, this classification may not be entirely accurate. However, the role of primary distinctiveness (i.e. the structure of the to-be-remembered stimulus list) in memory for typical and distinctive faces is not clear and hitherto has not been explored by researchers.

In a classic von Restorff effect experiment, distinctiveness is defined relative to the experimental context (i.e. there is nothing intrinsically more memorable about the isolated item). Clearly, a distinctive face embedded in a series of typical faces could be considered distinctive in both an 'absolute' and in a 'relative' sense. Of more interest, however, is the perception and recognition of a typical face embedded in a series of distinctive faces. Although not 'absolutely' distinctive, this face might look structurally dissimilar and therefore unusual relative to other faces in the set. Is it possible to reverse the conventional distinctiveness effect by manipulating the structure of the experimental list? We addressed this question some time ago and found tentative evidence that the superior recognition of distinctive faces compared to typical could be temporarily overridden by experimental context.

In our experiment, two presentation sets were constructed, each consisting of one critical item. The first comprised one distinctive face embedded in a series of fourteen typical faces, the second consisted of one typical face embedded in a series of fourteen distinctive faces. We hypothesized that if the distinctiveness effect is sensitive to list structure, then the single typical item in the second set should be considered distinctive relative to the context in which it is shown. Serial position of the critical item (typical or distinctive) in each set was also manipulated so that it appeared at the beginning, middle or end of the input list. One of the assumptions of the von Restorff effect is that the structure of the to-be-remembered items activates an overall conceptual organization and distinctive items are those which do not fit into this organization. This being the case, one would anticipate superior recognition of an isolated item placed towards the end of the list compared to one placed at the beginning of the list prior to the formation and organization of information.

At test, subjects were shown a series of face pairs consisting of a target face and a matched distracter face in a two-alternative-forced choice design. The data showed that the latencies to critical faces were significantly shorter than those to non-critical faces in both conditions (Figure 5.1), suggesting that the appearance of a face relative to other faces in the set affected speed of recognition which, as mentioned above, is a characteristic finding in experiments with distinctive facial stimuli. There was no reliable interaction between the type of the isolated face and the type of the background face. A rather unexpected result of this study was the failure to demonstrate a serial position effect which suggests the possibility that organizational effects exert their influence *post hoc* rather than 'on-line' (Hosie and Milne, 1992).

Clearly, a true test of the similarity between this effect and the von Restorff effect would require the inclusion of a control list constructed of faces of the same type (in this case, typical or distinctive) as the isolated or critical face. This would allow the estimation of the relative contributions of prior knowledge and current context to recognition performance.

This study represents a preliminary investigation of the relationship between facial distinctiveness and the von Restorff effect, and a more thorough exploration of these types of manipulation is required. However, even if few similarities are demonstrated between these two effects, the paradigm itself suggests a number of possible avenues of research. For example, what effect does the occurrence of a distinctive face have on memory for preceding and immediately succeeding faces? If distinctive

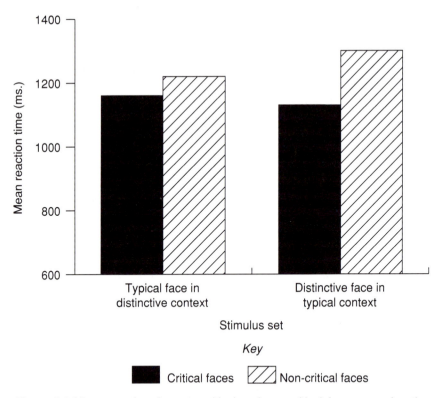

Figure 5.1 Mean reaction times to critical and non-critical faces as a function of stimulus set

faces undergo more elaborative processing then one might predict that memory for succeeding faces would be more disrupted by the presentation of a distinctive face compared to a typical face. This remains to be tested.

It is uncommon to construct lists such as those presented above. Instead, most studies of recognition memory use sets of faces comprising an equal number of typical and distinctive faces which are randomly mixed at presentation and at test (e.g. Light *et al.*, 1979; Shepherd *et al.*, 1991). In another study we manipulated the structure of the presentation lists of faces by comparing a standard randomized set (in which typical and distinctive faces are randomly mixed) with two sets which were identical in content but different in structure (i.e. a set consisting of the massed presentation of typical items followed by the massed presentation of distinctive items (typical–distinctive massed), and a second set in which this order of presentation was reversed (distinctive–typical massed)). A common test set was constructed for all three lists comprising typical and distinctive faces randomly mixed. Each target was associated with a distracter, matched in terms of its distinctiveness rating. In this experiment therefore, set content and variability were kept constant and the only difference between the presentation lists was the order of presentation of information.

A distinctiveness effect was observed for A' and for the proportion of false alarms. Distinctive faces were more accurately recognized and less likely to be misidentified than typical faces. However, analysis of false alarms also demonstrated an interaction between presentation list and distinctiveness, revealing a large and significant difference in false alarms to typical and distinctive faces in the random mixed list, followed by a progressively weaker effect in the typical-followed-by-distinctive mixed condition and no effect in the distinctive-followed-by-typical mixed condition (Hosie and Milne, 1993). These data appear to provide some evidence that the context provided by the experimental list can moderate the effect of distinctiveness on memory.

Perhaps one of the most important types of experimental manipulation in any investigation of memory is that of experimental design. Studies examining recognition memory for typical and distinctive faces have adopted a within-subjects mixed list design in which subjects are presented with a set of typical and distinctive faces randomly mixed at presentation and at test (Light *et al.*, 1979; Shepherd, *et al.*, 1991). There is one notable exception to this paradigm. Valentine (1991; Valentine and Endo, 1992) has demonstrated distinctiveness effects on memory for faces using a within-subjects, between-lists design in which subjects are shown and tested on a set of typical faces followed by a set of distinctive faces, or vice versa. Given that it is possible to manipulate distinctiveness in a variety of different ways (between versus within-subjects and/or mixed versus homogenous lists) one must consider whether the effects are independent of design.

One problem with the mixed list design is that it represents the optimal conditions for observing a distinctiveness effect. Distinctive faces in a mixed list are not only nominally distinctive but are also relatively distinctive in comparison to typical faces in the same set. As a result, we have carried out a number of experiments in which we have attempted to remove the relative component of distinctiveness by comparing a between-subjects comparison of memory for typical and distinctive faces (in which subjects are presented with typical or distinctive faces only at presentation and at test) with the more conventional within-subjects mixed list design. The data in these studies were analysed using a modified analysis of variance procedure (Erlebacher, 1977) specifically designed to test whether the effect of an independent variable (in this case distinctiveness) is different across a within- and between-subjects design. This type of procedure has been used successfully to investigate distinctiveness effects in other areas of memory research (e.g. McDaniel and Einstein, 1986).

The results of these studies showed that the effect of distinctiveness on memory is sensitive to experimental design and in particular, the difference in false alarm rate between typical and distinctive faces is reduced in a between-subjects design. Furthermore, this reduction in the distinctiveness effect was due to an increase in false alarms to distinctive faces in the between-subjects manipulation. However, these results may not be accounted for entirely by differences in discrimination accuracy. Analyses of response bias showed a lower response criterion for distinctive faces (i.e. an increased likelihood of attracting an 'old' response) in the between-subjects manipulation compared to the within-subjects mixed list condition. Indeed, in the mixed list condition the response criterion for distinctive faces was high (significantly higher than that to typical faces) indicating a more conservative response strategy for distinctive faces in this set. Interestingly, there was no response bias, or shifts in response bias, for typical faces in the mixed list and between-subjects design (Hosie and Milne, submitted).

The non-random distribution of false alarms in studies of face recognition has been of interest to psychologists in this area for many years (Goldstein et al., 1977). One of the preliminary findings emerging from manipulations of list structure and experimental design is that the false alarm rate to distinctive faces is more sensitive to these variables than the false alarm rate to typical faces or the overall hit rate to faces. This concurs with the results of Vokey and Read (1992), which have demonstrated that false positive responses are not due solely to context-free familiarity and must in part be due to episodic memory or specific familiarity.

Manipulations of list structure (at both encoding and recognition) may provide further insight into the contribution of experimental context to memory for typical and distinctive faces. The extent to which the organization or structure of the presentation set dictates recognition of typical and distinctive faces is not known. One interesting question relating to list structure is whether subjects are aware of fluctuations in the variability of a set of faces. For example, when subjects are presented with a block of typical massed items followed by a block of distinctive massed items, are they aware of a change in the level of variability? Is the representation of this list different from a purely random mixed list in which the level of variability fluctuates around some mean level? One obvious question which arises from changing the structure of a presentation list is whether knowledge of set variability is computed in relation to schematic memory or whether it is acquired 'on-line' as stimuli are presented or studied. There is some evidence for the on-line computation of variability in the construction of social categories (see Park and Hastie, 1987).

Experimental design is also important to understanding list structure effects. Results from a within-subjects design should be clarified (if possible) in a between-subjects design. A within-subjects design invites comparison between images in the same set and if one is trying to draw conclusions about how these images are processed then the influence of contrast effects must be considered. For example, there is evidence that subjects' perception of facial expressions is different depending on whether a within- or between-subjects presentation is used (Russell, 1994).

One hypothesis that we are currently investigating is that inter-item similarity or list variability might determine the level of detail that is encoded. In other words, when a target set is highly variable and inter-item similarity is low, representations may be coarsely encoded, but when a target set contains some highly similar items the 'granularity' of the representations may be much finer. Thus, when blocked typical or distinctive target sets are tested against distracters of the same level of variability, false alarm rates remain relatively constant, but when a mixed list is presented, the fineness of encoding necessary to discriminate between typical items in the target set results in a significant decrease in false alarm rate for distinctive faces.

By manipulating memorability directly, it is also possible to examine the contribution of different measures of discrimination accuracy and response bias. For example, Vokey and Read (1992) observed that in a true face recognition task involving the use of different photographs of the same individuals between study and test, ratings of general familiarity and memorability were related to overall response bias whereby an increase in familiarity was associated with a lowered response criterion, while an increase in memorability was associated with an increased response criterion. The effect of list structure and experimental design on shifts in encoding bias is likely to be highly informative about the way in which subjects encode sets of faces which vary in their degree of relative distinctiveness.

CONCLUDING REMARKS

The relationship between distinctiveness and memory is an intriguing one. Facial distinctiveness enhances memory performance for unfamiliar faces and facilitates recognition of familiar faces. In this chapter, we have concentrated on the former and have suggested that one fruitful area of research is the study of different types of laboratory manipulation of distinctiveness. Although we have suggested that faces can be distinctive or unusual in an 'absolute' (i.e. relative to everyday knowledge) or in a 'relative' sense (i.e. with respect to other faces in the immediately surrounding context), these two definitions are not mutually exclusive. Clearly, both contribute to recognition memory. However, the contribution of the latter has not been fully examined. Doubtless, semantic information affects perception and recognition of faces in the laboratory. However, memory for a face also depends on the specific episode of encounter and on the conceptual representation activated by the context in which it is presented. Although a face is 'tagged' as looking unusual or familiar based on semantic memory, subsequent recognition of it may depend more on the context (i.e. list of other faces) in which it is presented. It is for this reason that the effect of list structure and to some extent experimental design may contribute further to our knowledge of distinctiveness effects on memory.

REFERENCES

Bartlett, J.C., Hurry, S. and Thorley, W. (1984) Typicality and familiarity of faces. *Memory and Cognition,* 12, 219–228.

Benson, P. J. and Perrett, D.I. (1991) Perception and recognition of photographic facial quality caricatures: implications for the recognition of natural images. *European Journal of Cognitive Psychology,* 3, 105–135.

Brigham, J.C. (1990) Target person distinctiveness and attractiveness as moderator variables in the confidence-accuracy relationship in eyewitness identifications. *Basic and Applied Social Psychology,* 11, 101–115.

Bruce, V., Burton, M.A. and Dench, N. (1994) What's distinctive about a distinctive face? *Quarterly Journal of Experimental Psychology,* 47A, 119–141.

Cohen, M.E. and Carr, W.J. (1975) Facial recognition and the von Restorff effect. *Bulletin of the Psychonomic Society,* 6, 383–384.

Cross, J.F., Cross, J. and Daley, J. (1971) Sex, race, age and beauty as factors in recognition of faces. *Perception and Psychophysics,* 10, 399–396.

Ellis, H.D., Shepherd, J.W., Gibling, F. and Shepherd, J. (1988) Stimulus factors in face learning, in M.M. Gruneberg, P.E Morris and R.N. Sykes (eds), *Practical Aspects of Memory: Current Research And Issues: Vol.1. Memory in Everyday*

Life. Chichester, UK: John Wiley.

Erlebacher, A. (1977) Design and analysis of experiments contrasting the within- and between-subjects manipulation of the independent variable. *Psychological Bulletin,* 84, 212–219.

Going, M. and Read, J.D. (1974) The effect of uniqueness, sex of subject and sex of photograph on facial recognition. *Perceptual and Motor Skills,* 39, 109–110.

Goldstein, A.G., Stephenson, B. and Chance, J. (1977) Face recognition memory: distribution of false alarms. *Bulletin of the Psychonomic Society,* 9, 416–418.

Hosie, J.A. and Milne, A.B. (1992) The effect of temporal and contextual factors on memory for faces. Poster presentation at the XXVth International Congress of Psychology, Brussels, 19–24 July.

Hosie, J.A. and Milne, A.B. (1993) The effect of experimental design on the distinctiveness effect for faces. Paper presentation at the International Conference on Face Processing, British Psychological Society (Welsh Branch), 21–23 September.

Hosie, J.A. and Milne, A.B. (submitted for publication) The effect of experimental design on the recognition of typical and distinctive faces.

Johnston, R.A., Milne, A.B., Williams, C. and Hosie, J.A. (submitted for publication) Do distinctive faces come from outer space: an investigation of the status of a multidimensional face space.

Light, L.L., Kayra-Stuart, F. and Hollander, S. (1979) Recognition memory for typical and unusual faces. *Journal of Experimental Psychology: Human Learning and Memory,* 5, 212–228.

McDaniel, M.A. and Einstein, G.O. (1986) Bizarre imagery as an effective memory aid: the importance of distinctiveness. *Journal of Experimental Psychology: Learning, Memory and Cognition,* 12, 54–65.

Park, B. and Hastie, R. (1987) Perception of variability in category development: instance- versus abstraction-based stereotypes. *Journal of Personality and Social Psychology,* 53, 621–635.

Rhodes, G. and Moody, J. (1990) Memory representations of unfamiliar faces. *New Zealand Journal of Psychology,* 19, 70–78.

Rhodes, G., Brennan, S. and Carey, S. (1987) Identification and ratings of caricatures: implications for mental representations of faces. *Cognitive Psychology,* 19, 473–497.

Russell, J.A. (1994) Is there a universal recognition of emotion from facial expression? A review of the cross cultural studies. *Psychological Bulletin,* 115, 102–141.

Schmidt, S. (1991) Can we have a distinctive theory of memory? *Memory and Cognition,* 19, 523–542.

Shepherd, J.W., Gibling, F. and Ellis, H.D. (1991) The effects of distinctiveness, presentation time and delay on face memory. *European Journal of Cognitive Psychology,* 3, 137–145.

Valentine, T. (1991) A unified account of the effects of distinctiveness, inversion and race on face recognition. *Quarterly Journal of Experimental Psychology,* 43A, 161–204.

Valentine, T. and Bruce, V. (1986a) Recognizing familiar faces: the role of distinctiveness and familiarity. *Canadian Journal of Psychology,* 40, 300–305.

Valentine, T. and Bruce, V. (1986b) The effect of distinctiveness in recognizing and classifying faces. *Perception,* 15, 525–535.

Valentine, T. and Endo, M. (1992) Towards an exemplar model of face processing: the effects of race and distinctiveness. *Quarterly Journal of Experimental Psychology,* 44A, 671–703.

Valentine, T. and Ferrara, A. (1991) Typicality in categorisation, recognition and identification: evidence from face recognition. *British Journal of Psychology,* 82,

87–102.

Vokey, J.R. and Read, J.D. (1988) Typicality, familiarity and the recognition of male and female faces. *Canadian Journal of Psychology,* 42, 489–495.

Vokey, J.R. and Read, J.D. (1992) Familiarity, memorability and the effect of typicality on the recognition of faces. *Memory and Cognition,* 20, 291–302.

von Restorff, H. (1933) Über die Virkung von Bereichsbildungen im Spurenfeld. *Psychologie Forschung,* 18, 299–342.

Wallace, W.P. (1965) Review of the historical, empirical and theoretical status of the von Restorff phenomenon. *Psychological Bulletin,* 63, 410–424.

Winograd, E. (1981) Elaboration and distinctiveness in memory for faces. *Journal of Experimental Psychology: Human Learning and Memory,* 7, 181–190.

Chapter 6

Memorability, familiarity, and categorical structure in the recognition of faces

John R. Vokey and J. Don Read

INTRODUCTION

Natural categories such as faces are *structured*, meaning there is a more or less orderly relation among the exemplars such that it makes sense to say that some members are *better* or more *typical* exemplars of the category than are others, even if the basis of this relation is not readily apparent (cf. Wittgenstein, 1953; Rosch, 1973; Rosch and Mervis, 1975; Rosch *et al.*, 1976). Indeed, equivocating on the term, it is *natural* for people to rank or rate faces in terms of their typicality as exemplars of the category so that the distinction between a typical and an atypical face is obvious to most observers – to the point of being considered to be an *attribute* of the face, even though the source of the judgement is often difficult or impossible for most people to articulate. In turn, these ratings of typicality have been found to be related to many judgements people make about faces, including people's recognition of faces: the specific familiarity of atypical or unusual faces is better discriminated than that of typical faces on tests of item recognition (e.g. Going and Read, 1974; Cohen and Carr, 1975; Light *et al.*, 1979; Courtois and Mueller, 1981; Bartlett *et al.*, 1984). Typicality has been suggested to mediate similar effects on face recognition found for ratings of attractiveness and likeability, in that faces judged to be attractive or likeable are also more likely to be rated as typical (Light *et al.*, 1981; Mueller *et al.*, 1984). In this chapter, we address the issue of how this natural structure of faces – as indexed by people's judgements of facial typicality – comes to affect these judgements. We argue that these effects of the natural structure of faces are mediated by two components, which we refer to as memorability and general familiarity, functioning in opposition. Although we believe these components have much broader generality than that proposed here, we limit our discussion, by way of example, to how these two components can be seen to underlie the effects of rated typicality and rated attractiveness on the discrimination of specific familiarity on face recognition.

Attributing various effects to the natural structure of faces is to recognize that the relationships among faces in some hyper-dimensional similarity space or 'face space' are important determinants of how people process facial information and what they can do with it. As Valentine (1991; Valentine and Endo, 1992) has noted in a useful exposition of these ideas, acknowledging the importance of such structure in people's interactions with faces does not necessarily commit one to any particular model of that structure. Accordingly, none of the results discussed here help to discriminate between, for example, abstractive memory models such as facial prototypes as the embodiment of the structure on the one hand, and non-abstractive, distributive models such as memory for individual exemplars on the other, or, for that matter, some combination of the two. However, we do have some thoughts on the matter as a way of co-ordinating this work with the broader memory literature, which we raise towards the end of the chapter. First, however, we briefly review the research on typicality and face recognition, which suggests that at least two components are necessary to provide a complete account of the effects of typicality on the recognition of faces. We then summarize our recent work (Vokey and Read, 1992) that attempted to isolate these components. Following a summary of the Vokey and Read (1992) demonstration that these two components can provide a complete account of the effect of typicality on face recognition, we provide a new demonstration of how the same two components can be used to provide a complete account of the effects of attractiveness on the recognition of faces.

WHY TWO COMPONENTS ARE NECESSARY

The idea of inter-item similarity is inherent in the construct of 'distinctiveness', an earlier proposed basis for the mediation of categorical structure on face recognition (e.g. Going and Read, 1974). According to this proposal, atypical faces are better discriminated on tests of recognition because they are more distinctive than are typical faces; presumably, the greater distinctiveness of atypical faces results in greater distinctiveness in the encoding of these faces, and hence better subsequent retrieval (Winograd, 1981). In support of this idea that the effects of categorical structure are mediated by distinctiveness, Light *et al.* (1979) found that the rated inter-item similarity of faces was highly correlated with their rated typicality, and was, in fact, a better predictor of recognition discrimination than was typicality. Furthermore, they found that distinctive target faces benefited more from elaborative or more lengthy encoding tasks than did typical or non-distinctive target faces on subsequent tests of recognition, supporting the idea that the effect of distinctiveness and hence typicality is of primary benefit to the retrieval of distinctive faces.

The alternative to accounts based on distinctiveness has been to suggest that the effects of typicality on recognition are mediated by differences in structurally-induced, context-free familiarity. The principal idea here is that because of their high inter-item similarity, typical faces are a priori more familiar than atypical faces, and that for recognition these differences in context-free familiarity fail to be discriminated from differences in specific familiarity resulting from specific experience with a given face (see e.g. Bartlett *et al.*, 1984; Vokey and Read, 1988). Atypical faces are better discriminated than are typical faces on tests of recognition, according to this view, because the level of specific familiarity obtained from specific exposure as targets is easier to detect against the low background level of structurally-induced familiarity of atypical faces than the high background level for typical faces that may more often be confused with specific familiarity. In support of this hypothesis, both Bartlett *et al.* (1984) and Vokey and Read (1988), for example, found that unfamiliar atypical faces are judged to be less generally familiar than are typical faces. Bartlett *et al.* found further that pre-familiarizing the faces could reduce or even eliminate the effect of typicality on recognition in that familiarized atypical distracters no longer provide a discrimination advantage.

The weakness of both the distinctiveness and context-free familiarity accounts at least as usually construed is that neither one alone can account for the most notable aspect of the effect of typicality on face recognition, namely that facial typicality is one of a class of problematic recognition variables known as *mirror-effect variables* (Glanzer and Adams, 1985; 1990). Mirror-effect variables are so-called because they have opposite effects on the recognition rates of hits and false alarms. In general, the scale end of the variable associated with better recognition discrimination, such as atypical faces, is also associated with both higher hits *and* lower false alarms than the opposite end of the mirror-effect variable, such as typical faces. Thus, although the account of typicality effects in terms of encoded distinctiveness provides an explanation for the generally superior hit-rate – through increased retrieval – associated with the recognition of atypical faces, it fails to account for the corresponding lower rate of false alarms associated with these same faces as distracters. Similarly, although structurally-induced familiarity provides an account for the lower rate of false alarms to atypical faces, it fails to account for the often increased hit-rate of atypical faces when used as targets.

Putative accounts of typicality effects on face recognition should not be singled out for censure in this regard. As Hintzman *et al.* (1994) noted recently, mirror effects are not handled well by any current model of recognition. In most models, recognition decisions are represented in terms of signal detection, with a single criterion along a unidimensional decision axis, typically trace strength or familiarity. Although there are other ways of characterizing the problem (see Hintzman, 1994; Hintzman *et al.*, 1994), the principal difficulty as we see it is with the unidimensionality of the decision: only *one* criterion along a *uni*dimensional decision axis. Adding a *second* criterion (and an independent basis for setting it), for example, or, equivalently, adding a second independent decision axis (with its own criterion) would provide for the needed degree of freedom in accounting for mirror effects. We refer to this latter approach as recognizing the need for at least *two components* in any account of typicality effects on face recognition, although exactly how the two components are instantiated is subject to wide variation. For example, Bartlett *et al.* (1984) proposed that the familiarity arising from specific exposure is negatively related to the level of structurally-induced familiarity of a given face, a proposal very similar to that of Hintzman's (1988) multiple-trace model of the effects of word frequency (another mirror-effect variable) on item recognition. Here, the advantage for recognition discrimination of reduced structurally-induced familiarity of atypical faces or low-frequency words (resulting in reduced false alarms to these items as distracters) is further enhanced by an encoding advantage (presumably the advantage of encoding distinctiveness discussed earlier) for these same items as targets.

Hintzman *et al.* (1994) explicitly acknowledge three approaches to modifying current memory models to account for mirror effects. The first is to keep the original decision axis of familiarity or strength and supplement it with a second process that reverses the item-type distributions for target and distracter items along this axis. The second is to invoke a process that re-scales the decision axis itself, so that on the new scale the distributions of target and distracter items for the different item types are appropriately reversed. The third approach, the focus of the research in Hintzman *et al.*'s paper and a source of our own musings on these matters (Vokey and Read, 1992), is the memorability hypothesis of Brown *et al.* (1977), in which the evidential weight to attach to an item's familiarity as evidence of specific prior exposure is adjusted in light of the item's assessed memorability. In any case, two processes are required, which for the moment is all we mean to imply by the necessity of two components to account for typicality effects on face recognition.

Light *et al.* (1979) were the first to propose an account of the effect of typicality on the recognition of faces that required two components, which they explicitly identified on the one hand as structurally-induced, general familiarity responsible for the effect of typicality on false alarms, and on the other hand as a specific memory component arising from the distinctiveness of encoding of atypical and typical faces and responsible for the effect of typicality on hits. Note that both components are a function of the structure of face space, but that they reflect different, presumably independent aspects of it. In Vokey and Read (1992), we proposed a similar model, except we argued that the second component was better characterized as *memorability*. In our conception, the retrieval effects of encoding distinctiveness in the Light *et al.* model are only a part of the consequences of the memorability component. The memorability of a face also has consequences for its correct rejection as a *distracter*; that is, for the control of false alarms. As we see it, general familiarity and memorability usually work in opposition in determining recognition: general familiarity reduces discrimination by increasing false alarms while memorability enhances it by reducing false alarms and, if the encoding/retrieval advantages are sufficient, increasing hits. In this view, we were guided by Brown *et al.*s' (1977) conception of memorability as an explanation for the effect of word frequency in what they refer to as 'negative recognition' – the recognition that you have *not* experienced an item or event previously. Brown *et al.* reject as inadequate the common (and unidimensional) idea that negative recognition is just the absence of positive memory (i.e. retrieval). Instead, they argue that subjects also assess the memorability (or retrieval potential) of test items; the lack of specific retrieval for what should be an easily retrieved item is strong evidence that, in fact, the item had not been encountered previously.

TYPICALITY AS MEMORABILITY AND GENERAL FAMILIARITY

If the categorical structure of faces is mediated by general familiarity and memorability in people's judgements about faces, then these two components should be latent in the relationships among the judgements across faces. For example, although ratings of typicality would be expected to be a composite of general familiarity and memorability, and therefore would not be expected to provide a clean reflection of either component, ratings of facial memorability might be expected to be relatively little affected by general familiarity, and hence might be expected to provide a relatively pure reflection of variations of the memorability component across faces. Similarly, asking subjects for judgements about the general familiarity of otherwise unfamiliar faces should provide a relatively pure measure of that component, with little effect of the memorability component.[1] Both of the ratings of familiarity and memorability would then be expected to be moderately related to the corresponding ratings of typicality, but not substantially with each other. In fact, patterns such as these have been reported. Vokey and Read (1988), for example, found that false alarms in detecting repetitions of faces and judgements of the faces' context-free familiarity were both related to ratings of the faces' typicality, but not to each other. Similarly, Valentine and Bruce (1986) found for familiar faces that both typicality (i.e. distinctiveness ratings in this case) and rank order familiarity of the faces were significant predictors of the time required to identify the faces as known, but were unrelated to each other. More recently, Bruce *et al.* (1994) reported that the target and distracter ratings about whether a given face had been seen previously were both correlated with the face's ratings of typicality, but, again, were completely unrelated to each other (see also Bruce *et al.*, Chaper 7, this volume).

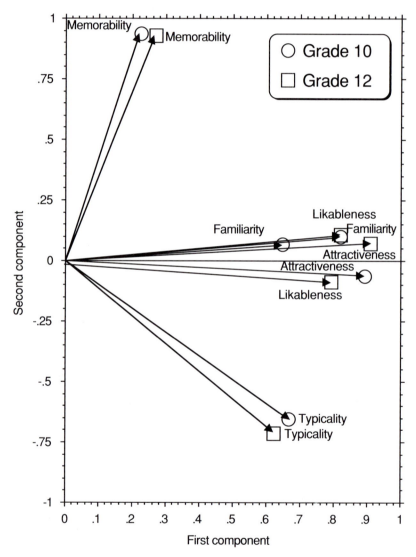

Figure 6.1 The vector plot of the projections of the five ratings variables on the first two varimax-rotated principal components for both the Grade 10 and the Grade 12 face sets in Vokey and Read (1992)

Such patterns of relationships suggest that it should be possible to decompose the ratings in general, and the typicality ratings in particular, into the two suggested components, along with the weighting or relative contribution of each component to each of the rating variables. This was essentially the logic of the approach we took in Vokey and Read (1992), except that we included in addition to typicality, memorability and general familiarity the ratings of two other facial attributes, attractiveness and likeability, also thought to be a function of categorical structure, in an attempt to stabilize the extraction of the two components. The complete procedure is given in Vokey and Read (1992). In summary, two sets of high school photographs, a Grade 10 set (students roughly 16 years of age) and a Grade 12 set (students roughly 18 years of age) of the same 180 faces, were given to two different groups of subjects to rate for typicality, attractiveness, likeability, general familiarity and memorability. The resulting ratings were then subjected, for each face set independently, to a principal components analysis (PCA) to extract the two components, and scores on both components were computed for each face within grade.

A vector plot of the projections of the five ratings variables on the first two varimax-rotated principal components for both the Grade 10 and the Grade 12 face sets in Vokey and Read (1992) is shown in Figure 6.1. As can be seen for both grades of face photographs, the first component, which we refer to as 'general familiarity', has high, positive loadings with the variables of familiarity, attractiveness and likeability, and virtually no relationship with ratings of memorability. The second or 'memorability' component has a high, positive loading with the memorability ratings, but is correlated not at all with the cluster of variables defining the general familiarity component. Typicality, as expected, lies along the diagonal, loading moderately and equally ($|\bar{r}| = .66$) with both components, positively with the component of general familiarity, and negatively with the memorability component. In fact, as the two components are orthogonal, the simple sum of the squared loadings indicates that the typicality ratings are effectively accounted for (roughly 90 per cent of the variance) by the two components. Figure 6.2 shows the regression of the general familiarity component scores on typicality for the Grade 12 faces; Figure 6.3 depicts the similar regression with the memorability component scores.[2]

In a subsequent experiment in Vokey and Read (1992), the same faces were used as targets and distracters in a recognition task. Figure 6.4 depicts the recognition discrimination for these faces as a function of the earlier typicality ratings, and shows the standard result for typicality: namely, that recognition discrimination drops as function of increasing typicality, from a very high logistic-d' of over 4.5 for the least typical face to a low average of virtually no discrimination at all (i.e. logistic-d' = 0) for the faces previously rated as the most typical. The key issue,

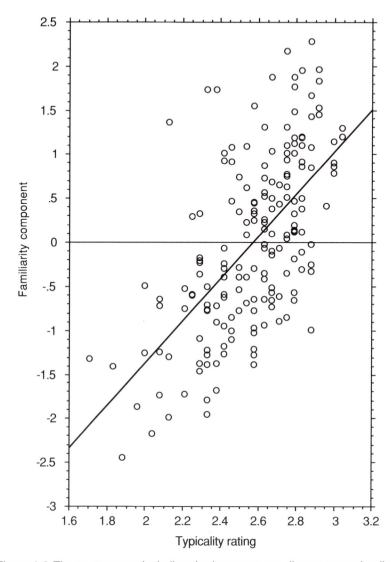

Figure 6.2 The scattergram including the least-squares, linear regression line of the regression of the familiarity component on typicality ratings for the Grade 12 face set from Experiment 1 of Vokey and Read (1992)

of course, is how this recognition discrimination relates to the putative mediators of the effect of typicality, general familiarity and memorability. Figure 6.5 shows the regression of recognition discrimination on the familiarity component scores. As can be seen, and as expected, recognition discrimination falls as a function of increasing general familiarity, but only at about one-half the rate of that shown for typicality. The

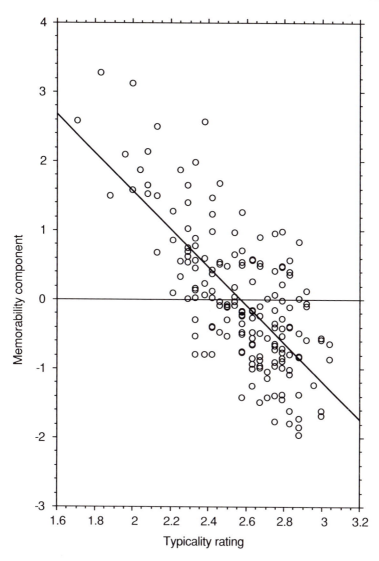

Figure 6.3 The scattergram including the least-squares, linear regression line of the regression of the memorability component on typicality ratings for the Grade 12 face set from Experiment 2 of Vokey and Read (1992)

other half is shown in Figure 6.6, which depicts the regression of recognition discrimination on the memorability component. Here, as expected, recognition discrimination increases as a function of increasing memorability. Figure 6.7 shows the regression on typicality of the residual recognition discrimination after the effects of the two components have been removed. As can be seen, there is no residual effect of typicality;

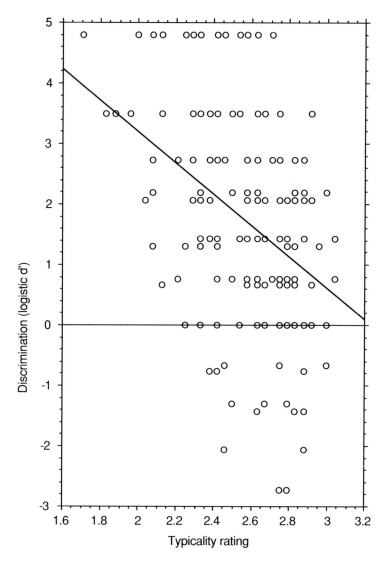

Figure 6.4 The scattergram including the least-squares, linear regression line of the regression of recognition discrimination (logistic d') on typicality ratings for the Grade 12 face set from Experiment 2 of Vokey and Read (1992)

its effect on recognition discrimination is accounted for completely by the simple additive effects of the general familiarity and memorability components working in opposition. These results have since been replicated by O'Toole *et al.* (1994) in a provocative extension of this work (see also O'Toole *et al.*, Chapter 8, this volume).

Two further results from the Vokey and Read (1992) experiments not

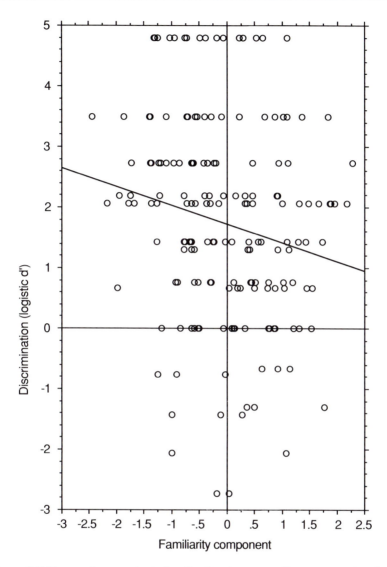

Figure 6.5 The scattergram including the least-squares, linear regression line of the regression of recognition discrimination (logistic d') on the familiarity component for the Grade 12 face set from Experiment 2 of Vokey and Read (1992)

shown in the preceding figures should be noted. First, the effect of the familiarity component was found strictly on false alarms, as suggested by the single-factor familiarity explanation for the typicality effect on the recognition discrimination of faces; variations in context-free familiarity had no effect on hits. Second, although there was an effect of memorability on hits, as expected by the single-factor encoding distinctiveness

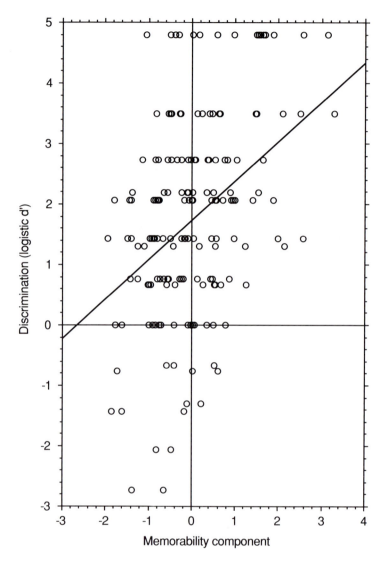

Figure 6.6 The scattergram including the least-squares, linear regression line of the regression of recognition discrimination (logistic d') on the memorability component for the Grade 12 face set from Experiment 2 of Vokey and Read (1992)

and retrieval explanation of the typicality effect, the bulk of the effect of the memorability component was also on false alarms; the primary effect of memorability, as anticipated by the memorability hypothesis of Brown *et al.* (1977), is to increase recognition discrimination by reducing false alarms to highly memorable faces. Thus, although the effect of memor-

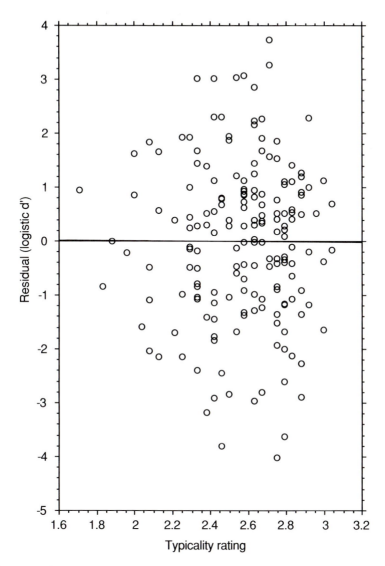

Figure 6.7 The scattergram including the least-squares, linear regression line of the regression on the typicality ratings of the residual recognition discrimination (logistic d') after the linear effects of the two components have been taken into account for the Grade 12 face set from Experiment 2 of Vokey and Read (1992)

ability is undoubtedly a retrieval-*time* phenomenon, only a small part (but a part often large enough to provide for the increased hits required by the other half of the mirror effect) of its effect would appear to be a function of enhanced encoding and subsequent increased retrieval of memorable targets.

ATTRACTIVENESS AS MEMORABILITY AND GENERAL FAMILIARITY

At least since Galton (1878) first presented his demonstration of and reasoning for the attractiveness of composite or averaged faces, facial attractiveness has been linked with the natural structure of faces, with average or typical faces being seen as more attractive than atypical faces. Recent work using computer-processed, digitized images has confirmed the attractiveness of facial composites or averages (Langlois and Roggman, 1990; Perrett *et al.*, 1994), and other work has shown that attractive faces are indeed rated as more typical (Light *et al.*, 1981). Most discussions of this phenomenon from Galton to the present day are couched in terms of it being a predictable or natural consequence of evolution and natural selection favouring non-deviant (or typical) mate choices (e.g. Perrett *et al.*, 1994), although others also stress that such a result is expected as an equally natural consequence of everyday cognitive processing favouring as attractive that which is high in structurally-induced familiarity (Light *et al.*, 1981; Langlois and Roggman, 1990). Thus, from both perspectives, attractiveness would be expected to track typicality quite closely. It follows that it would also be expected to evince similar relationships as those of typicality with other judgements that subjects are asked to make about faces, such as recognition. Light *et al.* (1981) reported that the rated attractiveness of faces is positively related to their rated typicality and, as with typicality, negatively related to their recognizability. In fact, Light *et al.* (1981) argued that the effects of attractiveness on recognition were mediated by typicality because they found no further contribution to facial recognition than that accounted for by typicality (or inter-item similarity). Accordingly, it is to be expected that attractiveness ratings should inherit many of the structural relationships, such as general familiarity and memorability, that we have shown to mediate the effects of typicality.

However, it is unlikely that facial attractiveness, and hence its relationship with recognition, are as simple as attractiveness being a proxy for typicality. First, although it is undoubtedly the case that average or typical faces are attractive, there is evidence that *highly attractive* faces are not average, and presumably not typical (see Alley and Cunningham, 1991; Perrett *et al.*, 1994). Second, along with unattractive faces, folk wisdom suggests that highly attractive faces should be easy to remember, rather than difficult to remember as suggested by the notion that the greater the attractiveness, the greater the typicality. The expectation from folk wisdom is that the relationship between facial attractiveness and accuracy of recognition may be described as U-shaped (i.e. positive quadratic), with faces of moderate or average attractiveness being relatively *more* difficult to remember than either very attractive or very unattractive faces.

Just such a result was reported by Shepherd and Ellis (1973) for recognition following a long, thirty-five-day delay, although shorter delays in the range common to most face recognition research showed no such effect, nor have many other studies. Light *et al.* (1981), for example, explicitly looked for a positive quadratic relationship between recognizability and attractiveness, but found it to be linear throughout their range of attractiveness ratings.

One possible explanation for the only rare appearance of a positive quadratic relationship of recognizability with attractiveness may be that most test sets contain few, highly attractive faces, so that all that can be observed is the left half or negatively sloped leg of the quadratic function. Another possibility is that the U-shaped function anticipated in folk wisdom may be related to only one of the two components mediating the effect of typicality, namely, memorability, which overlays the effect of decreasing recognizability with increased attractiveness that occurs as a function of the familiarity component. If so, then depending on the precise mixture of highly attractive, average and unattractive faces, the effects of the familiarity component on recognition could mask or prevent detection of the quadratic function related to the memorability component. Furthermore, if the quadratic relation is strictly a function of the memorability component, then it may also provide an explanation for the Shepherd and Ellis (1973) finding of a positive quadratic function between recognizability and attractiveness only with long delays. Given that one aspect of the effect of the memorability component is to enhance the retrieval of targets, it may be that a long delay is needed to reveal this effect against the background of enhanced response to all targets due to a temporary and slowly fading increase in their specific familiarity.

Regardless of the precise mechanisms, these speculations suggest that it should be possible to decompose attractiveness into the same two components as typicality, and that it should evince a similar positive relationship with the general familiarity component; however, with the memorability component, rather than the negative relationship found with typicality, attractiveness might demonstrate the U-shaped function suggested by folk wisdom. That is to say, typicality and attractiveness probably share the same structural mediators, but reflect their effects differently. We investigate these relationships using the data for the Grade 12 face set from Experiments 1 and 2 of Vokey and Read (1992).

Figure 6.8 shows the quadratic polynomial regression of the familiarity component on attractiveness. As can be seen, the familiarity component bears a strong, positive linear relationship with attractiveness, very similar to that with typicality. It also bears, however, a slight but significant *negative* quadratic component relationship with attractiveness: the strong, positive trend weakens at the high end of the attractiveness scale. Figure 6.9 depicts the quadratic polynomial regression of the memorability component on attractiveness. In this case, unlike the results for typicality, there was no significant negative linear relationship or, for that matter, any linear trend whatsoever. Rather, the whole of the effect was found in a significant positive quadratic trend: on average, both the extremes of attractiveness scored high on the memorability component, with faces of moderate or average attractiveness scoring low, just as anticipated by folk wisdom.

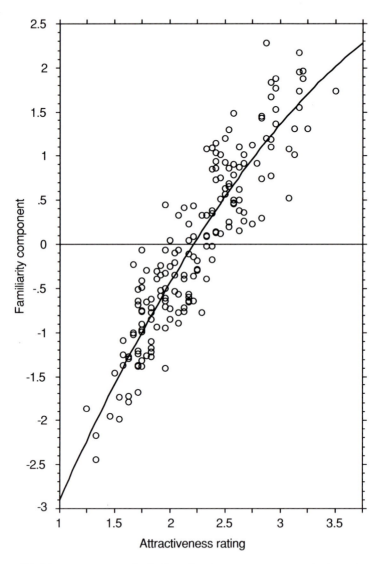

Figure 6.8 The scattergram including the least-squares, quadratic polynomial regression line of the regression of the familiarity component on attractiveness ratings for the Grade 12 face set from Experiment 1 of Vokey and Read (1992)

Figure 6.10 shows the quadratic polynomial regression of recognition discrimination on attractiveness. Although clearly not as robust a relationship as that with typicality (cf. Figure 6.4), as expected from the regressions of the components, recognition discrimination bore both a significant negative linear trend (similar to, although weaker than that

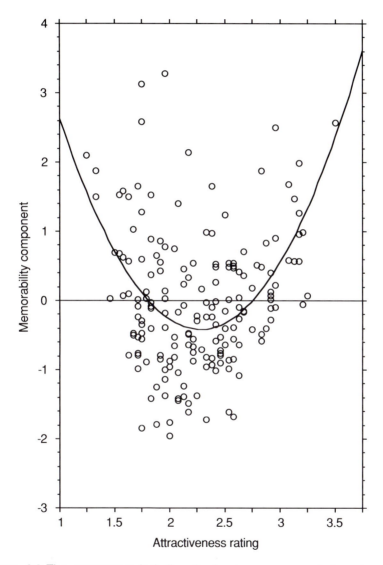

Figure 6.9 The scattergram including the least-squares, quadratic polynomial regression line of the regression of the memorability component on attractiveness ratings for the Grade 12 face set from Experiment 1 of Vokey and Read (1992)

with typicality) and a significant positive quadratic trend with attractiveness. Aside from vindicating the expectations of folk psychology, this last result provides one of the few demonstrations of this effect in the literature. The only other one we are aware of is that in a monograph by Sporer (1992).

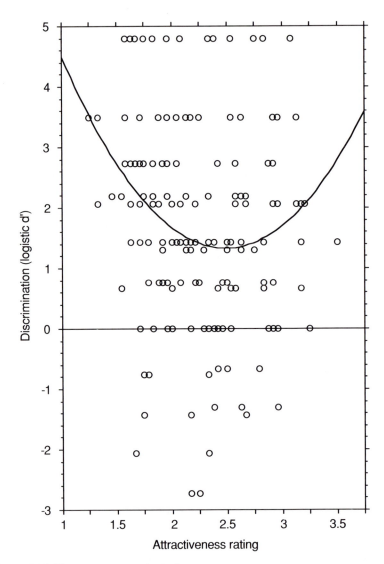

Figure 6.10 The scattergram including the least-squares, quadratic polynomial regression line of the regression of recognition discrimination (logistic d') on attractiveness ratings for the Grade 12 face set from Experiment 2 of Vokey and Read (1992)

The remaining question is whether the two components provide a complete account of the effects of attractiveness on recognition discrimination. Figure 6.11 shows the regression on attractiveness of the residual recognition discrimination after the effects of the two components have been removed. These are the same residuals that were previously regressed on typicality (see Figure 6.7). As with typicality, there is no residual effect of attractiveness; despite its different and somewhat complicated relationship with the components, the effect of attractiveness on recognition discrimination is accounted for completely by the simple additive effects of the general familiarity and memorability components.

GENERAL VIEW

The main point of this chapter was to demonstrate the utility and generality of a two-component model of the effects of natural structure on the recognition of faces. The point was *not* to provide a model of face recognition; indeed, as is apparent in any of the figures in this chapter that include recognition discrimination, the bulk of the recognition data is left unaccounted for, presumably reflecting at least in part the specific familiarity arising from exposure as targets that is the focus of so much memory research. What we have done is to provide a complete account of the effects of structure on recognition, at least as indexed by people's judgements of typicality and attractiveness. Still, we believe the approach taken here has much in common with the broader memory research. Already mentioned are such memory phenomena as the mirror effect and concepts such as Brown *et al.*'s (1977) memorability hypothesis, and recognition models such as Hintzman's (1986; 1988) Minerva II. Other phenomena and models could be mentioned, but the obvious link is with dual process theories of recognition such as those of Atkinson and Joula (1974); Gillund and Schiffrin (1984); Mandler (1980; 1991), or Jacoby (e.g. Jacoby and Dallas, 1981), or with any of the more recent attempts to divide memory performance into aware (or intentional) and unaware (or unintentional or automatic) component processes (e.g. Jacoby, 1991), although we do not believe that the distinction between aware and unaware component processes maps directly on to the memorability and general familiarity components we have described here.

For our way of thinking, however, the most useful connection is with those approaches and models that have attempted to forge a link between structural learning and recognition memory, particularly those that attribute the whole of the effects to a distributed or exemplar- (or episode-) based memory system (e.g. Brooks, 1978; 1987; Jacoby and Brooks, 1984; Whittlesea, 1987; Vokey and Brooks, 1992). Such models suggest two mechanisms for the influence of structure on recognition and classification without requiring that the structure itself be abstractly represented.

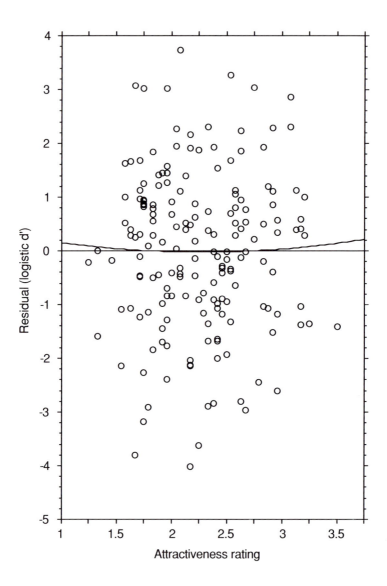

Figure 6.11 The scattergram including the least-squares, quadratic polynomial regression line of the regression on the attractiveness ratings of the residual recognition discrimination (logistic d') after the linear effects of the two components have been taken into account for the Grade 12 face set from Experiment 2 of Vokey and Read (1992)

The first of these mechanisms is a form of retrieval time pooling or 'chorus of instances' such as that given by the 'echo' in Hintzman's (1986; 1988) Minerva II, the summed similarity in Nosofsky's (1986) Generalized Context Model, and the 'computing norms on the fly' of Kahneman and Miller's (1986) Norm Theory. We suspect that something like this ganged retrieval of multiple instances (drawn from a lifetime of experience of such instances) when presented with a face at test is the source of the general familiarity component. In terms of face space, we would thus expect this component to be related to such geometrical measures as average distance (to all exemplars of the set) and distance from the average or prototypical face (of the set being interrogated). As such, if the face space is constructed from multidimensional featural descriptions (as in Bruce et al., 1994; Chapter 7, this volume) or pixel maps (as in O'Toole et al., 1994; Chapter 8, this volume), we would also expect the familiarity component to be related to the lower-order (i.e. first few eigenvectors or principal components) dimensions of covariation in this space – a result recently confirmed by O'Toole et al. (1994; Chapter 8, this volume).

The second mechanism, first proposed by Brooks (1978) as an explanation for structural effects in the absence of some central abstraction, is the retrieval of a similar or analogous specific prior instance in response to a test instance as the basis of responding. All of the models just cited, as well as parallel distributed memory models (e.g. McClelland and Rummelhart, 1985; Gluck and Bower, 1988; Whittlesea, 1988), have this additional characteristic of non-linear generalization gradients around prior instances so that the memory for a specific instance that is highly similar to the current probe can have a disproportionately large effect on the output of the memory system. In this way, memory for a specific item highly similar to the probe or test item can have strong effects on categorical and recognition judgements regardless of whether or not the probe is also similar to the average properties of the set; that is, regardless of whether or not the face, in this case, is also generally familiar (see Vokey and Brooks, 1992, for a similar argument concerning the learning of artificial grammars). We suspect that some such mechanism is responsible for the memorability component, although we would elaborate on it to include in the subject's judgement processes the *failure* to retrieve any specific prior instance as evidence that the specific test instance had not been encountered previously, as a way of countering false alarms that otherwise would be generated on the basis of general familiarity. Accordingly, again, if the face space is constructed from multidimensional featural descriptions or pixel maps, we would expect the memorability component to be related to the *higher*-order or individuating dimensions of covariation in this space – a result recently also confirmed by O'Toole et al. (1994; Chapter 8, this volume).

AUTHORS' NOTE

This chapter is based on a talk of the same title presented at The International Conference on Face Processing, 21 September 1993, in Cardiff, Wales. We thank Ms Janine Weir and Ms Lorna Moore whose assistance at various stages of this work has been invaluable. This work was funded in part by Natural Sciences and Engineering Research Council of Canada operating grants to each of the authors, and by funding from the University of Lethbridge Research Fund to the first author.

NOTES

1 Asking subjects for relatively pure judgements of general familiarity turns out to be more difficult than it might at first appear. Asked too generally, it becomes equivalent to a typicality rating, whereas asked too narrowly it becomes tantamount to a recognition judgement. Measures, such as false alarm rate when used as distracters, clearly reflect general familiarity, but also would be expected to be influenced to a large degree by memorability. Of the methods we have used, the most successful (Vokey and Read, 1992) has been to use completely unfamiliar faces, but to imply to the subjects that some of the faces should be familiar to them as fellow students from their classes and around campus. To provide a plausible explanation to the subjects as to why none of the faces strikes them as particularly familiar (as would be expected if they were actual classmates), we used photographs of the targets as high school students, many as far back as when the individual depicted was in Grade 10, in the hope that the subjects would attribute the relatively low level of specific familiarity of all the faces to that factor, rather than rejecting all of the faces as simply too unfamiliar. Any misrecognitions under these circumstances, then, would appear to a relatively direct measure of general or context-free familiarity, but even then would be expected to be sensitive only to the extremes. For this reason, we rarely rely on a single measure of general familiarity, preferring to extract it as the latent component of a positive manifold of multiple measures such as typicality, attractiveness, likeability, and the just described misrecognition variable to fix the orientation of the component vector among them. Other more indirect measures, such as perceptual identification or reaction time to identify as a face versus non- (or scrambled) face are plausible candidates, although we have not attempted them.

2 As similar structural relationships were evinced with the Grade 10 face set (see Vokey and Read, 1992), subsequent discussion is limited to presenting the results for the Grade 12 face set only.

REFERENCES

Alley, T. R. and Cunningham, M. R. (1991) Averaged faces are attractive, but very attractive faces are not average. *Psychological Science, 2,* 123–125.

Atkinson, R. C. and Joula, J. F. (1974) Search and decision processes in recognition memory, in D. H. Krantz, R. C. Atkinson, R. D. Luce and P. Suppes (eds), *Contemporary Developments in Mathematical Psychology: Vol. 1. Learning, Memory and Thinking.* San Francisco, California: Freeman.

Bartlett, J. C., Hurry, S. and Thorley, W. (1984) Typicality and familiarity of faces.

Memory and Cognition, 12, 219–228.

Brooks, L. R. (1978) Non-analytic concept formation and memory for instances, in E. Rosch and B. Lloyd (eds), *Cognition and Concepts*. Hillsdale, NJ: Erlbaum.

Brooks, L. R. (1987) Decentralized control of categorization: the role of prior processing episodes, in U. Neisser (ed.), *Concepts and Conceptual Development: Ecological and Intellectual Factors in Categorization*. Cambridge, England: Cambridge University Press.

Brown, J., Lewis, V. J. and Monk, A. F. (1977) Memorability, word frequency and negative recognition. *Quarterly Journal of Experimental Psychology*, 29, 461–473.

Bruce, V., Burton, A. M. and Dench, N. (1994) What's distinctive about a distinctive face? *Quarterly Journal of Experimental Psychology*, 47A, 119–141.

Cohen, M. E. and Carr, W. J. (1975) Facial recognition and the von Restorff effect. *Bulletin of the Psychonomic Society*, 6, 383–384.

Courtois, M. R. and Mueller, J. H. (1981) Target and distractor typicality in facial recognition. *Journal of Applied Psychology*, 66, 639–645.

Galton, F. (1878) Composite portraits. *Journal of the Anthropological Institute of Great Britain and Ireland*, 8, 132–142.

Gillund, G. and Shiffrin, R. M. (1984) A retrieval model for both recognition and recall. *Psychological Review*, 91, 1–67.

Glanzer, M. and Adams, J. K. (1985) The mirror effect in recognition memory. *Memory and Cognition*, 13, 8–20.

Glanzer, M. and Adams, J. K. (1990) The mirror effect in recognition memory: data and theory. *Journal of Experimental Psychology: Learning, Memory and Cognition*, 16, 5–16.

Gluck, M. A. and Bower, G. H. (1988) Evaluating an adaptive network model of human learning. *Cognitive Psychology*, 27, 166–195.

Going, M. and Read, J. D. (1974) The effect of uniqueness, sex of subject, and sex of photograph on facial recognition. *Perceptual and Motor Skills*, 39, 109–110.

Hintzman, D. L. (1986) 'Schema abstraction' in a multiple-trace memory model. *Psychological Review*, 93, 411–428.

Hintzman, D. L. (1988) Judgments of frequency and recognition memory in a multiple-trace memory model. *Psychological Review*, 95, 528–551.

Hintzman, D. L. (1994) On explaining the mirror effect. *Journal of Experimental Psychology: Learning, Memory and Cognition*, 20, 201–205.

Hintzman, D. L., Caulton, D. A. and Curran, T. (1994) Retrieval constraints and the mirror effect. *Journal of Experimental Psychology: Learning, Memory and Cognition*, 20, 275–289.

Jacoby, L. L. (1991) A process dissociation framework: separating automatic from intentional uses of memory. *Journal of Memory and Language*, 30, 513–541.

Jacoby, L. L. and Brooks, L. R. (1984) Nonanalytic cognition: memory, perception and concept formation. *Psychology of Learning and Motivation*, 18, 1–47.

Jacoby, L. L. and Dallas, M. (1981) On the relationship between autobiographical memory and perceptual learning. *Journal of Experimental Psychology: General*, 110, 306–340.

Kahneman, D. and Miller , D. T. (1986) Norm theory: Comparing reality to its alternatives. *Psychological Review*, 93, 136–153.

Langlois, J. H. and Roggman, L. A. (1990) Attractive faces are only average. *Psychological Science*, 1, 115–121.

Light, L. L., Hollander, S. and Kayra-Stuart, F. (1981) Why attractive people are harder to remember. *Personality and Social Psychology Bulletin*, 7, 269–276.

Light, L. L., Kayra-Stuart, F. and Hollander, S. (1979) Recognition memory for typical and unusual faces. *Journal of Experimental Psychology: Human Learning and Memory,* 5, 212–228.

McClelland, J. L. and Rummelhart, D. E. (1985) Distribute memory and the representation of general and specific information. *Journal of Experimental Psychology: General,* 114, 159–188.

Mandler, G. (1980) Recognizing: the judgment of previous occurrence. *Psychological Review,* 87, 252–271.

Mandler, G. (1991) Your face looks familiar but I can't remember your name: a review of dual process theory, in W. E. Hockley and S. Lewandowsky (eds), *Relating Theory and Data: Essays on Human Memory in Honor of Bennet B. Murdock.* Hillsdale, NJ: Erlbaum.

Meuller, J. H., Heesacker, M. and Ross, M. J. (1984) Likability of targets and distractors in facial recognition. *American Journal of Psychology,* 97, 235–247.

Nosofsky, R. M. (1986) Attention, similarity, and the identification–categorization relationship. *Journal of Experimental Psychology: General,* 115, 39–57.

Nosofsky, R. M. (1989) Further tests of an exemplar-similarity approach to relating identification and categorization. *Perception and Psychophysics,* 45, 279–290.

O'Toole, A. J., Deffenbacher, K. A., Valentin, D. and Abdi, H. (1994) Structural aspects of face recognition and the other-race effect. *Memory and Cognition,* 22, 208–224.

Perrett, D. J., May, K. A. and Yoshikawa, S. (1994) Facial shape and judgements of female attractiveness. *Nature,* 368, 239–242.

Rosch, E. (1973) Natural categories. *Cognitive Psychology,* 4, 328–350.

Rosch, E. and Mervis, C. B. (1975) Family resemblances: studies in the internal structure of categories. *Cognitive Psychology,* 7, 573–605.

Rosch, E., Simpson, C. and Miller, S. (1976) Structural bases of typicality effects. *Journal of Experimental Psychology: Human Perception and Performance,* 2, 491–502.

Shepherd, J. W. and Ellis, H. D. (1973) The effect of attractiveness on recognition memory for faces. *American Journal of Psychology,* 86, 627–633.

Sporer, S. L. (1992) *Das Wiedererkennan von Gesichtern.* Weinheim: Psychologie Verlags Union.

Valentine, T. (1991) A unified account of the effects of distinctiveness, inversion and race on face recognition. *Quarterly Journal of Experimental Psychology,* 43A, 161–204.

Valentine, T. and Bruce, V. (1986) Recognizing familiar faces: the role of distinctiveness and familiarity. *Canadian Journal of Psychology,* 40, 300–305.

Valentine, T. and Endo, M. (1992) Towards an exemplar model of face processing: the effects of race and distinctiveness. *Quarterly Journal of Experimental Psychology,* 44A, 671–703.

Vokey, J. R. and Brooks, L. R. (1992) Salience of item knowledge in learning artificial grammars. *Journal of Experimental Psychology: Learning, Memory and Cognition,* 18, 328–344.

Vokey, J. R. and Read, J. D. (1988) Typicality, familiarity and the recognition of male and female faces. *Canadian Journal of Psychology,* 42, 480–495.

Vokey, J. R. and Read, J. D. (1992) Familiarity, memorability and the effect of typicality on the recognition of faces. *Memory and Cognition,* 20, 291–302.

Whittlesea, B. W. A. (1987) Preservation of specific experiences in the representation of general knowledge. *Journal of Experimental Psychology: Learning, Memory and Cognition,* 13, 3–17.

Whittlesea, B. W. A. (1988) Selective attention, variable processing and distributed representation: preserving particular experiences of general structures, in R. G. M. Morris (ed.), *Parallel Distributed Processing: Implications for Psychology and Neurobiology.* Oxford, England: Oxford University Press.

Winograd, E. (1981) Elaboration and distinctiveness in memory for faces. *Journal of Experimental Psychology: Human Learning and Memory, 7,* 181–190.

Wittgenstein, L. (1953) *Philosophical Investigations.* Oxford, England: Basil Blackwell and Mott.

Chapter 7

Missing dimensions of distinctiveness

Vicki Bruce, A. Mike Burton and Peter J. Hancock

INTRODUCTION

A number of chapters in this volume describe how the psychological variable of rated 'typicality' or 'distinctiveness' of faces has reliable effects on how well faces can be remembered, and how easily different kinds of decision (e.g. is this a face? is this a familiar face?) can be made about faces (see Johnston and Ellis, Chapter 1, and Valentine *et al.*, Chapter 4). Tim Valentine (1991) describes how such effects can be accommodated within a framework where faces are represented within a psychological 'space' of variation, whose dimensions correspond to different salient physical dimensions along which faces vary. In Valentine's model, typical face exemplars cluster around the origins of the space and distinctive exemplars are located in sparsely populated distant regions of the space.

The face space framework has proved very useful in accounting for a variety of apparently rather disparate phenomena in the literature on face recognition, for example, the effects of race, and face inversion as well as distinctiveness (e.g. Valentine, 1991). However, the question of the nature of the dimensions which form the basis of the space has been relatively neglected. Valentine and Endo (1992) assume that 'any attribute which can serve to discriminate faces would form a dimension of the space', implying that any dimension along which faces vary, if visible, would be represented in the space. Such a view would imply that colour, texture, 3D shape and even more complex derived characteristics such as apparent age could form dimensions of the space.

In this chapter we first consider what is known about the representations which subserve face recognition in order to think about the possible nature of the dimensions of face space. We then go on to describe attempts to correlate the physical deviation of faces with the psychological variable of distinctiveness.

DIFFERENT SCHEMES FOR REPRESENTING FACES

Faces as pictures

In the psychological as well as the computer science literature there has been a tendency to treat the face as though it were a two-dimensional picture, within which key points or edges can be located and measured. Brennan's automatic caricature generator (Brennan, 1985; Rhodes *et al.*, 1987) represents faces in this way, and several attempts have been made to build automatic face retrieval systems by storing face images as sets of measurements, such as length of nose, distance between eyes, width of eyebrows, or ratios derived from such measurements. What we will here call the 'picture-based' approach is distinguished from other approaches to face image representation by the fact that neither the texture nor the pigmentation of the face is captured intrinsically by the measures made (although it might be coded separately in a forensic retrieval system such as the 'FRAME' system described by Shepherd, 1986), and that the three-dimensional shape of the face is not coded explicitly, although it might be reflected in some of the 2D measurements; for example, full lips might have a wider measured 2D thickness than thin lips.

A 'pictorial' approach which discards surface texture and colour, and codes 3D shape only implicitly from visible 2D features, appears to provide a remarkably good account of how we recognize basic level objects (Biederman, 1987; Hummel and Biederman, 1992). Moreover, such a system builds upon the kind of 'primal sketch' level representation that has been thought to be derived by early visual processing (e.g. Marr and Hildreth, 1980). Basic-level categorization of objects is accurate from line-drawings, and is affected rather little by surface texture or colour (Biederman and Ju, 1988; Price and Humphreys, 1989).

However, it can easily be demonstrated that the same is not true of face recognition. A simple outline drawing of a face – however detailed – is not a good representation for face recognition. Davies *et al.* (1978) compared the recognition of photographs of famous faces with the recognition of outline drawings obtained by tracing the face features, wrinkles and other prominent surface marks on the faces. Identification of the line-drawings was extremely poor (47 per cent) compared with that of the original images (90 per cent). It is not simply that drawings convey too little information for within-category discrimination. Black and white drawings of faces can be recognized well if information about the relative pattern of dark and light is preserved. If, in addition to tracing contours from the original image, relatively dark regions of the image are filled in as black areas in the drawing, identification of the drawings can be nearly as accurate as photographs (Bruce *et al.*, 1992). It appears that representations for face recognition need to convey information about the pigmentation and/or the shading of the face to be fully effective.

The dramatic effect that photographic negation has on face identification (e.g. Galper, 1970; Phillips, 1972) also suggests that recognition must be based upon more than just the simple layout of facial features, since this remains the same whether faces are shown in positive or negative versions. In recent data of our own we have found that recognition of famous faces which was almost perfect when shown in positive images (95 per cent correct) dropped to only 55 per cent correct when the same faces were shown in photographic negative (Bruce and Langton, 1994). Negation may have its effects because it reverses normal pigmentation values (e.g. a light-skinned person with black hair will appear to be a dark-skinned person with light hair) and also inverts patterns of shading in a way which is not interpretable as the actual surface shape even if lit from a different direction.

Changes in direction of lighting can disrupt the recognition and matching of faces (Johnston *et al.*, 1992; Hill and Bruce, 1994). Johnston *et al.* (1992) showed that familiar faces were more difficult to recognize when illuminated from below than from above, and Hill and Bruce showed that the accuracy of matching two different images of the same person's head (with hair concealed) was reduced when one of the images showed a face lit from above and another showed a face lit from below. This decrement in matching was observed even when the two images showed faces in coincident, profile views, where the invariant shape of the occluding contour could have been used to determine that the two images were of the same person.

Finally, in an extensive project of research investigating what information people used to decide whether (caucasian) faces were male or female, we found it difficult to account for a variety of data by assuming that the visual system used only simple 2D measures and ratios (Bruce *et al.*, 1993b; Burton *et al.*, 1993). In our project, a set of 185 photographs of young adult (clean-shaven) males and females were obtained, in which hair was concealed with a swimming cap. We found that subjects were 96 per cent correct at deciding whether these faces were of males or females. We then asked two related questions. First, by comparing how well different kinds of measurements could discriminate the two sets of faces, we asked what information *could* be used to distinguish male from female faces. Second, by observing the effects on sex discrimination accuracy of reducing or concealing information of different types from the face, we enquired what information *is* used by the human visual system to make this discrimination. These two investigations need not necessarily yield the same answers. For example, the average size of head is a good discriminator between male and female faces, but we can show that accuracy of sex discrimination performance is not affected when this cue cannot be used.

On the whole, we obtained converging answers to these two questions. To produce discriminant function analyses which differentiated the two sets of faces as accurately as humans, we found it necessary to incorporate measures of the 3D shape of the faces in addition to simple 2D distances and ratios. Measures which discriminate male from female faces are diverse and include the width and separation of the eyebrows, the 3D protruberance of the nose and cheeks, and the shape of the mouth. If the 3D shapes of 'average' male and female surfaces are compared, the surface of the male protrudes more, relative to the female, in the regions of the brow, nose and chin, and the female protrudes more in the region of the cheeks (Bruce *et al.,* 1993b). Human vision also appears to make use of a complex set of 2D and 3D measures. When different parts of photographs of faces are concealed with masks, performance degrades gracefully rather than catastrophically, suggesting that it does not depend on a single critical region. Moreover, when only information about the overall layout of the face in 2D and 3D is evident by showing face surface images derived from optical scanning (see Figure 7.1), performance is reasonably accurate in angled views which reveal most about the 3D structure of the face (see Table 7.1(a)), though it drops substantially if full face images are shown (Bruce *et al.,* 1993b).

It therefore appears that the dimensions which account for our discrimination between different individual faces, or between different classes of faces (e.g. males from females) include more than can be obtained by making measurements on a simple 'sketch' of a face.

Faces as surfaces

One possible alternative for the representation of faces, that has received little attention in the literature, is that the descriptions of structure which mediate face recognition describe the 3D as well as the 2D layout of the face surface. In such a representation, things such as the protruberance of a region (e.g. the bridge of the nose) would be coded in addition to 2D distances such as the distance between the eyebrows. On this view, simple line-drawings, or photographic negative images of faces, would be poor vehicles for recognition because they have discarded, or distorted, all information about shading and shadow which might be used by the visual system to derive 3D structure.

The idea that 3D shape is represented explicitly in the description which mediates recognition has been quite common in some approaches to object recognition (e.g. Marr and Nishihara, 1978), and the primitives which have formed the suggested building blocks of such representations have generally been volumetric primitives such as generalized cones. Such volumetric primitives seem rather inappropriate for describing the 3D shapes of faces (though see Pentland, 1986). In a recent project carried out in collaboration with researchers at University College London (e.g. Bruce *et al.*, 1993a) we investigated a surface-based descriptive scheme. The UCL team developed a laser range-finder for measuring the 3D surface of the human head, in order to acquire and analyse data before and after corrective facial surgery. The scanner records the 3D locations of a set of some 20,000 points on the surface of the face, and these points can be connected to form a wire-frame mesh and displayed using a simple lighting model (see Linney, 1992, for a full description).

Coombes *et al.* (1991) have developed a method of describing the surface of the face as a set of patches of different surface types (cf. Besl and Jain,

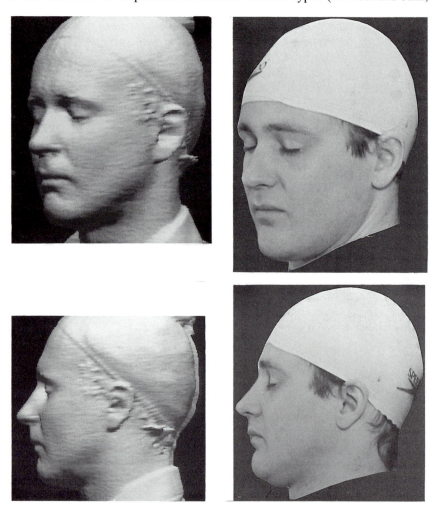

Figure 7.1 Surface images, based on laser scanning (left) and photographs of the same person taken under the same conditions as the laser scan (right)

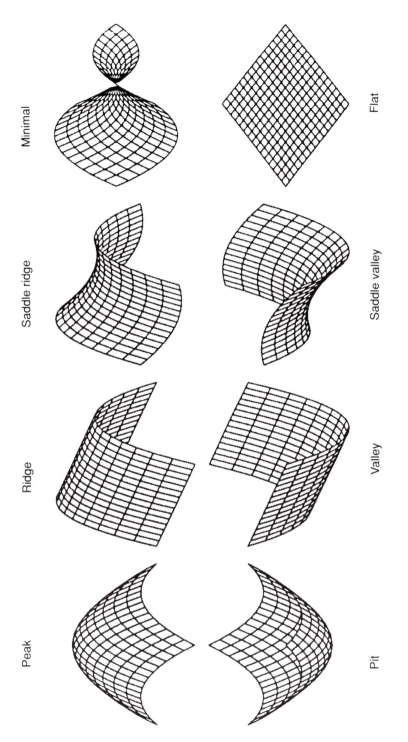

Figure 7.2 The eight fundamental surface types into which patches of surface can be classified on the basis of their curvatures

1988) defined by the surface curvatures (Gaussian and mean curvatures) at each point on the surface. Any region of surface can be classified as one of eight fundamental surface types depending upon the values of the surface curvatures at that point. The eight surface types are peak, pit, ridge, valley, saddle ridge, saddle valley, minimal and flat surfaces (see Figure 7.2). Different threshold values can be set for the Gaussian and mean curvatures so that at one extreme only the most curved parts of the face are described and, as the threshold is altered, so the less curved features are detected.

If the visual system describes face surfaces in the way captured by this classification into surface types, then we would expect to find a correlation between surface properties of the face and perceptual classification. Bruce *et al.* (1993a) provided some preliminary evidence for this. We asked a series of observers to decide whether pairs of surface images of heads were identical, or had slightly different nose shapes. Images of two different people's heads were shown in the course of the experiment, and we found people were considerably more accurate with one of the two heads used in the experiment than with the other. A description of the surface types and how they changed with variation in nose shape revealed that there was much greater variation in the amounts of different surface types for the head whose differences were easier to see than for the one whose differences were harder to see. This observation, along with some on correlations between surface deviation and face distinctiveness which we describe later, suggests that the human visual system is sensitive to aspects of the face to which the surface descriptive system is also sensitive.

However, while the surface description system may capture some aspects of human face representation, it is not by itself a sufficient account of the representations mediating recognition. Just as outline drawings prove difficult to recognize, so do the surface images obtained by laser measurement. Bruce *et al.* (1991) compared the recognition of familiar faces from laser surface images, with the recognition of photographs of the same people taken with eyes closed and hair concealed (i.e. as in the surface images), and found that recognition of the surface images was much poorer than the recognition of photographs, particularly for female faces (see Table 7.1(b)).

Thus both the pictorial and surface-based accounts of face representation seem to have shortcomings as descriptions of how we represent face identities. Although the surface-based description scheme captures aspects of the 3D structure of the face, it discards information about pigmentation and texture, which seems to play an important role in recognition. At the very least, we would have to articulate a face description scheme in which pigmentation and texture are represented alongside surface structure. However, there may be an alternative way to analyse faces in which information about the 3D shape of the face is captured implicitly via the analysis of image intensities.

Table 7.1   Classification of faces shown as photographs or surface images
(hair concealed for both)

(a) Per cent correct classification of male and female familiar faces as
male/female (chance = 50 per cent)

	View:	Profile		3/4	
	Sex:	male	female	male	female
Format:	surface	88	66	89	86
	photo	89	90	96	95

(b) Per cent correct identification of male and female familiar faces by name
from list of eighteen alternatives

	View:	Profile		3/4	
	Sex:	male	female	male	female
Format:	surface	55	13	73	25
	photo	83	88	85	88

Source: (a) Bruce *et al.*, 1993b; (b) Bruce *et al.*, 1991

Faces as images

An alternative way to conceive of the face representation problem is to
consider image-based schemes. On such schemes the layout of face
features in 2D and 3D is not described explicitly; rather, the face is
encoded and stored as a set of operations on the image intensity values
themselves. Image-based schemes implicitly capture information about
3D structure through shading patterns, as well as 2D layout of face
features.

The archetypal image-based approach to face recognition is that of
Kohonen (e.g. Kohonen *et al.*, 1981), who fed the raw image pixel values
into a large auto-associative neural net. This was capable of learning a
number of faces, and reconstructing them from partial input. The system
has no notion of faceness and could equally well learn an image of
anything else – indeed, it might perform better, since there would be
less overlap with other stored images. A similar pixel-based approach is
taken by WISARD (e.g. Stonham, 1986), which is implemented directly
in hardware. This gives it sufficient capacity and throughput to learn
many examples of each face, thereby achieving a measure of position
invariance.

Most image-based techniques attempt to reduce the volume of data,
typically by pre-processing with an array of local filters. Daugman (1993)
uses pairs of Gabor filters, which have desirable properties from an engineering point of view, and also resemble the sensitivity of cells in primary
visual cortex. The output of the filters forms the representation of the
face on which matching may be performed. This achieves a small measure
of position invariance, since movements much smaller than the scale of

the filter produce little change in response. Full position invariance requires some other intervention, and Daugman uses a template system to locate the eyes and mouth. A similar filtering method is used by von der Malsburg and associates (e.g. Buhmann *et al.*, 1991; see also Fiser *et al.*, 1995), but this system uses a graph-matching procedure to do position and some view independence after the filtering.

These systems are capable of impressive recognition performance, but it is not known whether they fail in the same way as humans do. They work, but may be using a quite different set of features from those used by people, and therefore might find quite different faces 'distinctive'.

The auto-associative technique introduced by Kohonen is formally equivalent to performing a principal components analysis (PCA) on the variations of intensity at different pixels across successive face images. PCA is a standard statistical technique for reducing large data sets, by finding projections through the data space which maximize the variance. Technically, PCA returns the eigenvectors of the correlation matrix of the input data, and the results of applying it to images of faces are therefore sometimes known as eigenfaces. This approach has some appeal as an explicit method for extracting the 'dimensions' from varying face images without requiring that the images be parsed or features measured. Like all pixel-based techniques, there is still a need for help with position invariance, such as aligning by the eyes. Given a set of suitably aligned pictures, the resultant eigenfaces are a set of ghostly images that capture the main components of variation in the image set (see Figure 8.5, Chapter 8, page 175, this volume, for examples of eigenfaces). Typically, the first component appears to have something to do with the presence of hair around the ears and neck. O'Toole *et al.* (1994, and Chapter 8, this volume) found a second component that seemed to relate to the sex of the individual, in face shape as well as hair length. The technique has been used both for face recognition (Cottrell and Fleming, 1990; Turk and Pentland, 1991) and for sex identification (Golomb *et al.*, 1991).

The PCA account raises the interesting possibility that the 'dimensions' of face space might coincide with the principal components of variation extracted from the variations in sets of face images, which has led to investigations of whether the PCA approach can provide a psychologically plausible account of the distinctiveness and memorability of faces. O'Toole *et al.* (Chapter 8, this volume) describe one project, and later in this chapter we discuss some of our own recent data on this.

The difficulty with schemes based entirely upon the analysis of 'raw' images, however, is that methods for separating face from background and for achieving size and position invariance must be considered. In some image analysis systems there is a pre-processing stage where patterns corresponding to faces are extracted from their background by searching for 'face-like' templates (e.g. Turk and Pentland, 1991). Achievement of viewpoint and lighting invariance is also not trivial using image-based schemes, and it is not clear what the best method will be for solving this. Despite these problems, as we will see in the next section, image-based schemes do a reasonably good job of accounting for aspects of human performance data in face recognition.

PHYSICAL BASIS OF FACIAL DISTINCTIVENESS

The discussion above has shown that consideration of the nature of the dimensions of 'face space' raises some quite complex issues. Nevertheless, whatever the nature of these dimensions, we should expect that the measured deviation of faces from average should correlate with their psychological distinctiveness and with their objectively determined memorability.

An unpublished study by Ellis and Shepherd (1987) first attempted to discover a set of physical predictors of the 'memorability' of faces. They used a set of 240 pictures of young adult faces, and for each face obtained an objective measure of its memorability using a distracter-free recognition study. In other work they showed strong correlations between this measure of memorability and distinctiveness (Shepherd et al., 1991).

Seventeen anthropometric measures of 2D dimensions such as nose length and mouth width were available for each of the 240 faces in the set, and it was therefore possible to compute for each face an index of its 'eccentricity' by summing the (unsigned) z-scores across all seventeen dimensions for each face. Thus a face with several dimensions with large deviations from the norm would have a higher sum-of-z-scores than a face whose dimensions were all very similar to the norm. However, the eccentricity scores gave a correlation of only 0.14 with objectively determined memorability, accounting for only a tiny proportion of the variance in these memorability scores.

This result was disappointing, since it implies that *psychological* distinctiveness cannot be captured by straightforward *physical* deviation. However, there are several possible reasons why the Ellis and Shepherd study may have resulted in low correlations (see Bruce et al., 1994 for discussion). The most important one to note here is that the memorability of the faces was assessed from images showing full hairstyles, but the set of seventeen measurements included nothing about hairstyle except hair length. Given the importance of hairstyle in the recognition of unfamiliar faces, it may be that effects of hairstyle have swamped more subtle effects of face variation. In work conducted subsequently (Bruce et al., 1993a; Bruce et al., 1994) we have got around this problem by using faces with no visible hair. Here we will review the results of these investigations.

Preliminary study of surface-based scheme

Bruce *et al.* (1993a) used surface images acquired by laser scanning to see whether faces which were rated as distinctive had more 'deviant' surface types than those rated as more typical in appearance. A set of scans was obtained from eighteen volunteers: nine men and nine women. Surface images derived from these scans were rated for distinctiveness on a ten-point scale by a set of observers, and from these ratings it was possible to select a distinctive male (mean rating 7.2), a distinctive female (7.0), a typical male (4.3) and a typical female (4.3). The male surface images and the female surface images were averaged to provide a composite surface for the 'average' male and 'average' female. We then investigated whether distinctive exemplars deviated more from the average than did typical exemplars. This comparison was made separately for the male and the female exemplars.

To do this, the six sets of surface data (average male/female; distinctive male/female; typical male/female) were encoded into surface types and graphical representations produced to describe the amount (area) of each surface type, at a number of different thresholds. Graphs were produced for three different regions of the face across each of the eight surface types (see Figure 7.3). In several, though not all, of the comparisons there were greater deviations of the distinctive compared with the typical faces from the average. For example, in the region of the lower face, the distinctive faces had less flat surface and more pit surface region than did typical faces.

Across all the comparisons made we were able to show that there was a statistically significant tendency for distinctive exemplars to deviate more from the average than typical exemplars. Although in a way this result might seem somewhat circular – we have merely demonstrated that a face surface that is rated as distinctive is more deviant from average than a less distinctive one – this result should be viewed against the rather negative initial results reported by Ellis and Shepherd. One possibility is that the use of 3D shape measures may give a better handle on distinctiveness than the 2D measurement set used earlier. However, this seemed an unlikely explanation given the compelling demonstrations of automatic caricaturing (see chapters 2 and 3 by Stevenage and Rhodes, this volume) derived entirely from 2D control points. We therefore decided to repeat Ellis and Shepherd's study, with some crucial variations.

Face measurement project

The preliminary study described above suggested that distinctive faces may deviate more overall from the 'average' surface shape than more typical faces. However, this study was limited by the very small number

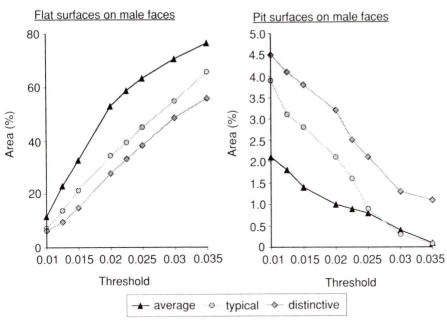

Figure 7.3 Two examples of the analysis of surface types for average, distinctive and typical facial exemplars. The graphs illustrated show analysis of male exemplars for the lower region of the face images. At all threshold levels studied, the distinctive exemplar deviates more from the average than does the typical exemplar for both pit and flat surface types. The direction of this greater deviation is also sensible. The distinctive exemplar shows a greater proportion of pit surface and a lower proportion of flat surface compared with the typical

Source: Bruce *et al.*, 1993a

of heads which had been scanned from which to select 'typical' and 'distinctive' exemplars, necessitated by the very intensive nature of the measurement and description of these faces.

At about the same time as we were analysing the surface shape descriptions of this small sample, we were also collecting a set of measurements made by hand on photographs of a much larger set of individuals (Bruce *et al.*, 1994).

A set of photographs was collected of eighty-nine male and eighty-six female faces, all aged between 18 and 30 years old, without glasses, cosmetics, or facial hair. Photographs were taken simultaneously of these faces from two cameras at the same fixed distance from full face and profile. This enabled measurements made on full face to be co-ordinated with those made on profile so that crude measures of 3D co-ordinates could be obtained. A series of photographs was taken of each subject, including pictures with hair visible, with hair concealed with a swimming cap, and with a series of marks drawn on the face with cosmetic pencil to highlight equivalent points in full face and profile images.

A digitizer was used to recover the co-ordinates of a set of seventy-three points from the full face pictures and thirty-four points from the profiles. Measurements of 2D distances, angles and 3D distances were then derived from these measured points.

The faces were rated for distinctiveness by two sets of subjects. The first set of subjects rated the faces for distinctiveness with hair visible. The second set rated faces with hair concealed. This second set of subjects also provided objective data on the memorability of the faces with their hair concealed. After rating half the faces for distinctiveness, each subject in the second set was then shown all the faces in the set and asked to rate, for each, whether or not they thought they had seen it earlier. This meant that for faces shown with hair concealed, three different measures were obtained: (1) the rated distinctiveness of the face; (2) rated familiarity of the face when it *had* been studied earlier, which we term its 'memorability', and (3) the rated familiarity of the face when it had *not* been studied earlier, which we term its 'context-free familiarity'. The 'memorability' measure reflects the tendency to score a 'hit' to the face in recognition memory, and the context-free familiarity measure reflects the tendency to make a 'false positive' response.

Table 7.2 summarizes the four sets of ratings obtained to the faces, separately for the male and female exemplars. The two sets of distinctiveness ratings are moderately correlated with one another, and each is

Table 7.2 Pearson correlation coefficients between different distinctiveness ratings and memory ratings (r=0.28 is significant at 0.01, 2-tailed)

(a) Female faces

	Distinctiveness ratings		Memory ratings	
	Hair visible	Hair concealed	Memorability	Context-free familiarity
	1	2	3	4
1		0.46	0.37	−0.09
2			0.51	−0.37
3				−0.02

(b) Male faces

	Distinctiveness ratings		Memory ratings	
	Hair visible	Hair concealed	Memorability	Context-free familiarity
	1	2	3	4
1		0.33	0.28	−0.31
2			0.41	−0.46
3				−0.02

Source: Bruce *et al.*, 1994

correlated with the familiarity ratings. Correlations between distinctiveness ratings obtained with hair concealed, and familiarity ratings, are
generally higher than for distinctiveness ratings with hair visible, as we
might expect. Correlations between distinctiveness and memorability are
positive, and those between distinctiveness ratings and context-free familiarity are negative, as expected, and significant except in one case. Table
7.2 reveals a more puzzling finding in addition, however. While ratings of
distinctiveness are correlated positively with memorability, and negatively
with context-free familiarity, the two latter ratings are not correlated one
with another. Thus distinctive faces are easier to remember, and less likely
to be falsely recognized, than typical faces, but there is *zero* correlation
between the tendency of a face to be well remembered when it was
studied, and the tendency for the face to be falsely recognized when it
was not. We have subsequently replicated this pattern of intercorrelations
using a new set of male faces studied with hair visible (Hancock *et al.*, in
preparation).

Although this pattern of intercorrelations is puzzling, it is consistent
with other demonstrations in the literature by Vokey and Read (1993),
and more recently by O'Toole *et al.* (1994) (see Chapter 6 by Vokey and
Read and Chapter 8 by O'Toole *et al.* in this volume). These authors have
obtained sets of ratings of typicality/distinctiveness, memorability and
familiarity to faces and examined their intercorrelations. Vokey and Read
(1992) did not assess memorability and apparent familiarity using a study
test procedure of the kind described here; rather, subjects were asked to
make each of these ratings independently to each face when it was seen
for the first time, i.e. how typical/distinctive does it look; how memorable;
and how familiar (on the pretence that the faces may have been seen
around campus). Examining the pattern of intercorrelations, rated typi-
cality/distinctiveness correlated positively with rated memorability and
negatively with rated familiarity, but there was no correlation between
the memorability and the familiarity ratings. Vokey and Read suggest that
memorability and familiarity represent orthogonal dimensions which
together produce all the effects of the 'typicality' dimension. Moreover,
these two independent components together accounted for variation in
recognition memory performance for the same faces, whether tested in
same or different pictures.

At first glance, such a result seems difficult to reconcile with Valentine's
face space model, since one would expect that a face located in the sparse
regions of face space should be rated as distinctive, be well remembered
when it has been encountered before, and unlikely to be recognized
falsely. Conversely, one located in the dense area of space should be rated
as typical, be difficult to remember correctly but likely to be recognized
falsely. One possible way of accounting for such data is to suggest that it
is variation on some dimensions that accounts for a face's memorability,

and variation on other dimensions that accounts for its apparent familiarity – perhaps memorable faces have idiosyncratic local features, for example. This account is related to that offered by O'Toole *et al.* (1994) and to Vokey and Read (1992). Using the measurements which we had made on the faces we then went on to investigate whether distinctiveness was correlated with the total deviation of the face from average measures, and how well such deviations could account for the separable factors of memorability and context-free familiarity of the faces.

In one set of correlations we used the same set of sixteen '2D' measures[1] which had been used in the earlier study by Ellis and Shepherd (1987). In other correlations we added to these sixteen measurements a further twenty-five measurements which included ratios, angles and 3D distances derived from profile as well as full face views of the faces (see Bruce *et al.*, 1994, for details). We were interested to see whether the inclusion of a more complex set of measurements improved the observed correlations. We computed a total eccentricity score for each measurement set and for each face in the database by adding the modulus z-scores across each of the measurements in the set. We then investigated the correlations between these physical eccentricity scores and our psychological distinctiveness ratings and memory scores.[2]

Table 7.3 shows the table of Pearson correlations between the total deviation scores and each of our measures for male and female faces separately. The first thing to note is that the correlations between physical deviation and rated distinctiveness are quite high and significant when we consider distinctiveness ratings obtained with hair concealed, but much lower to distinctiveness with hair visible. Indeed, the non-significant correlation of only 0.176 between the male distinctiveness ratings with hair, and physical deviation, is comparable to that obtained by Ellis and Shepherd.[3] It seems that to account for any reasonable proportion of the variance in distinctiveness it is much better to exclude aspects of facial appearance which cannot be captured by measurements.

The next thing to note is that adding in a set of measurements additional to the sixteen '2D' distances makes remarkably little difference to the strength of the correlation. This may be because the additional set contributes little, or it may be because the more measures there are added, the more small variations add 'noise' to the overall measure of eccentricity.

To see whether the additional measurements really made a difference to the predictive power of the physical deviations, we conducted multiple linear regressions (MLR) between variations in the physical measurements and the distinctiveness and memory measures. Table 7.4 shows the results of these MLR studies, where we can see that the predictive power is increased by the addition of the additional measures. Moreover, the best correlation achieved with R=0.6 accounts for a quite reasonable 36 per

Table 7.3 Pearson correlation coefficients between the summed z-scores over sixteen simple 2D measures, and a larger set of forty-one including ratio, angles and 3D measures ($r=0.28$ is significant at 0.01, two-tailed)

(a) Female faces

	2D measures	All measures
Distinctiveness (hair visible)	0.29	0.25
Distinctiveness (hair concealed)	0.38	0.35
Memorability	0.16	0.16
Familiarity	− 0.02	− 0.16

(b) Male faces

	2D measures	All measures
Distinctiveness (hair visible)	0.18	0.24
Distinctiveness (hair concealed)	0.53	0.56
Memorability	0.36	0.45
Familiarity	− 0.41	− 0.41

Source: Bruce *et al.*, 1994

Table 7.4: Multiple R scores displayed as in Table 7.3 (note that all multiple Rs are positive; the direction of prediction is given by the sign of the predictor variables)

(a) Female faces

	2D measures	All measures
Distinctiveness (hair concealed)	0.46	0.55
Memorability	NS	0.35
Familiarity	NS	0.47

(b) Male faces

	2D measures	All measures
Distinctiveness (hair concealed)	0.55	0.64
Memorability	0.46	0.60
Familiarity	0.37	0.45

cent of the variance in distinctiveness. Considering that our measurements cannot capture aspects of face texture, pigmentation or minor blemishes, asymmetries and so forth, this performance is quite reasonable.

Face distinctiveness in PCA-based system

In the first part of this chapter we suggested that an image-based coding of faces might implicitly convey all the other possible ways of measuring face structure, and that the principal components of variation of face images may provide a way to describe 'face space'. O'Toole *et al.* (1994) (see also Chapter 8, this volume) have found that a measure of facial 'distinctiveness' derived from PCA-coding (how well a novel face can be reconstructed using a set of eigenvectors derived from a different set of faces) provided a better predictor of the accuracy of face memory than did any ratings of these faces made by human subjects. One advantage of an image-based description scheme is that we no longer have to worry about the hair – whatever is there for the subjects is also present in the images which form the basis of the measurement system. Indeed, it is possible that the very high correlations between PCA-based distinctiveness and recognition memory may be accounted for by the very great range of hair-styles and lengths present in the set of faces used by O'Toole *et al.,* where both male and female exemplars were contained in the same set.

In recent work at the University of Stirling, we have also been investigating correlations between PCA-based descriptions of faces, human ratings of their distinctiveness, and their memorability and apparent familiarity assessed using a similar procedure to that of Bruce *et al.* (1994). The set of face images we have been studying are much more closely standardized than those used by O'Toole *et al.* A set of 174 male faces, normalized for inter-ocular distance and position, were divided into two groups and rated for distinctiveness (how easy would it be to spot this person at a station?) on a scale of 1–10 by seventeen subjects each. The first fifty PCs were computed from the complete set of images. This gives a vector of length 50 to represent each image. Multiple linear regression was performed between these vectors and the distinctiveness ratings. One of the two groups gave a correlation of 0.72, the other 0.5, and when combined the complete set gave a correlation of 0.56. This compares well with a typical intercorrelation of about 0.6 between two sets of subjects rating the same faces, and is also very similar to the best correlation we achieved between explicit measurements and rated distinctiveness (Table 7.4). Furthermore, consistent with our earlier work using explicit measurements, the correlations between the PCA vectors and distinctiveness of faces were higher than correlations with either 'memorability' or 'context-free familiarity' measures obtained with the same faces, suggesting that distinctiveness may be tapping aspects of faces which make them correctly remembered as well as those which make them falsely remembered (for further details see Hancock *et al.,* in preparation).

CONCLUSIONS

The overall conclusion is that it is quite feasible to obtain correlations between the physical deviation of faces and their psychological 'distinctiveness'. This is an unsurprising result, but none the less reassuring, given the apparently mysterious quality of face memorability found by Ellis *et al.*

Moreover, it seems that however faces are measured, this same result is found. Thus correlations were observed between rated face distinctiveness and deviation of 3D surface types (Bruce *et al.,* 1993b), 2D measurements (Bruce *et al.,* 1994), combined 2D and 3D measures (Bruce *et al.,* 1994) and PCA-based deviation (Hancock *et al.,* in preparation). Thus face space does indeed seem to comprise all the possible salient dimensions of variation. The power of the image-based approach is that it captures all possible 'features' without requiring that they are located and measured, and the statistical model of face space provided by the PCA method seems to provide a good initial model with which to implement Valentine's face space. However, the observation that strong correlations can be obtained between any kind of measure of face deviance and psychological distinctiveness means that these studies do not in themselves discriminate between one or other model of the face representation process. Decisions between, say, a picture-based, surface-based or image-based model of face representation will have to be made on other grounds. The earlier part of this chapter reviewed effects of surface detail, negation and lighting on face recognition, which strongly suggest that an image-based approach such as PCA may be more psychologically valid than approaches based on the explicit extraction and measurement of face 'features'.

What is also not clear at present is how any of the face description systems we have reviewed can allow us to explain the rather counter-intuitive lack of correlation between what we have labelled 'memorability' and 'context-free familiarity'. One possible way round this is to suggest (cf. Vokey and Read, 1992) that remembering something that has been seen before depends on idiosyncratic associations made at the time of encoding ('looks like Uncle Harry', 'looks attractive', whatever), while the tendency to falsely remember an actually unseen face relies primarily on overall resemblance to other faces. However at present this does not readily explain why the best correlations between physical deviation (whether measured by hand or by PCA) and psychological variation seem always to arise between physical variation and 'distinctiveness' rather than with context-free familiarity or false positive rates. Our current explorations of a PCA-based face space are attempting to address this issue in more detail.

ACKNOWLEDGEMENTS

Research cited in this chapter has been supported in the past by the ESRC and SERC, and is currently supported by SERC grants GR/H/93828 (to Vicki Bruce and Mike Burton at Stirling) and GR/J/04951 (to Ian Craw at Aberdeen). Our work on surface images of faces was conducted in collaboration with Alf Linney, Anne Coombes and associates at University College London. We thank Anne Coombes for providing figures 2 and 3. This chapter was drafted at ATR Human Information Processing Research Laboratories in Japan. We thank Shigeru Akamatsu for his hospitality and facilities.

NOTES

1 Of the seventeen measures, one was inter-ocular distance which we used to normalize for size before computing deviations, leaving a set of sixteen measures standardized for head size.
2 We explored the correlations using both parametric and non-parametric techniques, faces not standardized for size as well as standardized by inter-ocular distance, and sum-of-squared z-scores as well as sum-of-zs. The pattern of results was similar across all these various manipulations, and here, as in Bruce *et al.* (1994), we summarize just one set of analyses.
3 Ellis and Shepherd used a memory measure rather than distinctiveness, but their measures were derived using a distracter-free paradigm not directly comparable with either our memory measure or our context-free familiarity measure. We must be cautious about making too much of the similarity between their obtained correlation between eccentricity and memorability and our own between eccentricity and distinctiveness.

REFERENCES

Besl, P.J. and Jain, R.C. (1988) Segmentation through variable-order surface fitting. *IEEE Transactions PAMI,* 10, 167–192.
Biederman, I. (1987) Recognition-by-components: a theory of human image understanding. *Psychological Review,* 94, 115–147.
Biederman, I. and Ju, G. (1988) Surface versus edge-based determinants of visual recognition. *Cognitive Psychology,* 20, 38–64.
Brennan, S.E. (1985) The caricature generator. *Leonardo,* 18, 170–178.
Bruce, V. and Langton, S. (1994) The use of pigmentation and shading information in recognizing the sex and identities of faces. Manuscript under revision for *Perception.*
Bruce, V., Hanna, E., Dench, N., Healey, P. and Burton, M. (1992) The importance of 'mass' in line drawings of faces. *Applied Cognitive Psychology,* 6, 619–628.

Bruce, V., Healey, P., Burton, M., Doyle, T., Coombes, A. and Linney, A. (1991) Recognizing facial surfaces. *Perception*, 20, 755–769.

Bruce, V., Coombes, A. and Richards, R. (1993a) Describing the shapes of faces using surface primitives. *Image and Vision Computing*, 11, 353–363.

Bruce, V., Burton, A.M., Hanna, E., Healey, P., Mason, O., Coombes, A., Fright, R. and Linney, A. (1993b) Sex discrimination: how do we tell the difference between male and female faces? *Perception*, 22, 131–152.

Bruce, V., Burton, A.M. and Dench, N. (1994) What's distinctive about a distinctive face? *Quarterly Journal of Experimental Psychology*, 47A, 119–141.

Buhmann, J., Lange, J., von der Malsburg, C., Vorbruggen, J.C. and Wurtz, R.P. (1991) Object recognition in the dynamic link architecture: parallel implementation of a transputer network, in B. Kosko (ed.), *Neural Networks for Signal Processing*. Englewood Cliffs, NJ: Prentice-Hall.

Burton, A.M., Bruce, V. and Dench, N. (1993) What's the difference between men and women? Evidence from facial measurement. *Perception*, 22, 153–176.

Coombes, A.M., Moss, J.P., Linney, A.D. and Richards, R. (1991) A mathematical method for the comparison of three-dimensional changes in the facial surface. *European Journal of Orthodontics*, 13, 95–110.

Cottrell, G.W. and Fleming, M.K. (1990) Face recognition using unsupervised feature extraction. *Proceedings of the International Conference on Neural Networks*, 322–325.

Daugman, J.G. (1993) High confidence visual recognition of persons by a test of statistical independence. *IEEE Transactions on Pattern Analysis and Machine Intelligence*, 15, (11), 1148–1161.

Davies, G. M., Ellis, H.D. and Shepherd, J.W. (1978) Face recognition accuracy as a function of mode of representation. *Journal of Applied Psychology*, 63, 180–187.

Ellis, H.D. and Shepherd, J.W. (1987) *Analysis of mechanisms by which Human Observers Acquire Knowledge of Faces*. Final report on grant C00232260 from the Economic and Social Research Council.

Fiser, J., Biederman, I. and Cooper, E.E. (1995) Test of a two-layer network as a model of human entry-level object recognition. *Proceedings of the Third Annual Computational Neuroscience Meeting*. Kluwer, in press.

Galper, R.E. (1970) Recognition of faces in photographic negative. *Psychonomic Science*, 19, 207–208.

Golomb, B.A., Lawrence, D.T. and Sejnowski, T.J. (1991) Sexnet: a neural network identifies sex from human faces, in D.S. Touretzky and R. Lippman (eds), *Advances in Neural Information Processing Systems 3*. San Mateo, CA: Kaufman.

Hancock, P., Burton, A.M. and Bruce, V. (1994) Manuscript in preparation.

Hayes, A. (1988) Identification of two-tone images: some implications for high- and low-spatial frequency processes in human vision. *Perception*, 17, 429–436.

Hayes, T., Morrone, M.C. and Burr, D.C. (1986) Recognition of positive and negative bandpass-filtered images. *Perception*, 15, 595–602.

Hill, H. and Bruce, V. (1994) Effects of lighting on face matching. Manuscript submitted for publication. Abstracted in *Perception, 22S, 22–23 (ECVP '93)*.

Hummel, J.E. and Biederman, I. (1992) Dynamic binding in a neural network for shape recognition. *Psychological Review*, 99, 480–517.

Johnston, A., Hill, H. and Carman, N. (1992) Recognizing faces: effects of lighting direction, inversion and brightness reversal. *Perception*, 21, 365–375.

Kohonen, T., Oja, E. and Lehtio, P. (1981) Storage and processing of information in distributed associative memory systems, in G.E. Hinton and J.A. Anderson (eds), *Parallel models of associative memory*. Hillsdale, NJ: Erlbaum.

Linney, A. (1992) The use of 3D computer graphics for the simulation and prediction of facial surgery, in V. Bruce and M. Burton (eds), *Processing Images of Faces*. Norwood, NJ: Ablex.

Marr, D. and Hildreth, E. (1980) Theory of edge detection. *Proceedings of the Royal Society of London*, B207, 187–216.

Marr, D. and Nishihara, H.K. (1978) Representation and recognition of the spatial organisation of three-dimensional shapes. *Proceedings of the Royal Society of London*, B200, 269–294.

O'Toole, A., Deffenbacher, K.A., Valentin, D. and Abdi, H. (1994) Structural aspects of face recognition and the other-race effect. *Memory and Cognition*, 22, 208–224.

Pentland, A.P. (1986) Perceptual organisation and the representation of natural form. *Artificial Intelligence*, 28, 292–331.

Phillips, R.J. (1972) Why are faces hard to recognize in photographic negative? *Perception and Psychophysics*, 12, 425–426.

Price, C.J. and Humphreys, G.W. (1989) The effects of surface detail on object categorisation and naming. *Quarterly Journal of Experimental Psychology*, 41A, 797–828.

Rhodes, G., Brennan, S. and Carey, S. (1987) Identification and ratings of caricatures: implications for mental representations of faces. *Cognitive Psychology*, 19, 473–479.

Shepherd, J.W. (1986) An interactive computer system for retrieving faces, in H.D. Ellis, M.A. Jeeves, F. Newcombe and A. Young (eds), *Aspects of Face Processing*. Dordrecht, NL: Martinus Nijhoff.

Shepherd, J.W., Gibling, F. and Ellis, H.D. (1991) The effects of distinctiveness, presentation time and delay on face recognition. *European Journal of Cognitive Psychology*, 3, 137–145.

Stonham, J. (1986) Practical face recognition and verification with WISARD, in H. Ellis, M.A. Jeeves, F. Newcombe and A. Young (eds), *Aspects of Face Processing*. Dordrecht, NL: Martinus Nijhoff.

Turk, M. and Pentland, A. (1991) Eigenfaces for recognition. *Journal of Cognitive Neuroscience*, 3, 71–86.

Valentine, T. (1991) A unified account of the effects of distinctiveness, inversion and race on face recognition. *Quarterly Journal of Experimental Psychology*, 43A, 161–204.

Valentine, T. and Endo, M. (1992) Towards an exemplar model of face processing: the effects of race and distinctiveness. *Quarterly Journal of Experimental Psychology*, 44A, 671–703.

Vokey, J.R. and Read, J.D. (1992) Familiarity, memorability and the effect of typicality on the recognition of faces. *Memory and Cognition*, 20, 291–302.

Chapter 8

A perceptual learning theory of the information in faces

Alice J. O'Toole, Hervé Abdi, Kenneth A. Deffenbacher and Dominique Valentin

The study of human face processing has advanced considerably in recent years, from consisting of a collection of isolated empirical facts and anecdotal observations to a relatively coherent view of the complexity and diversity of the problems tackled by a human observer when confronted with a face. This rapid progress can be traced to the proposal of comprehensive theories of face processing (cf. Ellis, 1975, 1986; Hay and Young, 1982; Bruce and Young, 1986), which have provided a theoretical framework for investigating human face processing within functional subsystems. These models have had much to say about the kinds of tasks subserved by the human face processing system (e.g. naming faces, extracting visual categorical information such as sex and age, etc.), and about the co-ordination of processing among these tasks (e.g. Young *et al.*, 1986). They have also provided important constraints for making sense of neuropsychological data on patients with various face processing deficits (e.g. Bruyer, 1986). Despite the success of these models in guiding research efforts into many aspects of human face processing, they have provided somewhat less guidance in understanding the immensely complicated problems solved by the perceptual system in extracting and representing the richness of the perceptual information available in human faces. In recent years, it has been primarily from computational models that the difficulty of this problem and its importance to understanding human face processing abilities has come to be appreciated.

In the present chapter, we concentrate entirely on the problem of quantifying and representing the information in human faces. We propose a quantifiable theory of the perceptual information in faces and propose a simple statistical/neural network model to simulate the learning of this information. We believe that perceptual learning provides a useful analogy for the problem of selecting and 'learning' the information in faces that is most useful for performing a given task. In many ways, acquiring expertise in processing human faces seems similar to learning many of the kinds of stimuli for which we typically call on perceptual learning as a theoretical construct. For example, how do we listen to music and extract features that enable us to accurately distinguish among different composers? Of primary importance is experience. Both the amount and diversity of experience we have with music constrain the kinds of distinctions we can make. While many people can distinguish a previously unheard Mozart piece from a previously unheard Prokofiev piece after hearing only a few different examples of Mozart and Prokofiev, the problem of distinguishing Mozart and Haydn pieces may require a great deal more experience and considerably more sophisticated distinctions. Second, explicit verbal instructions in learning seem to be little used and of little use. Someone is more likely to tell you that Prokofiev is 'gentler' or 'rounder' than Stravinsky than they are to give you a list of objective musical features for distinguishing the two. Also analogous to the face processing problem is the recognition/naming dissociation – the perceived familiarity of a piece of music is a compelling experience that occurs frequently even when we are unable to recall anything else about it, such as who wrote it, or where we heard it.

What seems to make faces similar to the kinds of stimuli to which we apply perceptual learning theory is the elusiveness of a feature list with which they can be described in a precise and globally agreed upon language. This intuition is supported by empirical evidence indicating that verbalizing a detailed physical description of faces can actually impair later recognition of the described faces (Schooler and Engstler-Schooler, 1990). As with music, human observers seem to be surprisingly comfortable applying abstract language to convey information about faces. We often describe faces using language such as 'mean-looking' or 'perky' which, oddly enough, most of us seem to find helpful in distinguishing among faces, and which some studies have found to be beneficial for recognizing faces (e.g. Bower and Karlin, 1974).

While we believe a perceptual learning theory is applicable to learning faces in many respects, what makes faces very different from these other kinds of stimuli is the sheer quantity of experience we have with them and the strong importance they play in social interaction. In these ways, learning human faces is perhaps comparable to some aspects of natural language learning. We will develop this analogy shortly in the context of learning same- versus other-race faces.

The perceptual learning or statistical structure theory we propose represents faces using 'features' derived from the statistical structure of a *set* of learned faces. With perceptual learning, the information most useful for distinguishing among faces within a learned set emerges as an optimal code. We propose to model this learning process with a computational autoassociative memory that operates on image-based codings of faces. This 'memory' implements principal components analysis, which is a statistical procedure used for expressing a set of correlated variables in terms of a (smaller) set of uncorrelated variables (Hotelling, 1933). Further, the model we propose can be viewed in standard neural network terms as a parallel distributed processing system (McClelland and Rumelhart, 1988). It is important to note that we do not view this model as a replacement for current face processing models (Hay and Young, 1982; Bruce and Young, 1986; Ellis, 1986), but rather as a perceptual 'front end'[1] to these more comprehensive systems. We would argue, however, that the nature of this front-end has strong implications for the efficiency and accuracy with which different face processing tasks can be performed. In fact, we believe that many robust empirical findings concerning faces are due, at least in part, to difficulties that can be understood in terms of perceptual constraints on the problem.

As a psychological model of processing the perceptual information in faces, autoassociative memories have several appealing properties that have to do primarily with the distributed nature of the storage mechanism in the model. Since faces share the same storage space, the representations of similar faces can interfere with each other in relatively natural ways. This is another way of saying that the memory is context-sensitive and so its performance will depend on similarity relationships within the entire set of faces on which it is trained. *At the level of individual faces*, this model makes interesting predictions about the distinctiveness of individual faces. *At the level of sets of faces*, the model's ability to act as a statistical analysis tool that operates on physical codings of sets of faces allows for some interesting explorations of the effects of the heterogeneity of the faces learned on the model's recognition and classification abilities.

Before proceeding, it is perhaps worth mentioning the goals of such a model. Any psychological model of the information in faces should meet the following criteria. First, it should be adequate to support the diversity of face processing tasks that humans achieve. Additionally, with a psychologically relevant, quantifiable model of the information in faces, it should be possible to predict the quality of information available for any given task (e.g. sex classification or recognition). While these criteria are very far from being met by any current model, including the one we propose, we believe that much can be learned by exploring the extent to which informational or perceptual constraints alone can account for some well-known phenomena associated with human face processing. Hence, one goal of testing this model will be to determine where cognitive or semantic factors must be postulated to account for these phenomena.

This chapter is organized as follows. First, we outline a sample of approaches that have been used for specifying the information in faces. Second, we give a brief definition of the autoassociative neural network model. In the next section we demonstrate, first, that the computational model is capable of solving some useful face processing tasks. We then review some recent studies suggesting its potential psychological relevance. Finally, we discuss the relationship of a perceptual learning representation to the approaches discussed in the representational issues section.

REPRESENTATIONAL ISSUES

An overview of the psychological and computational literature on face processing reveals a variety of attempts to 'specify' the kinds of physical information in human faces. Unfortunately, while several of these approaches are related, it is often very difficult to make concrete comparisons between them (and sometimes even within an approach), due to differences in the way definitions have been operationalized or to differences in the kinds of data they have been used to describe. In this section of the chapter, we outline a sample of the approaches that are commonly found in the literature and point out common threads in these approaches. While concrete comparisons are not possible in many cases, it seems unreasonable to ignore the important ways in which the approaches may be tapping similar kinds of coding principles. With that caution in mind, our primary purpose in this endeavour is to lay a foundation for comparing the proposed perceptual learning approach to these other well-studied approaches.

In the psychological literature, the most frequently encountered distinction made concerning the kinds of information in faces is a qualitative one drawn between *feature-based* and *configural* information. As noted by Bartlett and Searcy (1993), this is perhaps better described as a family of distinctions that have been referred to variously as component (piecemeal) versus configural (e.g. Carey and Diamond, 1977), global versus local (Navon, 1977), and isolated features versus second-order relational information (Rhodes *et al.*, 1993). Bruce (1988) defines a feature as 'a discrete component part of a face such as a nose or a chin', whereas configural information refers to the 'spatial interrelationship of facial features' (p. 38). The primary practical difficulty encountered in testing the relative importance of feature-based versus configural information in face processing concerns the problem of selectively varying the two sources of information. Thus, while it seems possible to selectively alter facial configuration, it is not clear that it is possible to selectively vary feature-based information. As noted by Sergent (1984), changes in the features of faces, such as switching the noses of two faces, necessarily change some properties of the configuration. In fact, Rhodes *et al.* (1993) note that even simple configuration changes can alter the dimensions of what may be plausibly considered isolated features (e.g. moving the mouth up or down in a face changes a feature such as upper lip length).

In practice, the manipulation of configural information has been operationally defined in experiments in a wide variety of ways. For example, Young *et al.* (1987) distorted configural information in composite faces[2] by horizontally misaligning the top and bottom halves of the faces. Additionally, inversion of the eyes and mouth in an upright face, the primary manipulation in the Thatcher Illusion (Thompson, 1980), is generally considered a disruption of configural information (See Stevenage, Chapter 2, this volume). While both manipulations disrupt the spatial configuration of the features, intuitively they seem to be very different kinds of manipulations. Additionally, both entail some change to the facial features. Aligning and misaligning the top and bottom halves of faces changes the shape of individual features in the centre of the faces – such as the nose and ears. Likewise, the inversion of the mouth and eyes in an upright 'Thatcherized face' changes the form of the eyes/mouth to the point of grotesqueness. Selective configuration manipulations are most closely approximated in studies that move features relative to one another (e.g. Sergent, 1984; Bartlett and Searcy, 1993). Interestingly, what seem to operationally bind all three of these manipulations together are the measurable differences in human performance with these faces inverted, as opposed to upright. We will discuss some aspects of the effects of inversion in the final section of this chapter. What has been gained by using a configural/feature-based dichotomy is the understanding that for a human observer, the face is clearly more than the sum of its parts. This has provided insight into the nature of the perceptual unit comprised by a face and has been useful in linking face studies to the larger literature on processing visual features.

A second approach to describing the information in faces that has been explored in psychological studies is a quantitative analysis of the spectral information in face images. As imaged on the retina, faces are two-dimensional spatial patterns of light intensities that can be measured using standard Fourier analysis. The appeal of quantifying the information in faces in this way is twofold. First, converging evidence in neurophysiology and psychology is consistent with the notion that the visual system analyses input at several spatial resolution scales (cf. Shapley *et al.*, 1989 for a thorough review). Thus, spatial frequency pre-processing of faces is consistent with what is known about early visual processing. Like the principal components analysis model that we propose, spatial frequency analysis represents an image as a weighted combination of basis functions – specifically, trigonometric (sine and cosine) functions of different frequencies, amplitudes, and phases. High frequencies carry finely detailed information, whereas low frequencies carry coarse, shape-based information. This continuum of low to high frequency information is in some ways related to the feature-based versus configural dichotomy in that the low frequency information *tends* to capture global form information, whereas the high frequency information tends to capture local information.

A second advantage of the spatial frequency analysis is that it is an objective physical measure and hence can be assessed directly in individual faces and varied selectively. While this information must be specified with respect to faces rather than in visual angle dimensions (i.e. cycles per face rather than cycles per degree of visual angle), within this context it can serve as a useful tool for objectively quantifying the information in faces. Although most early work using a spatial frequency quantification of faces was aimed at discovering the minimal spectral information for recognizing faces (e.g. Harmon, 1973; Ginsburg, 1978), the primary contribution resulting from studies that have varied spatial frequency content in faces has been the realization that different kinds of information may be optimal for different face processing tasks. For example, Sergent (1986) showed that human observer performance in the tasks of face identification, male/female categorization, and a semantic categorization (whether the familiar face was a professor, graduate student, etc.) interacted with spatial frequency content and visual hemisphere field of presentation, thus indicating the necessity of considering the task when evaluating the importance of different kinds of information in faces.

The spatial frequency approach to quantifying the information in faces forms a bridge between the qualitative feature-based versus configural distinction and the focus on the *functional* value of information that is common in computational modelling approaches. We review computational modelling approaches only briefly here since very recent, thorough reviews of both non-connectionist (Samal and Iyengar, 1992) and connectionist (Valentin *et al.*, 1994b) models are available. Typically, computational models have been designed to solve only a single face processing task. For example, the neural network models of Brunelli and Poggio (1992) and Golomb *et al.* (1991), as well as the discriminant analysis model of Burton *et al.* (1993),[3] were designed to classify faces by sex. In the models of Burton *et al.* (1993) and Brunelli and Poggio (1992), the features used were those that seemed likely to be informative for the task. In fact, one focus of the Burton *et al.* study was to apply the discriminant analysis for evaluating the utility of individual features for this purpose. Using both feature-based and configural codings derived from two- and three-dimensional face representations yielded reasonable levels of accuracy. Unfortunately, however, in all of their coding attempts, model misclassifications of individual faces by sex were unrelated to human misclassifications, indicating that the information used by humans may be quite different from that used by the model. Likewise, Brunelli and Poggio (1992) used measures of the dimensions of faces, including thickness of eyebrow, breadth of the face, and six chin radii (i.e. the length of lines drawn at varying angles from the centre point of the mouth to the chin contour). These features were input to a radial basis function network that learned to classify faces by sex. Even though these representations have been useful for accomplishing the specific task for which they have been designed, the facial representations they employ are perhaps not optimal for other tasks, such as face recognition.

One problem with pre-selected feature sets is that they often discard important information about the texture and internal shape contours of the face. The autoassociative model we propose and several other related computational models (e.g. Sirovich and Kirby, 1987; Cottrell and Fleming, 1990; Golomb *et al.*, 1991; Turk and Pentland, 1991) have used a normalized, pixel-based coding of faces. This is unabashedly a 'kitchen-sink' approach to the problem that has both advantages and disadvantages. The primary advantage is that no information is discarded a priori. Thus geometric representations are coded implicitly, but in addition, detailed texture and shape information are preserved. For faces we believe that this kind of pixel-based code is a reasonable approach for two reasons: first, theoretical, and second, practical. From a theoretical point of view, when we consider face recognition by comparison to object recognition, it becomes evident that we mean different things by 'recognition'. The processes implied by face recognition are operating at a different level of the processing hierarchy. Specifically, in most object recognition applications, the goal of the task is to identify a subset of pixels in an image as an instance of a particular object; for example, a chair. In standard cognitive psychology terminology, this task is a basic level category classification (Rosch and Mervis, 1975). Little importance is placed on the chair being a particular chair, for example, one you know or have sat in previously. For faces, the identification of a subset of pixels in the image as a face represents only the first step of the process. Additionally, you would like to know if the face is one you know. To approach a person in order to begin a conversation, you would often wish to know the age, sex and even current mood of the person. To accomplish these latter tasks, internal shading and texture information is likely to be very useful. In fact, if the object recognition task were aimed at this level of information, a re-evaluation of the coding schemes generally used for object recognition would be in order. So, for example, if your task were to be the identification, not of a car, but of *your* car, from among a parking lot full of similar models, you would need to consider subtle textural information, including 'dings' and the dirt layer texture, and so on.

The primary disadvantage of a pixel-based approach is that it does not create a translation or view-invariant representation. From a practical point of view, however, good algorithms exist for finding a face in an image (Turk and Pentland, 1991), and the computational problem of scaling and aligning faces (necessary for processing faces in the present approach) is easy to solve. Using a pixel code therefore allows modellers to concentrate on the problems of recognition and visual categorization that make faces a qualitatively different kind of visual stimulus from the other kinds of objects with which we interact.

AUTOASSOCIATIVE MODEL DEFINITION

In this section we will give a very brief definition of the autoassociative memory model and will show how faces can be described as a weighted sum of the eigenvectors extracted from the autoassociative matrix. A very detailed presentation of this model and its application to face processing can be found elsewhere (e.g. Valentin *et al.*, 1994a; for a tutorial presentation see Abdi, 1994b).

An autoassociative memory matrix is constructed as the sum of outer-product (i.e. cross-product) matrices for a set of stimuli coded as vectors:

$$\mathbf{A} = \sum_i \mathbf{f}_i \, \mathbf{f}_i^T \qquad [1]$$

where $\mathbf{f}_i$ is the *i*-th face, coded as a pixel vector consisting of the concatenation of the rows of the face image, and where the faces are assumed to be normalized vectors (i.e. $\mathbf{f}_i^T \mathbf{f}_i = 1$). Simply stated, A contains a measure of the covariance of all possible pairs of pixels in the set of learned faces. Recall of the *i*-th face from this matrix is achieved as follows:

$$\hat{\mathbf{f}}_i = \mathbf{A} \, \mathbf{f}_i \qquad [2]$$

where $\hat{\mathbf{f}}_i$ is the system estimate of $\mathbf{f}_i$. The quality of the output face estimate is measured by comparing the 'retrieved' (reconstructed) image with the original image, using the cosine (i.e. normalized correlation) of the angle between the vectors $\hat{\mathbf{f}}_i$ and $\mathbf{f}_i$.

Like any positive semi-definite matrix, the matrix **A** can be expressed as a weighted sum of the outerproducts of its eigenvectors:

$$\mathbf{A} = \sum_i \lambda_i \mathbf{e}_i \mathbf{e}_i^T \qquad [3]$$

where λ_i is the *i*-th eigenvalue and $\mathbf{e}_i$ is the *i*-th eigenvector of *A*. Retrieval of a face vector from this matrix can be illustrated by rewriting Equation 2 and substituting Equation 3 for **A** as follows:

$$\hat{\mathbf{f}}_i = \lambda_1 (\mathbf{f}_i \cdot \mathbf{e}_1) \mathbf{e}_1 + \lambda_2 (\mathbf{f}_i \cdot \mathbf{e}_2) \mathbf{e}_2 + \ldots + \lambda_n (\mathbf{f}_i \cdot \mathbf{e}_n) \mathbf{e}_n \qquad [4]$$

where the weights are $(\mathbf{f}_i \cdot \mathbf{e}_j)$, which is equal to the dot product between the *i*-th face vector and the *j*-th eigenvector, and where *n* is the rank of the matrix. In other words, each retrieved face can be represented by a weighted sum of eigenvectors, and thus individual faces are made by putting together these 'eigen-images' in different weighted combinations.

The storage capacity of an autoassociative matrix can be improved by applying error correction in the form of the Widrow-Hoff or delta rule (Duda and Hart, 1973) during learning of the faces. Error correction can be implemented iteratively as follows:

$$\mathbf{A}_{t+1} = \mathbf{A}_t + \gamma \, (\mathbf{f}_i - \mathbf{A}_t \mathbf{f}_i \,) \mathbf{f}_i^{\,T} \qquad [5]$$

where γ is a learning rate parameter. Simply seen, the matrix $\mathbf{A}$ is updated at time $t+1$ by calculating the 'error', or difference between the actual face and the model estimate at time t, $(\mathbf{f}_i - \mathbf{A}_t \mathbf{f}_i \,)$, and re-teaching this 'difference' vector to the model via the outer-product rule (Equation 1). This process is repeated for all faces over many iterations. The learning parameter γ can be set to be very small or can decrease exponentially such that finer and finer changes are made to the matrix over time. From the principal component point of view, the effect of this error correction is equivalent to dropping the eigenvalues from Equation 4 (cf. Abdi, 1994a).

DEMONSTRATIONS OF THE MODEL'S ABILITY TO PERFORM USEFUL FACE PROCESSING TASKS

Recognition

How can this model be applied to the problem of distinguishing learned from new faces? In general, we have begun by training a model with a large number of full-face images. The model can then be tested by 'recalling' both learned and novel faces using Equation 2. We can then evaluate the 'quality of the representation' for any given learned or new face by computing the cosine between the original and model-reconstructed faces. The higher this cosine, the more faithful the autoassociative memory's representation of the face. This cosine measure is a sort of model resonance or 'feeling of familiarity' with the face. To test the model's ability to recognize faces, we would like to show that the model's 'feeling of familiarity' is higher for learned than for new faces. We have used signal detection theory (SDT) methodology for this purpose. With this procedure, we define the signal+noise distribution as the OLD or learned faces and the noise distribution as the NEW or unlearned faces. Using the cosine between the original and reconstructed faces, the procedure assigns each face to the category of OLD or NEW as follows. If the cosine for a given face exceeds some criterion, the face is assigned to the OLD face category; otherwise, the face is assigned to the NEW face category. Faces, then, can be categorized as hits, false alarms, misses, and correct rejections. To select the criterion we generally use the 'ideal observer' criterion, midway between the mean of the cosines for the OLD and NEW faces. A d' is then calculated in the standard manner.[4] A complete ROC curve can be calculated simply by sliding the criterion along the cosine histogram (cf. O'Toole *et al.*, 1991b).

On the average, cosines for the learned faces exceed those for the novel faces, indicating that the model, within capacity limits, can distinguish the learned from the novel faces (O'Toole *et al.*, 1988; O'Toole *et al.*, 1991b; and O'Toole *et al.*, 1993). We will discuss the relationship between model and human recognition performance in the section considering the application of the model to psychological issues.

Visually-derived semantic categorization

Variations of the present model have been used for the categorization of faces along the visually derived semantic dimensions of race and sex. O'Toole *et al.* (1991a) have shown that when a heterogeneous set of male and female, Japanese and Caucasian faces is learned by the model, information about the race and sex of faces can be found in a single or small subset of eigenvectors. As noted previously, a face can be represented by the set of weights needed to combine the eigenvectors to reconstruct it. Figure 8.1 shows the weight profiles of the faces divided by race. As can be seen, the weight on the second eigenvector appears to provide good information about the race of a face. We tested this formally by taking the mean of the mean weights for the Japanese and Caucasian faces and using this grand mean as a criterion. Race membership predictions were made by assigning faces with weights exceeding the criterion to one race and faces with weights less than this criterion to the other race. Using only the weights for the second eigenvector yielded correct race predictions for 88.6 per cent of the faces.[5] One advantage of this approach is that the present model is not trained explicitly to classify by race, but rather is trained to recognize faces. Hence, the classification information is a natural part of the information used in the recognition task.

DEMONSTRATIONS OF THE FEASIBILITY OF APPLYING THE MODEL TO PSYCHOLOGICAL ISSUES

The other-race effect

It is well known that people are better at recognizing faces of their own race than faces of other races. While a variety of explanations have been proposed, a very simple one can be framed in terms of perceptual learning. By this account, long-term repeated exposure to the many faces of one race allows the perceptual system to make effective use of subtle variations in the form and configuration of the facial features of the

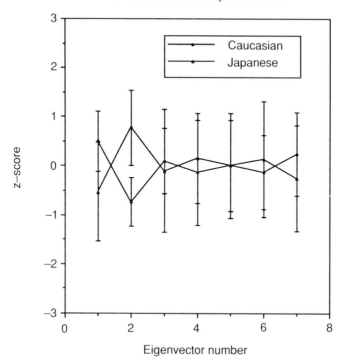

Mean coefficient profiles
for Caucasian and Japanese faces

Figure 8.1 Mean coefficient z-score profiles of Caucasian and Japanese faces. Error bars show the standard deviations of the z-scores. The best race separation is achieved with the second eigenvector

'same-race' faces (i.e. those learned). Unfortunately, other-race faces are not well characterized by these highly specialized features, and so we are less accurate at recognizing such faces. This account of the other-race effect is not unlike what is known about learning one's own native language. With a great deal of exposure to a single language, people become adept at processing the features of the language that are most useful for distinguishing between speech sounds in that language. This occurs at the cost of losing an ability to distinguish speech sounds that are important in other languages but are not particularly useful in one's own language.

Using Japanese and Caucasian faces, we (O'Toole *et al.*, 1991b) simulated a 'face history' by training a neural network to recognize a large number of faces of one race (a 'majority' race), and a lesser number of faces of another race (a 'minority' race). We found that the model 'perceived' or represented novel faces from the minority race with codings that were more similar to one another than the codings with which it represented novel majority faces. This is reminiscent of the oft-noted feeling that other-race faces 'all look alike' and is consistent with Bruce's (1988) and Shepherd's (1981) suggestion that other-race faces are less recognizable because they are perceived as more similar to one another. Both authors suggested that the higher perceived interface similarity for other-race faces is due to the fact that the dimensions of the similarity space are determined mostly by same-race faces. We also found that the model recognized majority faces more accurately than minority faces in an episodic memory task.[6] This is the classic 'other-race effect' phenomenon.

Typicality and recognizability

The relationship between rated typicality and recognizability of faces has been demonstrated by a number of investigators (e.g. Light *et al.*, 1979). This relationship has been interpreted in terms of the existence of a facial prototype, with typical faces being less well recognized than unusual faces. Recent findings by Vokey and Read (1992), however, indicate that rated typicality is a more complicated concept than had been thought previously. Applying a principal components analysis[7] to faces rated by human subjects for typicality, memorability (i.e. 'one that the observer thought would be easy to remember'), familiarity (i.e. 'a face that they believe they may have seen around campus'), attractiveness, and like-ability, they show that the rated typicality of faces is composed of two orthogonal components: (1) a *general familiarity* component consisting of a positive manifold of typicality, familiarity, attractiveness, and like-ability; and (2) a *memorability* component showing typicality inversely related to the rated memorability of a face. This suggests that human observers are basing their typicality ratings on two independent aspects of the faces, dissociable via their independent relationship to attractive-ness, likeability and familiarity, on the one hand, and to memorability on the other hand.

While the data of Vokey and Read (1992) are robust and replicable (O'Toole *et al.*, 1994), little is understood about what makes a face typical versus atypical with respect to the two orthogonal components. Recently, we (O'Toole *et al.*, 1994) have extended the two-component typicality results of Vokey and Read (1992) by adding a variable derived from the autoassociative memory to the coding for each face in the principal compo-nents analysis. Specifically, we added to the human rating and recogni-tion data the model's 'feeling of familiarity' measure (cosine) for each face. We then applied principal components analysis to the combined performance, rating and model data for the faces. The results indicated a separation of the multidimensional space into performance and rating subspaces. The rating subspace replicated the typicality component results found by Vokey and Read (1992). The performance axes were inter-pretable as a criterion ('*indictability*') axis and an *accuracy* axis. The cosine measure taken from the autoassociative memory loaded more strongly on the accuracy axis than did *any* of the observer ratings. In other words, the model measure related *more* strongly to human performance accur-acy than did any of the human ratings. Additionally, by looking at particu-lar faces that contributed strongly to the different typicality components, the model gave insight into the reason for the separation of the typicality components in the human data. Faces that contributed strongly to the memorability component were characterized by a distinctive localized feature such as an unusual mouth expression, for example, a grimace, whereas faces important for the familiarity component were characterized by more global deviations, such as unusual face shapes.

These results suggest the importance of considering faces as perceptual stimuli that provide observers with very rich, elaborate information that they use quite effectively, but which they cannot capture very well in discrete verbal ratings.

Recognition and the perception of visually-derived semantic information

Interestingly, a good likeness of a face can be captured using only a subset of the eigenvectors, those with larger eigenvalues (cf. Sirovich and Kirby, 1987). While this representation is optimal in a least squares error sense for approximating the face, we have noted that in eliminating eigen-vectors from the reconstructed faces, the likeness or general perceptual quality of the face decreases more by eliminating ranges of eigenvectors with smaller eigenvalues than by eliminating the 'more important' eigen-vectors, those with larger eigenvalues (O'Toole *et al.*, 1993). For example, Figure 8.2 displays an original face and the appearance of the face produced by eliminating different ranges of eigenvectors.

This observation, in combination with the results indicating the impor-tance of the eigenvectors with larger eigenvalues for determining visual category information from faces (O'Toole *et al.*, 1991a), motivated us to examine the importance of different ranges of eigenvectors for recogni-tion and sex categorization. O'Toole *et al.* (1993) trained the model with a large number of male and female young adult Caucasian faces and reconstructed both the learned faces and a second set of faces not learned by the model, while varying the range of eigenvectors used in the reconstruction. The model was tested for recognition using SDT methodology. The d' for discriminating learned and new faces across this range appears in Figure 8.3 and shows that the discriminability of the image information provided by the model peaks bimodally, with the most useful information found in the eigenvectors with smaller eigenvalues.

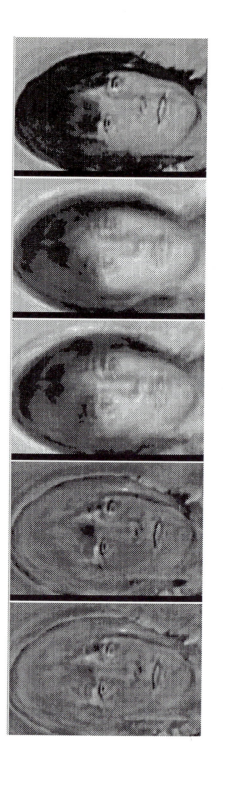

Figure 8.2 From left to right: (a) the original face; reconstructions using (b) the first twenty eigenvectors; (c) the first forty eigenvectors; (d) all but the first twenty eigenvectors; (e) all but the first forty eigenvectors

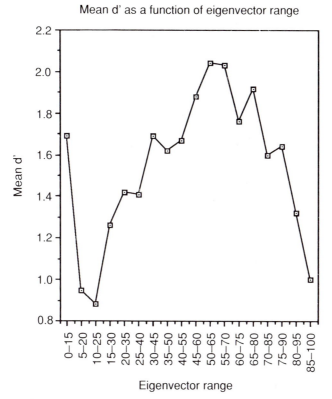

Mean d' as a function of eigenvector range

Figure 8.3 Mean **d'** peaks in two separate ranges of eigenvectors, with best performance in a range of eigenvectors with smaller eigenvalues

This indicates that the least squares error minimization strategy is perhaps not the best one for the purposes of recognition.

We then carried out a test of the model's ability to classify faces by sex across the eigenvectors. We did this for each eigenvector by computing point biserial correlations between the eigenvector weight for each of the faces and the face sex.[8] Figure 8.4 shows the cumulative proportion of explained variance for sex classification across the eigenvectors.[9] As can be seen, the best information for predicting face sex is found in the eigen-vectors with the largest eigenvalues. The second eigenvector was particu-larly useful ($r = 0.66$) as is demonstrated in Figure 8.5 (O'Toole *et al.*, 1993). From left to right, the figure shows the first eigenvector, the second eigen-vector, the first eigenvector plus the second eigenvector, and the first eigenvector minus the second eigenvector. Adding the second eigenvector to the first produces a masculine looking face, whereas subtracting the second eigenvector from the first produces a feminine looking face. This is particularly striking in that, at first glance, the second eigenvector reveals little information that would appear to be relevant to the sex of the face.

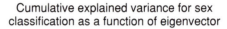

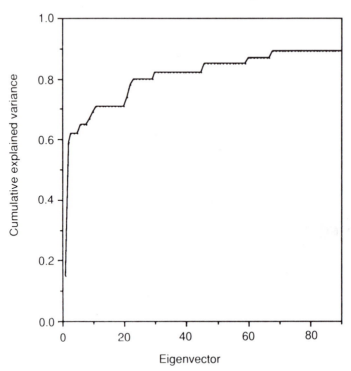

Cumulative explained variance for sex classification as a function of eigenvector

Figure 8.4 Weights on the eigenvectors with larger eigenvalues account for most of the explained variance in sex classification

Combined, the data from the recognition and sex categorization tasks show that the model contains information for both tasks, but that the optimal information for each task is found in different ranges of eigenvectors. For the visually derived semantic classification by sex, the eigenvectors with larger eigenvalues provide the best information. For the recognition task, the eigenvectors with smaller eigenvalues provide the most useful information.

REPRESENTATIONAL ISSUES REVISITED

In this section, we present some ways in which the statistical structure/perceptual learning theory of the information in faces can be related to all three representational approaches discussed previously: (1) the configural versus feature-based distinction; (2) the spatial frequency approach, and (3) the functional emphasis of computational models. We stress, again, that while concrete comparisons are not possible,

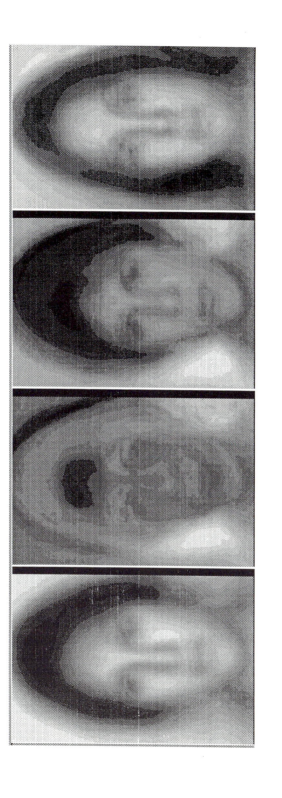

Figure 8.5 From left to right: (a) first eigenvector; (b) second eigenvector; (c) a + .4b; (d) a − .4b. Positive weights of the second eigenvector give rise to faces that appear masculine, whereas negative weights give faces that are feminine in appearance

it seems unreasonable to ignore important ways in which the approaches may be related. We do this with the goal of building links that may enable a more coherent view of representational issues found in the literature.

To begin, the informational components of the perceptual learning/statistical structure theory are eigenvectors. Each eigenvector can be measured in terms of its 'importance' to the general face representation system as the proportion of variance it explains in the pixel-by-pixel autoassociative matrix. A primary aspect of this concept is that 'importance' for any given eigenvector can come from two sources, which can be described in intuitive terms as follows. First, not too surprisingly, eigenvectors that are useful for making distinctions relevant for many faces will explain relatively larger proportions of variance than eigenvectors useful for making distinctions relevant for only a few faces. Major visually based categorical distinctions such as sex, race and age are examples of distinctions relevant for many/all faces. This is likely to be one reason that we have found the eigenvectors most related to the sex and race of a face to have relatively large eigenvalues.

A second source of 'importance', which is perhaps less obvious, concerns the relative *intensity* of different kinds of information in faces. By contrast to the first source, which is related to the *number* of faces for which a particular eigenvector is important, this source is related to properties of the face image *per se*, and becomes evident when the computational problem is viewed in terms of a spatial frequency description of faces. The statistical structure of natural images, of which faces are an example, is such that low spatial frequency components generally have higher amplitudes than high spatial frequency components.[10] An analogy to auditory stimuli may prove helpful for understanding the point. The amplitude of a spatial frequency component is like the 'loudness' of a frequency component in an auditory stimulus. For face images, the 'loudest' components tend to be the lower frequency, shape-based properties of faces rather than the higher frequency details. In a principal components analysis, therefore, low frequencies will generally account for more variance than high frequencies and hence will be associated with eigenvectors with larger eigenvalues (i.e. be more important). In fact, a face reconstructed with different subsets or ranges of eigenvectors from a principal components analysis (cf. Figure 8.2) appears to vary systematically in spatial frequency content. While we have not confirmed this formally, principal components analysis on faces would appear to naturally implement some aspects of spatial frequency filtering – primarily as a function of the relative intensities of the different frequency components.

To what extent does the relative amplitude relationship of different frequencies impact performance on face processing tasks? Returning to questions concerning the optimality of different information for different tasks, some previous findings become more clear. The higher amplitude of lower frequency components[11] should make the global configural information easier to detect and also be detectable/resolvable from a further distance. Additionally, as Sergent (1986) has illustrated, using psychological experiments varying the spatial frequency content of faces, and as the principal components model tends to confirm computationally, these low frequency, higher amplitude components seem to be particularly useful for visually based categorizations such as sex and race categorizations. It is possible that the difference in the intensity of these components explains some of the reasons why sex classification can be achieved more quickly than other semantic categorizations and identifications (Sergent, 1986).

The particularly useful nature of the high amplitude, low frequency, global information for making sex and race classifications is likely to be a second reason why we have found eigenvectors useful for these classifications to have relatively large eigenvalues. Presumably, however, the *number* and *intensity* factors are independent. Intuitively, we might imagine these factors dissociating in a problem like classification by age, where low intensity, high frequency, texture information such as wrinkling might actually be useful for large-scale distinctions among many faces. We have not yet explored this problem.

The perceptual learning and spatial frequency approaches are different, however, in the sense that spatial frequency analysis measures the information in a *single* face image, whereas principal components analysis measures the information in a *set* of face images. The representation of faces that emerges is therefore sensitive to the model's face history. This is a useful component of any computational model interested in simulating human face processing phenomena like the effects of face typicality and the 'other-race effect'. A good example of how the properties of the set of faces affect model reconstructions of faces can be found in Valentin *et al.* (in press; 1994a; 1994b).

A final common thread we wish to explore concerns the puzzle of human observers' difficulties in representing and processing inverted faces. Psychologists have been fascinated by the effects of face inversion since Yin's original paper in 1969. Perhaps the principal lesson that has been learned from these effects is that as amazingly accurate and flexible as our abilities with faces seem to be, the representation of faces we employ is not without limits. From a computational point of view, the surprise has been that the inversion transformation, technically speaking, discards no information.

From a perceptual point of view, Rock (1974) has argued that the key to understanding inversion effects with faces is twofold. First, faces are highly complex and similar to one another, containing many small nuances that are important for distinguishing among similar faces. The second factor is the large differential in experience that human observers have with upright rather than inverted faces – faces are typically mono-oriented in space. The combination of these two factors is in many ways typical of the problems we have in acquiring the subtle features of some classical perceptual learning stimuli. Returning to our original example of distinguishing the music of two composers, the complexity of musical phrasing and interrelation of subcomponents in music creates a perceptual experience that is difficult to 'subdivide' into simple parts. Likewise, a phoneme in language, while serving as a perceptual unit of sorts (perhaps not unlike the eyes, nose and mouth of a face), is strongly affected both perceptually and computationally by contextual factors. It is for this reason that the phonemic unit has proved somewhat less useful than expected for quantifying speech streams. Both faces and these auditory stimuli are: (1) highly complex, and (2) mono-oriented with respect to a (some) physical dimension(s) – specifically, the x and y dimensions of space for faces and the time dimension for language and music. Inversion of a face might be considered similar to inverting time in a speech stream or musical composition; that is, playing a tape of a sentence or a Mozart piece backwards. Clearly, all of the physical information remains present in this kind of a transformation (e.g. Fourier spectrum). We are, none the less, completely unable to identify words or musical phrases with such a transformation.

The inversion of faces constitutes a much less extreme transformation than the inversion of time in an auditory stimulus due to the fact that faces can be inverted in space naturally, whereas music and speech cannot be inverted naturally in time (at least not at less than the speed of light! (Einstein, 1918)). In fact, most of us have some limited experience with upside-down faces and much more experience with recognizing less complicated inverted objects (cups, chairs, etc.). Additionally, all of us have experience in observing objects undergoing spatial inversion (watching an object being turned upside-down).

The face representation used in the perceptual learning model would be likely to perform very badly on inverted faces. Just how badly would depend primarily on the proportion of inverted to upright faces the model learns. From a perceptual learning point of view, this suggests that the problem we have recognizing inverted faces is similar to the problem we have recognizing other-race faces. The experience differential with upright versus inverted faces yields a representation optimal for coding upright faces in ways that make them optimally distinctive. Inverted faces, like other-race faces, should appear more similar to each other than upright faces – this may be related to the fact that a face and its 'Thatcherization' appear very dissimilar upright, but much more similar inverted (Bartlett and Searcy, 1993).

Despite coding principles in the perceptual learning model that might predict some aspects of the effects of inversion, we do not expect that it will provide a complete account of the various inversion phenomena. In

particular, the model does not have general knowledge about the statistical structure of non-face objects, nor does it have access to general pro-
cedures that we seem to be able to call on successfully for general object
recognition (e.g. mental rotation – Shepard and Metzler, 1971).
Understanding how these more general purpose object recognition tools
work may eventually be useful, perhaps even necessary, for understanding
face inversion phenomena.

In summary, we believe that many problems in face processing can be
understood, at least in part, at the level of the perceptual constraints on
face processing. This indicates the importance in psychological and computational models of taking into account the kinds of perceptual problems
posed by the statistical structure of faces as visual stimuli. The model we
propose is far from answering many important questions about the kinds
of information we derive from faces. It falls particularly short in giving
insight into how we accomplish view transformations and in how the representation of an unfamiliar face changes with additional and more diverse
experience with the face, for instance over time and through motion. While
the former may reasonably be attacked by enriching the quality of three-
dimensional information available to the model, the latter will likely
require much more sophisticated modelling techniques than the ones we
are currently employing.

NOTES

1 A term we borrow from Bruce (1988).
2 Faces made by combining two faces; in this case, the top half of one face and
   the bottom half of a second face.
3 While presented by these authors as a statistical discriminant model, the
   analysis is formally equivalent to a perceptron type of neural network
   (Rosenblatt, 1958; cf. Abdi, 1994a for equivalence proof).
4 See Turk and Pentland (1991) for another recognition algorithm.
5 Note that for visually based classifications (e.g. sex) it is possible to achieve
   100 per cent correct categorizations of the learned faces by combining all
   eigenvector weights. Performance on new faces, while less than perfect, is well
   above what can be achieved with a single eigenvector (cf. Abdi *et al.*,
   submitted). Additionally, while using the weights on all eigenvectors allows
   for perfect performance on the learned faces, only the eigenvectors with relatively larger eigenvalues contribute to the model's ability to generalize sex
   information to unlearned faces (Abdi *et al.*, submitted).
6 Both Japanese and Caucasian faces served alternately as the majority and
   minority race faces for tests yielding conclusions 1 and 2. Due to a shortage
   of Japanese faces for the episodic recognition task, this was tested with only
   Caucasian faces as the majority race faces.
7 This principal components analysis was applied to subject judgements, not to
   a representation of the stimuli. Note also that a Varimax rotation was applied
   to the space after the principal components analysis.
8 As defined by 0 and 1 for male and female faces, respectively.
9 Only eigenvector weights that correlated significantly (significance of r test, p

<.05) are included. One hundred per cent of the variance would be explained if all eigenvectors were included.

10   This 'energy' differential between high and low frequency information in faces is one of several factors outlined by Sergent (1989) as potentially accounting for diverging conclusions on human studies of the importance of spatial scale information in face processing.

11   Even in light of the modulation transfer function of the eye (cf. Cornsweet, 1970), the intensity difference between the lowest and highest frequency information in faces is very large (unpublished observations).

REFERENCES

Abdi, H. (1994a) *Les réseaux de neurones.* Grenoble: Presses Universitaires de Grenoble.

Abdi, H. (1994b) A primer of neural networks. *Journal of Biological Systems, 2,* 247–281.

Abdi, H., Valentin, D., Edelman, B. and O'Toole, A. J. (submitted) More about the difference between men and women: evidence from linear neural networks and principal components approach.

Bartlett, J. C. and Searcy, J. (1993) Inversion and configuration of faces. *Cognitive Psychology, 25,* 281–316.

Bower, G. H. and Karlin, M. B. (1974) Depth of processing pictures of faces and recognition memory. *Journal of Experimental Psychology, 103,* 751–757.

Bruce, V. (1988) *Recognizing Faces.* Hillsdale, NJ: Erlbaum.

Bruce, V. and Young, A.W. (1986) Understanding face recognition. *British Journal of Psychology, 77,* 305–327.

Brunelli, R. and Poggio, T. (1992) HyperBF networks for gender classification, in *Proceedings of the DARPA Image Understanding Workshop,* San Mateo, CA: Morgan Kaufmann.

Bruyer, R. (1986) *The Neuropsychology of Face Perception and Facial Expression.* Hillsdale, NJ: Erlbaum.

Burton, A. M., Bruce, V. and Dench, N. (1993) What's the difference between men and women? Evidence from facial measurement. *Perception, 22,* 153–176.

Carey, S. and Diamond, R. (1977) From piecemeal to configurational representation of faces. *Science, 195,* 312–314.

Cornsweet, T. (1970) *Visual Perception.* New York: Academic Press.

Cottrell, G.W. and Fleming, M.K. (1990) Face recognition using unsupervised feature extraction. *Proceedings of the International Neural Networks Conference.* Dordrecht: Kluwer.

Duda, R. O. and Hart, P.E. (1973) *Pattern classification.* New York: John Wiley & Sons.

Einstein, A. (1918) *Mein weltbild.* Berlin: Ullstein Verlag.

Ellis, H. D. (1975) Recognizing faces. *British Journal of Psychology, 66,* 409–426.

Ellis, H. D. (1986) Processes underlying face recognition, in R. Bruyer (ed.), *The Neuropsychology of Face Perception and Facial Expression.* Hillsdale, NJ: Erlbaum.

Ginsburg, A. (1978) Visual information processing based on spatial filters constrained by biological data. Ph.D. thesis, University of Cambridge (Published as AFAMRL Technical Report TR–78–129).

Golomb, B. A., Lawrence, D. T. and Sejnowski, T. J. (1991) Sexnet: a neural network identifies sex from human faces, in R. Lippmann, J. Moody and D. S. Touretsky (eds), *Advances in Neural Information Processing Systems 3.* San

Mateo, CA: Morgan Kaufmann.

Harmon, L. D. (1973) The recognition of human faces. *Scientific American, 227*, 71–82.

Hay, D. C. and Young, A. W. (1982) The human face, in A.W. Ellis (ed.), *Normality and Pathology in Cognitive Functions*. New York: Academic Press.

Hotelling, H. (1933) Analysis of a complete set of variables into principal components. *Journal of Educational Psychology, 24*, 417–441.

Kleiner, K. A. (1987) Amplitude and phase spectra as indices of infant's pattern preferences. *Infant Behaviour and Development, 10*, 49–59.

Light, L. L., Kayra-Stuart, F. and Hollander, S. (1979) Recognition memory for typical and unusual faces. *Journal of Experimental Psychology: Human Learning and Memory, 5*, 212–228.

McClelland, J. and Rumelhart, D. (1988) *Explorations in Parallel Distributed Processing*. Cambridge, MA: MIT Press.

Navon, D. (1977) Forest before trees: the precedence of global features in visual perception. *Cognitive Psychology, 9*, 353–383.

O'Toole, A. J., Millward, R. B. and Anderson, J. A. (1988) A physical system approach to recognition memory for spatially transformed faces. *Neural Networks, 1*, 179–199.

O'Toole, A. J., Abdi, H., Deffenbacher, K. A. and Bartlett, J. (1991a) Classifying faces by race and sex using an autoassociative memory trained for recognition. *Proceedings of the Thirteenth Annual Conference of the Cognitive Science Society*. Hillsdale, NJ: Erlbaum.

O'Toole, A. J., Deffenbacher, K. A., Abdi, H. and Bartlett, J. A. (1991b) Simulating the 'other-race effect' as a problem in perceptual learning. *Connection Science Journal of Neural Computing, Artificial Intelligence and Cognitive Research, 3*, 163–178.

O'Toole, A. J., Abdi, H., Deffenbacher, K. A. and Valentin, D. (1993) A low dimensional representation of faces in the higher dimensions of the space. *Journal of the Optical Society of America A, 10*, 405–411.

O'Toole, A. J., Deffenbacher, K. A., Valentin, D. and Abdi, H. (1994) Structural aspects of face recognition and the other-race effect. *Memory and Cognition, 22*, 208–224.

Rhodes, G., Brake, S. and Atkinson, A.P. (1993) What's lost in inverted faces? *Cognition, 47*, 25–57.

Rock, I. (1974) The perception of disoriented figures. *Scientific American, 230*, 78–85.

Rosch, E. and Mervis, C. B. (1975) Family resemblance studies in the internal structure of categories. *Cognitive Psychology, 7*, 573–605.

Rosenblatt, F. (1958) The perceptron: a probabilistic model for information storage and organization in the brain. *Psychological Review, 65*, 386–408.

Samal, A. and Iyengar, P.A. (1992) Automatic recognition and analysis of human faces and facial expression: a survey. *Pattern Recognition, 25*, 65–77.

Schooler, J. W. and Engstler-Schooler, T. Y. (1990) Verbal overshadowing of visual memories: some things are better left unsaid. *Cognitive Psychology, 22*, 36–71.

Sergent, J. (1984) An investigation into the component and configural processes underlying face recognition. *British Journal of Psychology, 75*, 221–242.

Sergent, J. (1986) Microgenesis of face perception, in H.D. Ellis, M.A. Jeeves, F. Newcombe and A. Young (eds), *Aspects of Face Processing*. Dordrecht, NL: Martinus Nijhoff.

Sergent, J. (1989) Structural processing of faces, in A.W. Young and H. D. Ellis (eds), *Handbook of Research in Face Processing*. Amsterdam: Elsevier Science Publishers (North-Holland).

Shapley, R., Caelli, T., Grossberg, S. Morgan, M. and Rentschler, I. (1989) Computational theories of visual perception, in L. Spillman and J. S. Werner (eds), *Visual Perception: The Neurophysiological Foundations.* San Diego, CA: Academic Press.

Shephard, R. N. and Metzler, J. (1971) Mental rotation of three-dimensional objects. *Science,* 171, 701–703.

Shepherd, J. (1981) Social factors in face recognition, in G. Davies, H. Ellis and J. Shepherd (eds), *Perceiving and Remembering Faces.* London: Academic Press.

Sirovich, L. and Kirby, M. (1987) Low-dimensional procedure for the characterization of human faces. *Journal of the Optical Society of America A,* 4, 519–518.

Thompson, P. (1980) Margaret Thatcher: a new illusion. *Perception,* 9, 483–484.

Turk, M. and Pentland, A. (1991) Eigenfaces for recognition. *Journal of Cognitive Neuroscience,* 3, 71–86.

Valentin, D., Abdi, H. and O'Toole, A. J. (in press) Principal component and neural network analyses of face images: explorations into the nature of information available for classifying faces by sex, in C. Dowling, F. C. Roberts and P. Theuns (eds), *Progress in Mathematical Psychology.*

Valentin, D., Abdi, H. and O'Toole, A.J. (1994a) Categorization and identification of human face images by a neural network: a review of linear autoassociative and principal components approaches. *Journal of Biological Systems,* 2, 413–429.

Valentin, D., Abdi, H., O'Toole, A. J. and Cottrell, G. (1994b) Connectionist models of face processing: a survey. *Pattern Recognition,* 27, 1209–1230.

Vokey, J.R. and Read, J.D. (1992) Familiarity, memorability and the effect of typicality on the recognition of faces. *Memory and Cognition,* 20, 291–302.

Young, A. W., Hellawell, D. and Hay, D. C. (1987) Configural information in face perception. *Perception,* 16, 747–759.

Young, A. W., McWeeny, K. H., Hay, D. C. and Ellis, A. W. (1986) Access to identity specific semantic codes from unfamiliar faces. *Quarterly Journal of Experimental Psychology,* 38A, 271–295.

Chapter 9

A manifold model of face and object recognition

Ian Craw

INTRODUCTION

In this chapter we describe a rather general geometric model of object recognition, and discuss the implications of this model for the associated problem of object representation. Our main concern is with the problem of intra-class discrimination, in which the aim is to distinguish between many rather similar examples of an object, and in order to be concrete, we place our model in the context of face recognition. Our main theoretical conclusion is that representations are naturally neither unique nor universal, and that existing theories which require either property should be re-examined carefully. In practice we are led to particular coding strategies which have proved successful in a machine recognition context.

We go on to discuss the associated problems of object recognition and representation in terms of the task demands, and review a number of existing theories from this viewpoint. We then show how the task demands suggest a differentiable manifold model of recognition, and we explore the general implications of this assumption. This leads on to a particular type of object representation which is consistent with our model, and we describe it in detail. We then compare the resulting model of face recognition with existing theories; our approach is consistent with current theories, but a greater generality of description allows us to highlight certain crucial assumptions in a number of detailed existing models. A further investigation of our suggested coding yields practical recognition results, and we will be reviewing these. We finally explore the implications of our model for more general recognition tasks, suggesting that the model is not specific to faces, and indeed moves smoothly between intra-class and inter-class discrimination, yielding what seems to be a parametrized version of geon-based recognition in the latter case.

RECOGNITION

We consider the process of image-based recognition, where the aim is to pass from visual input to 'recognition', perhaps by retrieving previously stored information, of the associated object. At the heart of the problem are the demands imposed by the requirement of invariance: we need to recognize the object itself, rather than a particular image of the object. In other words, we need to ignore the 'accidental' properties of the image, and concentrate on the 'essential' features. Some of these accidental features are common to most images, be they of faces or hammers; we wish to be able to recognize the object under different lighting conditions, from different angles, both of the object and the viewer, and perhaps when partially occluded, so that the visual information is incomplete. And there are much more subtle invariance requirements that the human vision system handles easily: a face is still recognized when seen with different expressions, and even after transformations such as ageing have occurred over significant periods of time.

Coding methods

It is essentially tautological that recognition takes place by comparing a representation derived from the image against various stored representations; recognition occurs when a suitable match is found. At its simplest, the process will be the same as if the images were being stored or 'remembered'. A memory trace is calculated, and compared with existing traces; a close enough match is then accepted as recognition. This is the familiar 'instance based' theory, with different imaging conditions giving rise to different instances in memory, which are then identified as belonging to the same object during the learning phase. It provides a complete explanation; but at the expense of passing the problems associated with how invariance is implemented to the next higher level of processing. The enormous size of the store of 'instances' against which matching takes place is also a problem. However, simple face recognizers have been built using such a mechanism (Stonham, 1986), different images of the same individual simply being linked by this common property.

At the other extreme, it may be that the incoming image is processed to achieve a unique fully invariant representation; recognition is then simply a matter of seeing whether this representation is already being stored; otherwise the object is recognized as new. Such a methodology has been successful in machine vision applications where there is the need to recognize a simple machine part, as a demonstrator for the 'bin picking' problem (Porrill et al., 1987). However, problems arise as the objects become more complicated, when it becomes increasingly difficult to give a canonical description and there seems to be no example of this strategy being used for computer face recognition. This suggests that such 'fully invariant single trace' or model-based representation is probably too simple in general; there seems no reason to assume a unique representation of an object, placing all the recognition burden on initially extracting invariant memory traces.

Between these extreme theories are a number of attempts at a compromise. One such is the theory of 'canonical views' in which a limited number of views of the object are stored, with recognition corresponding to recognition of one instance. Such a methodology aims to achieve view invariance, and again has been used successfully with the machine vision domain. Other invariances can be approximated in a similar way, again at the expense of an increased number of images against which matching is to be done. In extreme cases, with either a unique or a large number of views, this just reduces to one of the previous two methods.

Another way to reduce the size of the recognition space is via a theory of sub-objects, in which an object is described in terms of its component parts. A useful invariant definition of such parts is challenging, but following the rather unconstrained 'generalised cylinders' of Brooks (1981), the geons of Biederman (1987) seems promising; we discuss this further on page 199.

Representations

Whichever theory is adopted, incoming codes derived from the image are matched against stored codes. There are thus natural questions about the nature of the codes or representations. We can ask if the code is unique, or at least defined in some global way, and also whether it is comprehensible. To illustrate the variety of possible answers, we consider the same question as applied to modern databases. That experience certainly suggests that representation questions are difficult: an output table is simply one view of the data; the internal representation is deliberately hidden, and indeed in a distributed database, held on a number of machines, may vary with the machine. Questions about comprehensibility are not even well posed: the form of storage needed for rapid retrieval, perhaps a multi-level list of hash tables, need have no direct connection with the items being processed yet, at another level of discourse, we have just given such a 'comprehensible' description.

Our discussion of the actual codings used in existing systems aimed simply at handling viewpoint invariance suggests that there are no clear answers to the more general problems. As such, our approach is to discuss the requirements abstractly, postponing a consideration of an appropriate representation for as long as possible.

A MANIFOLD MODEL OF RECOGNITION

A common way to postpone a choice of representation is to argue geometrically, and in this section we discuss recognition in this language. Consider the set of all faces together with the collection of transformations on the set, arising from changes such as movement, expression or ageing which transform a face into a different one of the same individual. For the purposes of recognition, all these transformations leave the underlying identity invariant, and so formally we wish to identify, or unify, the orbits in the space of faces under the action of all such transformations. As these transformations are in general invertible, running time backwards in the case of ageing, an appropriate model is that of a space on which a *group* of transformations acts. Our aim then is to study the set of faces, modulo the subgroup of identity-preserving transformations.

Such a situation is familiar in modern geometry where, for example, symmetry is usually studied as an invariant of a suitable group of transformations, and we borrow from that experience an appropriately general model, namely a (possibly infinite dimensional) manifold on which our transformations, considered as a Lie group, act. Such a description is sufficiently abstract to postpone problems such as how to parametrize our faces, while at the same time it is sufficiently specific to have formal consequences. Of course such a model is not new; related ideas based on Lie groups have been suggested on a number of occasions, for example by Hoffman (1966 and 1978), and more recently by Townsend and Thomas (1993).

We thus explore the structure of a (not necessarily connected) manifold; the points of which are all possible faces. It seems unreasonable to conjecture connectedness because of different genotypes; it is not clear whether, for example, a European face can be smoothly transformed into an Oriental one, passing only through points which are themselves recognizably faces. Acting on this large *face* manifold M_0 is the group of all transformations, including those such as gaze direction, changing facial expression, smiling or ageing which must be factored out before recognition can take place. Note that these are all transformations on the manifold; at any stage under one of these transformations, the resulting object remains a face. Factoring out by the subgroup of identity-preserving transformation maps leads to the identity manifold M_i, in which each point is the equivalence class of all faces which constitute one individual.

Parallel to this structure are the face image manifolds, and associated to each pair consisting of a face in M_0 and an imaging method in some set V, we get a point in *face image space* I_0. Many of the apparent ambiguities in this space can be removed by factoring out transformations induced by V such as viewpoint or lighting which come from the imaging method rather than the underlying point in M_0. This gives equivalence classes I_1. However, recognition can only occur when we pass to the image of M_i, which we denote as I_i. We can summarize this structure with the commutative diagram:

$$
\begin{array}{ccccccc}
& \pi_2 & & & & & \\
V \times M_0 & \to & M_0 & \to & M_i & \to & G \\
\downarrow & & \downarrow & & \downarrow & & \downarrow \\
I_0 & \to & I_1 & \to & I_i & \to & I_G
\end{array}
$$

in which we denote by π_2 the projection to the second factor, the vertical arrow is induced from the imaging process, and for completeness, we have included the map to the genotype G and its two-dimensional representation I_G. The face description or recognition problem can be described as that of lifting the map $I_0 \to I_i$ to a map $I_0 \to M_i$ which recognizes an individual from an image.[1] This analysis makes the point that recognition does not *necessarily* pass through a lifting to M_0 itself, although that is the process we described as 'fully invariant' recognition, and certainly not via a lifting to $V \times M_0$, corresponding to the 'instance-based' recognition paradigm described above. Note also that the 'canonical views' paradigm can be regarded as lifting to some intermediate space.

We have distinguished between the two rows of the above diagram in order to make explicit the variations due to imaging conditions. However, in many ways the structures are parallel, and it is sometimes convenient, particularly during the discussion of other theories of face recognition on pages 193–195, to confuse the two.

An important property of a manifold is that in general there is no privileged co-ordinate system with which to describe the whole of the manifold; rather, there are a collection of local diffeomorphisms, or charts, none in any way unique, which collectively cover the whole manifold. Indeed, the aim of the theory is to study intrinsic properties, such as differentiability, which can be defined in a way that does not depend on the choice of chart.[2]

An example may make the concept clearer: there are many ways of mapping part of the earth's surface on to a piece of paper in a smooth (although not isometric) way, and none is the 'right' one; yet there is a need for the local approach, since the whole surface cannot be so mapped with a single chart.[3] Typical choices in practice may be a Mercator, or Orthographic projection. The analogy is worth pursuing, because we are familiar with the choices involved: a small-scale chart can indicate the relative positions of countries, while a large-scale plan may be used to position the walls of a house; there is no one scale that is 'right'. Varying the scale is not the only choice; political and contour maps give very different types of information, even at the same scale. In practice, our choice of chart is governed by the task in hand, and we cope with the complexities of the lack of a unique representation.

And we can distinguish between an intrinsic property, such as being an island, from one dependent on the mapping conventions, such as being coloured red.

Thus our choice of structure involves a deliberate rejection of a unique representation *per se*. The simplest example of a manifold, indeed of a Lie group, is Euclidean space itself. It has the special property that there *is* a single global chart; however, even in this case, there is no preferred co-ordinate system or scale, so choices still have to be made. Whether a given manifold *is* Euclidean space is thus seen as a purely empirical question; but without the more general language, this question becomes essentially impossible to formulate.

This point is fundamental to the argument we present in this chapter. We suggest that the main advantage of the more sophisticated model described here is the recognition of the importance of this distinction. This brings an improved clarity in distinguishing what is really there as part of the structure of the problem from what is the result of an essentially arbitrary choice; certainly fundamental properties should not depend on an arbitrary choice unless they remain constant, when a different choice is made. Without a natural co-ordinate system, there is no natural metric. The underlying topology – the neighbourhood structure – is an invariant, and there are a number of conditions, such as paracompactness, under which the space is metrizable, but there is no way of doing this canonically, and hence there is no significance in metric properties *per se*.

In order to be concrete, we have given a specific model. The various assumptions, such as smoothness, may be too optimistic, and can be relaxed without changing the nature of the model; indeed, relaxing these will make the situation even less controlled compared with Euclidean space, and our main point is that such a Euclidean structure should not be taken as axiomatic. What is of more interest is that our model suggests certain natural constructions and questions which should be investigated. In particular, there is a fundamental distinction between local properties, for which our charts still give an inherited Euclidean structure, and global ones, for which this is absent. We thus focus first on local questions which can be discussed in relatively simple terms, while global questions may be much harder to address.

CHOOSING A REPRESENTATION

General properties

In order to perform calculations we need to pick local co-ordinates on the manifold. By analogy with the examples above, this can be thought of as a non-linear warping in order to locally flatten the space. The process of selecting local charts mapping to a genuine Euclidean space is the one in which an actual representation is obtained. Our theoretical description gives no information about possible charts, but they do have specific properties which enable candidates to be recognized. Given a chart, i.e. a local diffeomorphism on to, say, an open ball in $\mathbf{R}^n$, we can perturb a point in the image by a suitably small amount, and (since the map is on to) stay within the image; and we can average two points in the image, and again stay within the image (using the local convexity, and *a fortiori* the existence of an addition). We can thus recognize representations as possibly implementing such a local diffeomorphism by whether they have these properties. We now describe one method of constructing representations which has these properties. Although not 'obvious', its importance has already been recognized in a number of different contexts, and we thus explore it further.

Shape-free faces

We describe a representation of faces in which two faces can be added together, or averaged, and yield a representation of another face. An example where this fails may clarify the point: face images themselves can

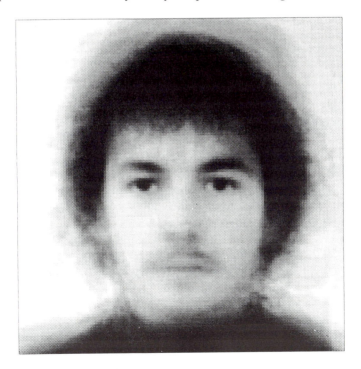

Figure 9.1 Mean of twenty face images

be considered as lying in a linear space of the underlying pixels, but an average image, such as that shown in Figure 9.1, is far from representing a face.[4] The difficulty is that we are trying to average unlike things; in our proposed solution, we first separate out the shape and the image grey levels or texture of the face, perform the averageing separately, and then combine the result.

One way to do this first locates landmarks on the face, and the average location of the landmarks within a suitable ensemble of similar faces is found. Each face image is then distorted to have the same shape by an appropriate morph or texture map. A second more global way, in which the average is assumed known – perhaps simply a 'typical' face or proto-type – computes a local distortion to get the best local fit between the current image and the reference image. These distortions then specify the shape change, while the distorted image has the shape of the prototype. Such local distortions are biologically very plausible; we return to this when we discuss net-based methods on pages 192–193.

We describe the resulting face image, having its own recognizable texture but with the average shape, as a *shape-free face*. We argue that this combination of landmark locations or distortions and shape-free face *does* give a suitable representation in which similar faces can be averaged, and the result is another face which is not recognizable as either of the original faces. We describe this process diagramatically in Figure 9.2, using a figure taken from Craw and Cameron (1992), where the representation was described for its use in recognition.

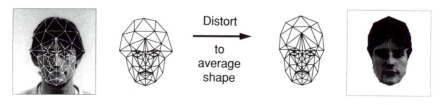

Figure 9.2 Control points are located and the mesh mapped to the average shape; the grey levels follow, giving a shape-free face or texture vector

Principal component analysis

Our manifold model of recognition has led, via the passage to a shape-free face, to a (not necessarily unique) local parametrization, and hence to a local description as points in some high dimensional Euclidean space. A natural question at this point is whether the full dimension of the parameter space is required for the recognition task in hand, or whether we can reduce the dimensionality of the co-ordinate patch locally diffeo-morphic to the manifold without significant loss. An obvious way to do this is to select a sample of the points, or faces, in the neighbourhood that are to be distinguished, and simply work in the (much lower dimensional) space spanned by this sample. We thus choose to ignore those factors which fail to differentiate between members of our reference set or ensemble. Indeed, a further reduction of dimension is possible using principal component analysis in which only the most important of the remaining dimensions are retained. Note that the use of principal component analysis arises in this context in a very natural way; it is a linear theory, and we have appropriately located its application to a linear space.

Accepting these arguments, we have thus arrived at a description of how a face may be coded. We first have a non-linear warping stage in which the manifold is locally co-ordinatized; this is then followed by a principal component analysis in which the dimensionality of the co-ordinate patch is reduced. Each of these stages uses a distinguished reference collection of faces or *ensemble*, which describes our expectation or the range of variability that can be expected. The combination of these two processes gives a suitable parametrization for recognition.

We now describe this procedure in less abstract terms.

- The first step is to locate the process at a typical point f_0 in the face manifold. It seems likely that this point is found by some grosser form of recognition; our assumption that face space is a manifold then gives some neighbourhood N of f_0 which is diffeomorphic, under φ, say, to a ball in some $\mathbf{R}^n$, i.e. which can be consistently parametrized. We now describe how intra-class discrimination is done for faces which are in the neighbourhood N, and by implication similar to f_0.

- Factor out the shape of each $f \in N$, in order to locally linearize face space at f_0. Any such procedure is an approximation: we describe one based on landmarks in detail. First, choose a suitable number of landmarks on f_0, typically the location of the eyes, mouth, etc.; locate each landmark on each $f \in N$, and deform all such faces to have the same shape as f_0.

- The dimension of the resulting image space is still large; next, choose a representative set of faces in N, the *ensemble*, and perform a principal component analysis on the resulting images. Coding the whole of the neighbourhood N simply in terms of an appropriate linear combination of the resulting eigenfaces then gives a representation which, although an approximation, is succinct; by adding in the locations of the landmarks of each face in N as part of our coding scheme, we then obtain the required approximation φ to the local diffeomorphism that was sought. The resulting parametrization has the property that a small perturbation away from $\varphi(f_0)$ is in fact the repre-sentation of some face image which lies in the neighbourhood N.

A natural representation

Although we have argued for this representation from a particular abstract viewpoint, a number of authors have in practice used the resulting para-metrization. Note first that a rather crude approximation to the local linearization can be obtained simply by translating and scaling all face images so that both eyes on each face occur at the same position on all images. Indeed, in the language of shape theorists, this is the shape represented in terms of Bookstein co-ordinates (Bookstein, 1991). Performing a principal component analysis on a collection of images normalized in this way has then been described by Sirovich and Kirby (1987), and Kirby and Sirovich (1990), who argued for such a succinct representation as useful for describing face images, and showed that each image in their ensemble of 100 could be represented with an error of at most 3.68 per cent using only fifty components. A similar representation, couched in the language of neural nets, goes back to Kohonen et al. (1981). More recently, such codes have been used for recognition (Turk and Pentland, 1991), while the full coding, passing to the more elaborate shape-free face is used for recognition of faces (Craw and Cameron, 1992), and eyes alone (Shackleton and Welsh, 1991). The passage to a full shape-free face is relatively commonplace when performing manipulations with face images, being the standard way of morphing between faces. It is also used when performing image carica-tures (Benson and Perrett, 1991), precisely because moving away from the actual landmarks on a face still generates faces which appear realistic, and thus satisfies the perturbation test described on pages 188–189. Finally, we note that many of the theoretical consequences of our model fit well with existing theories of face recognition; we return to this below.

A net-based method?

The description of our proposed method of coding objects does not address the question of implementation because it is irrelevant to the central thesis of this chapter. Nevertheless, it is of interest that imple-mentation can be done in many biologically plausible ways and that, in particular, both steps involved; the non-linear warping and subsequent linear analysis via principal component analysis are routine operations in neural net technology. The non-linear warping step, frequently observed and well understood (e.g. Hertz et al., 1991: 235), is already being suggested as an essential ingredient of a working net-based face recogni-tion system (Lades et al., 1993). The subsequent principal component analysis is essentially the function performed by linear neural nets (Linsker, 1986). The combination of steps is thus sufficiently net-like that it may actually be used in net-based face recognizers. Of course, learning the need for the non-linear warp will require much training, hence in practice at present, systems that do the warp directly have a computational advantage.

EXISTING MODELS OF FACE RECOGNITION

A number of models of face recognition have been proposed to account for the body of experimental work. The most influential is probably the Bruce–Young model which is a process or box model (Bruce and Young, 1986). However, at a finer level dealing with initial recognition, many experiments bear on the issue of coding; they suggest that distinctive unknown faces are easier to recognize, that inverted faces are harder to recognize – although less so in young children – and that other-race faces are treated differently from own-race faces. These results have led a number of authors to propose that faces are coded in terms of one or more prototypes (Ellis, 1981; Valentine and Bruce, 1986) or norms (Rhodes *et al.*, 1987), or in terms of schema (Goldstein and Chance, 1980). Caricatures provide further evidence of prototype extraction (cf. Rhodes *et al.*, 1987); a caricature is recognized faster for line-drawings, as would be expected if faces were coded as deviations from a prototype. This persists with grey scale caricaturing (Benson and Perrett, 1991); it is of interest that the relevant manipulations were implemented with the coding described on page 191.

Valentine's model of face space

In an attempt to produce a more computationally specified theory, Valentine (1991) suggests these arguments for prototype extraction can be phrased in terms of a knowledge of the population of faces previously encountered. He goes on to propose a mechanism, by which this knowledge influences subsequent recognition, in which faces are coded as points in some (high-dimensional) linear space, as deviations either from exemplars, or from a norm or prototype based on experience.

Specifically he assumes that 'a location in Euclidean multidimensional space provides an appropriate metaphor for the mental representation of a face'. One model codes all faces as deviations from some global norm, prototype or mean, and treats recognition in terms of a nearest neighbour matching; the other is essentially the same, except that the space is affine, so has no distinguished zero, and the faces themselves, rather than deviations, are coded.

This model is then used to discuss recognition and classification. Since a typical face is one which lies in an area of high exemplar density, it is likely that there are near neighbours which are different faces. Thus the model predicts that typical faces are harder to recognize than are distinctive ones. The reverse effect occurs if the task is simply to classify the input as a face, because there are many close neighbours against which to judge category membership. Similar arguments are suggested for other observed effects.

From our viewpoint the essential observation is that the properties used are all local properties of the space, and so the arguments apply equally to a space that is locally Euclidean. In this sense, while more general, our model makes the same predictions as Valentine's. However, the theories differ: Valentine predicts that a given face has a unique coding, at least for an individual at a given time, although presumably this changes with time as the experience or current prototype changes. In contrast, we explicitly reject a unique coding, suggesting that the coding used for recognition is chosen to suit the task in hand and is purely temporary. The difference in the two approaches is that we expect to get valid results only with faces which are relatively similar to those for which the local averages are obtained. In contrast, although Valentine's theory assumes global coding, we are not aware that this assumption has been examined experimentally.

The assumption that all faces can be coded with a single Euclidean space has strong consequences:

- there is a natural co-ordinate structure which is pre-eminent;
- Euclidean space comes equipped with certain global constructs which may not be useful in the context of faces; for example, the sum of two objects may not make sense, and scaling may not be a natural operation; and
- globally, the geometry may appear counter-intuitive if the dimension of the space is high; for example, if a collection of faces is distributed uniformly within a ball of Radius 1, then essentially all of them ($\geq$ 99.999 per cent) have length between 0.999 and 1 when the dimension of the space exceeds 12,000. This is by no means unreasonably large given the variability of faces!

Eigenface models

We have chosen to discuss Valentine's model in detail because the underlying geometrical assumptions are spelled out. Of course, much more modelling of face space has been done with the aim of describing and predicting the body of experimental work on face recognition. Rather than go into more detail, we refer the reader to the other chapters in this volume. But it is important for our purposes to discuss one other body of theory, which goes back to Kohonen *et al.* (1981). In a series of papers (O'Toole *et al.*, 1991a; O'Toole *et al.*, 1991b; O'Toole *et al.*, 1993; O'Toole *et al.*, 1994), a rather different theory has been suggested to account for a number of the phenomena that Valentine seeks to explain with his multidimensional face-space model. Modelling is done in the context of a linear associative neural net, in the tradition of Kohonen *et al.* (1981). Starting with a fixed ensemble of faces, each of which has a common position and scale, so that to a first approximation they are 'shape-free' in our terminology, they perform principal component analysis in order to extract the eigenfaces. Subsequent faces are coded in terms of this collection of eigenfaces. Formally the ensemble is described as the training set for the associative memory, but as noted in O'Toole *et al.* (1994), such a training set, learned using the Widrow-Hoff error correction rule, is exactly the same as coding in terms of the corresponding eigenfaces. They are thus coding face images in the same way as is described here, but for rather different reasons.

It is thus interesting that they report their codings to be psychologically relevant. When a new face f is coded in terms of eigenfaces, a measure is available describing how well the face is represented. We can take this as a measure of how suitable the ensemble is to represent the new face, or the accuracy of the assumption that $f \in N$. They report in O'Toole *et al.* (1994) that, using a Caucasian ensemble, this accuracy measure was a better predictor of human recognition accuracy for Caucasian faces than any of the observer face ratings they used. O'Toole *et al.* (1993) explore in more detail the 'meaning' of the individual eigenface loadings; in terms of an ensemble, in which both sexes are equally represented, they find that the loading on an early eigenface, typically the second, is a good predictor of sex. Similarly, when the ensemble is of mixed race, they are able to get a good predictor of race in terms of eigenface loadings. In our language this is interpreted as saying that the particular local approximation used is accurately able to describe both sex and race differences. In a similar vein, and coding in the same way, using separately white and black male faces as ensemble faces, Pentland *et al.* (1993) were able to get recognition rates of 95 per cent and 90 per cent, although with a corresponding Asian ensemble, arguably less homogeneous, the recognition rate was 80 per cent.

RECOGNITION RESULTS

We have argued on general grounds for our coding scheme, combining shape information from the warp to a shape-free face, together with a coding of the shape-free face image, co-ordinatized in terms of the eigenfaces derived from some ensembles of faces which provide background knowledge, and which represent the current experience of faces. In this section we describe briefly some results which suggest that this is a useful *practical* procedure for achieving a degree of invariant face recognition. The results described here were presented in part in Craw and Cameron

(1992). A total of 150 faces was chosen from the Aberdeen face database, gathered in 1982 for work on mugshot retrieval. The collection was a simulation of such a mugshot database (Shepherd, 1986); subjects were photographed in a uniform way, ensuring that differences such as background and lighting were effectively eliminated. The images were subsequently digitized in as uniform a manner as possible, with location and scale fixed so that each left eye and each right eye occupied a common position, and normalized to the same mean intensity. The landmarks were located on each image by hand, and the corresponding shape-free face was stored.

Three of the faces in the original collection, chosen because modern images of these faces could be obtained, were selected as targets. A set of ninety-seven faces was chosen at random to form the pool with the three targets. The remaining fifty faces formed the ensemble used to calculate the eigenfaces. Photographs of the three targets (we refer to them as

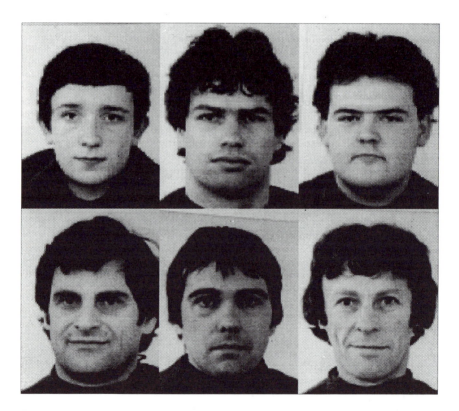

Figure 9.3 Six images from the pool of one hundred, including images of the targets Ian, Ken and Harry taken nearly ten years before those in Figure 9.4. The images in the bottom row are the three targets

Ian, Ken and Harry) taken in 1991 were obtained, with no attempt made to imitate the conditions in the original collection. We show these images in Figure 9.4, and the originals in Figure 9.3, together with the images of three other faces from the collection, to give an idea of the variation between images in the pool.

Figure 9.4 Modern images of Ian, Ken and Harry, used as cue to search the database

Each of the three cues was used in turn to test recognition. Both the cue and each face in the pool was projected on to the subspace spanned by the most significant twenty eigenfaces obtained from the (totally disjoint) ensemble. The dot product between the twenty byte representations of the cue and each image in the pool was calculated, and the magnitude used as (naive) notion of similarity to rank the images in the pool as matches for the corresponding cue image. Table 9.1 gives these rankings. Experiments with different subsets of one hundred as the pool, using the other fifty faces as ensemble, produce no effect on the results. In a second set of tests, we excluded the hair from the analysis and

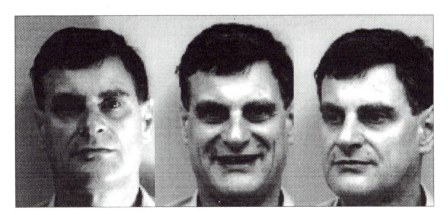

Figure 9.5 Modern images of Ian, sidelit, smiling and angled

matching. Thus the ensemble of fifty faces used to generate the eigen-faces was also restricted in this way; after normalising the eigenvalues we were left with twenty-one eigenfaces (rather than twenty) which were used for coding the face portion of the images in the pool and the cues. The rest of the procedure was as before, and again Table 9.1 gives the rankings. Following these tests, a further set of images of Ian was collected (in 1992) under deliberately varied conditions, with the aim of exploring the robustness of the recognition process. One image was taken with lighting obviously from the side, one with a smile, and the third delib-erately from an angle. These three images are shown in Fig 9.5.

The same recognition tests were then performed with each of these images as cue, and the earlier (1982) image of Ian as cue. The results are also shown in Table 9.1.

Table 9.1 Matching shape-free faces in the reduced eigenface representation. The rank, from a pool of a hundred faces, of the match between a cue face and the corresponding target, is shown. The target for each of the last four cues is the same.

Cue face	Full face (20 cmpts)	Ignoring hair (21 cmpts)
Ken now	27	2
Harry now	10	1
Ian now	1	1
Ian sidelit	3	1
Ian smiling	6	1
Ian angled	1	1

A problem with any test of this type occurs when 'accidental' factors assist the matching. For this reason, much of our work has been with a pool consisting of faces gathered under conditions which were as similar as possible without special treatment of any of the targets. The results for the first three cues, with flat lighting and a neutral expression, were reported in Craw and Cameron, 1992, although a larger area of the face has now been defined as hair (and hence excluded for the 'ignoring hair' results). The fact that recognition remained under quite large changes in the imaging conditions of the cue, represented by the last three rows of Table 9.1, suggests that our earlier results were robust.

We believe our coding scheme has promise, and that the extra compli-cation of passing to the shape-free face greatly improves the robustness of the recognition. It is clear how the passage to the shape-free version removes some of the image differences associated with both the smile and the angled face; small variations in angle can be removed effectively without the need to use a full 3-D model. Recognition across lighting

change seems more surprising; we suggest it may be a consequence of
our standardized ensemble, and that there was nothing in the eigenface
vocabulary which allowed the lighting differences to be coded. Indeed,
other tests we have done suggest that lighting invariance can be achieved
more easily in this form than in many other testing regimes, and that
recognition can easily follow the lighting condition rather than the individual in a situation in which the lighting in the pool has not been stan-
dardised. For this reason we have taken particular care to ensure that
our ensemble consists of essentially similar faces, and that all the images
in the pool were taken under the same conditions. We thus believe it
is a useful test that recognition occurred when the cue was taken under
very different conditions, and was performed across an age difference
of something like ten years, and it seems likely that the coding scheme
is able to abstract features which are a function of the face itself, rather
than a particular image of the face. Because of this need for standard-
ization, we have only been able to vary the condition of the cue in these
tests, and are unable to explore the effect of varying target conditions.
We are currently building a modern face database in order to extend
this investigation.

MORE GENERAL RECOGNITION MODELS

In the preceding section we have discussed how a manifold model of face
recognition leads to a re-examination and extension of existing models
of face recognition. In fact our model is much more general, and deals
in a unified manner with both inter- and intra-class discrimination.
Connectedness is one way to discuss categorical distinctions. Just as the
genus of a surface the (integer-valued) number of handles is a continuous
invariant of surfaces, so we can describe coarse distinctions (the number
and type of geons) within this description as well as making fine distinctions.

It is not clear how this explanation of intra-class discrimination, or
second-order shape differences, links with contemporary descriptions of
inter-class discrimination such as the theory of geons, due to Biederman
(1987). In contrast a manifold theory has a natural progression between
the two extremes, depending on what part of the representation is considered as significant. It is here that the choice of ensemble is an indication of what variety is to be encountered, and as such, what discrimination
is needed. If we have objects from very different parts of the recognition
manifold, then coarse discriminants suffice, and indeed are all that are
available, since finer ones are only able to work in a particular neighbourhood. The concept of eye shape is irrelevant in distinguishing between
a face and a hammer, but could be vital when differentiating between
different individuals. In contrast, in theories of intra-class representation,

there is some sort of 'ensemble' available which may be used to form an average or mean shape, against which intra-class differences are measured.

We now describe geon theory more carefully. Biederman (1987) argued for a general theory of human object recognition based on the assumption that objects could be best represented and described in terms of a relatively small set of components, parts or geons, distinguished only categorically from each other, by properties which were viewpoint invariant. The primitive representation of the object was to be scale translation and orientation invariant and composed of simple convex or singly concave parts. This geon description was to be available from the object itself, and a qualitative description of the component geons together with a categorical description of their relationships was to permit fast access to a database of object models.

In one sense, this theory could be regarded as a categorical version of the generalized cylinders of Binford (1982). At about the same time, a similar approach, with parts also from a more restricted vocabulary than generalized cylinders, but explicitly parametrized, was introduced by Pentland (1986). In each case, the aim has been to build a representation which is simple enough to be derived early in the processing chain, while having enough power to describe a wide variety of real world objects. Although geons were originally introduced as a theory of the human visual process, and backed by psychophysical experiments, attempts have subsequently been made to use them in the machine object recognition world, with systems like PARVO (Bergevin and Levine, 1993) designed to work from line-drawings, and going via a geon-based intermediate description. Experience of this endeavour seems to suggest the need for a finer level of description for some tasks, with additional quantitative information available during the recognition process. One such hybrid system, using both a qualitative geon-based segmentation and a parametric shape-fitting stage, has worked successfully with real imagery (Dickinson *et al.*, 1993).

CONCLUSIONS

We have argued for a particular abstract description of the recognition process based on the needs of invariance, and have been led to theories which are similar to existing ones but from a more general viewpoint. In particular, we have argued that an important distinction should be drawn between local properties, valid for all faces in some neighbourhood of a given one, and global properties, which are valid for all faces.

NOTES

1 We should perhaps have resisted the temptation to call this the identity map!
2 Those familiar with tensor analysis may recognize the aphorism 'Differential geometry is the study of properties invariant under change of notation!'.
3 The word 'chart' is standard terminology, and is used to avoid confusion with 'map', a ubiquitous synonym for function. There is no intention to confine charts to the sea, and 'geographical map' would be a useful alternative metaphor.
4 This is a situation in which we ignore the differences between the two lines in the commutative diagram on page 187; we refuse to try to illustrate a face itself.

REFERENCES

Benson, P.J. and Perrett, D.I. (1991) Perception and recognition of photographic quality facial caricatures: implications for the recognition of natural images. *European Journal of Cognitive Psychology*, 3, 105–135.

Bergevin, R. and Levine, M.D. (1993) Generic object recognition: building and matching coarse descriptions from line drawings. *IEEE Transactions on Pattern Analysis and Machine Intelligence*, 15, 19–36.

Biederman, I. (1987) Recognition-by-components: a theory of human image understanding, *Psychological Review*, 94, 115–146.

Binford, T.O. (1982) Survey of model-based image analysis systems. *International Journal of Robotics Research*, 1, 18–64.

Bookstein, F.L. (1991) *Morphometric Tools for Landmark Data*. Cambridge, UK: Cambridge University Press.

Brooks, R.A. (1981) Symbolic reasoning among 3-D models and 2-D images. *Artificial Intelligence*, 17, 285–348.

Bruce, V. and Young, A.W. (1986) Understanding face recognition. *British Journal of Psychology*, 77, 305–327.

Craw, I. and Cameron, P. (1992) 'Face recognition by computer', in D. Hogg and R. Boyle (eds), *British Machine Vision Conference 1992*. London: Springer-Verlag.

Dickinson, S.J., Bergevin, R., Biederman, I., Eklundh, J.-O., Munck-Fairwood, R. and Pentland, A. (1993) The use of geons for generic 3-d object recognition. *Proceedings of the Thirteenth International Joint Conference on Artificial Intelligence, Vol.2*. Los Alos, CA: Morgan Kauffman.

Ellis, H.D. (1981) 'Theoretical aspects of face recognition', in G.M. Davies, H.D. Ellis and J. Shepherd (eds), *Perceiving and Remembering Faces*. London: Academic Press.

Goldstein, A.G. and Chance, J.E. (1980) Memory for faces and schema theory. *Journal of Psychology*, 105, 47–59.

Hertz, J. Krogh, A. and Palmer, R. G. (1991) *Introduction to the Theory of Neural Computing*. Computation and Neural Systems Series. Redwood City, CA: Santa Fe Institute and Addison Wesley.

Hoffman, W.C. (1966) The lie algebra of visual perception. *Journal of Mathematical Psychology*, 3, 65–98 (errata: ibid., 4, 348–349).

Hoffman, W.C. (1978) The Lie transformation group approach to visual neuropsychology, in E.L.J. Leeuwenberg and H.F.J.M. Buffart (eds), *Formal Theories of Visual Perception*. Chichester: Halstead Press.

Kirby, M. and Sirovich, L. (1990) Application of the Karhunen-Loève procedure for the characterisation of human faces. *IEEE: Transactions on Pattern Analysis and Machine Intelligence*, 12, 103–108.

Kohonen, T., Oja, E. and Lehtiö, P. (1981) Storage and processing of information in distributed associative memory systems, in G. Hinton and J. Anderson (eds), *Parallel Models of Associative Memory*. Hillsdale, NJ.: Erlbaum.

Lades, M., Vorbrüggen, J., Buhmann, J., Lange, J., v. d. Malsburg, C., Würtz, R. and Konen. W. (1993) Distortion invariant object recognition in the dynamic link architecture. *IEEE: Transactions on Computers*, 42, 100–311.

Linsker, R. (1986) From basic network principles to neural architecture: emergence of orientation columns. *Proceedings of the National Academy of Sciences*, 83, 8779–8783.

O'Toole, A.J., Abdi, H., Deffenbacher, K.A. and Bartlett, J.C. (1991a) Classifying faces by race and sex using an autoassociative memory trained for recognition, in K.J. Hammond and D. Gentner (eds), *Proceedings of the Thirteenth Annual Conference of the Cognitive Science Society*, Hillsdale, NJ.: Erlbaum.

O'Toole, A.J., Deffenbacher, K.A., Abdi, H. and Bartlett, J.C. (1991b) Simulating the 'other-race' effect as a problem in perceptual learning. *Connection Science: Journal of Neural Computing, Artificial Intelligence and Cognitive Research*, 3, 163–178.

O'Toole, A.J., Abdi, H., Deffenbacher, K.A. and Valentin, D. (1993) Low-dimensional representation of faces in higher dimensions of the face space. *Journal of the Optical Society of America*, 10, 405–411.

O'Toole, A.J., Deffenbacher, K.A., Valentin, D. and Hervé, A. (1994) Structural aspects of face recognition and the other race effect. *Memory and Cognition*, 22, 208–224.

Pentland, A. (1986) Perceptual organisation and the representation of natural form. *Artificial Intelligence*, 28, 293–331.

Pentland, A., Starner, T., Masoiu, N., Oliyide, O. and Turk, M. (1993) 'Experiments with eigenfaces', in A. Pentland (ed.), *Looking at People: Recognition and Interpretation of Human Action*, IJCA I93. Proceedings of IJCA I93 workshop W28 in Chambéry, France.

Porrill, J., Pollard, S.B., Pridmore, T.P., Bowne, J.B., Mayhew, J.E.W. and Frisby, J.P. (1987) TINA: a 3d vision system for pick and place. Alvey Vision Conference (AVC), University of Sheffield Printing Unit.

Rhodes, G., Brennan, S. and Carey, S. (1987) Identification and ratings of caricatures: implications for mental representations of faces. *Cognitive Psychology*, 19, 473–497.

Shackleton, M.A. and Welsh, W.J. (1991) Classification of facial features for recognition. *Proceedings of the IEEE Conference on Computer Vision and Pattern Recognition (CVPR–91)*. New York: IEEE.

Shepherd, J.W. (1986) 'An interactive computer system for retrieving faces', in H.D. Ellis, M.A. Jeeves, F. Newcombe and A. Young (eds), *Aspects of Face Processing*. Dordrecht: Martinus Nijhoff.

Sirovich, L. and Kirby, M. (1987) Low-dimensional procedure for the characterization of human faces. *Journal of the Optical Society of America*, 4, 519–524.

Stonham, T.J. (1986) 'Practical face recognition and verification with WISARD', in H. Ellis, M. Jeeves, F. Newcome and A. Young (eds), *Aspects of Face Processing*. Dordrecht: Martinus Nijhoff.

Townsend, J.T. and Thomas, R.D. (1993) 'On the need for a general quantitative theory of pattern similarity', in S.C. Masin (ed.), *Foundations of Perceptual Theory. Advances in Psychology, Vol. 99*. Amsterdam: North Holland/Elseiver.

Turk, M. and Pentland, A. (1991) Eigenfaces for recognition. *Journal of Cognitive Neuroscience*, 3, 71–86.

Valentine, T. (1991) A unified account of the effects of distinctiveness, inversion and race in face recognition. *Quarterly Journal of Experimental Psychology*,

43A, 161–204.

Valentine, T. and Bruce, V. (1986) Recognizing familiar faces: the role of distinctiveness and familiarity. *Canadian Journal of Psychology*, 40, 300–305.

Chapter 10

Perspectives on face perception
Directing research by exploiting emergent prototypes

Philip J. Benson

WHAT PRICE FACE-LIKENESS?

The concept of 'faceness' or 'face-like' is one which should cause us some concern. This is perhaps one of the most fundamental perceptions we experience when dealing with this well-known class of homogeneous objects. It is the very self-similarity between exemplars within the domain of faces which has caused a great deal of our visual system (and perhaps beyond) to appear to have specialized and thus fine-tuned itself with the apparently express intent of providing an efficient capacity to judge, discriminate and remember. That is, memory for faces must be organized in a manner sympathetic to the potential and continued circumstances of our encounters with novel instances. Not only is the storage of the markers of identity and associated qualities for a few thousand faces necessary, but also the retrieval of other specific information must be made efficient. After all, while we are consciously unaware of the levels of neural processing involved in making a particular decision about a given face, if we pause to reflect on the magnitude and complexity of the cognitive search just performed then we should be intrigued and even impressed by our capabilities.

There are a great many levels at which we may process the facial image. As I have suggested, face-like is perhaps the most basic. Giuseppe Arcimboldo made intelligent light of this fact by constructing facial portraits from other classes of objects such as fruit, vegetables or species of vertebrates and invertebrates. Facial simulacra is familiar to us by way of our perception of faceness in naturally formed patterns observed in cloud formations, brief configurations of flames, or even in the bark of trees. In this instance, particular higher-order areas of our visual system 'erroneously' signal the presence of a face in the optic array, such is our bias towards perceiving the presence of a face. Not all observers will report the same perceptions, and this is thus perhaps the first indication of individual differences in face perception; even neonates will tend to pursue (by eye- or head-tracking) schematized facial stimuli (Bushnell *et al.*, 1989; Morton and Johnston, 1991; see Johnston (1994) for a recent review). While there is evidence to suggest that some degree of neural architecture for dealing with the facial image is innate, it is clear that the system takes time to develop and finally mature into one of the most powerful and adaptable recognition systems known to us.

Given that each of us share this construct, it is perhaps surprising to note that very little research has been conducted on the subject of *faceness*. The question arising is simply, how much information is required to signal the presence of face-likeness in the visual field? Here, I make no attempt to define what I mean by the term 'information', though it is clear that some semantic must be imposed on the spatial arrangement of extracted features which are considered and thus it is simply not just visual *data* we are concerned with. The visual system imposes some order and constraint upon the input pattern; it searches for patterns of structure, and faceness emerges at an early stage. Faceness is thus a significant contributing factor to the perception of the facial image and is not as trivial a point as might first appear. To what extent this notion of like-ness can vary and outwith what bounds does perception and recognition of facial qualities break down is not known. I will return to this subject later.

The costs of employing an apparently dedicated neural subsystem for face perception might appear to outweigh the benefits of such specializa-tion; after all, a specialized system is one which may be chronically disrupted leaving the host unable to operate to the expected standards of performance (for a recent review of prosopagnosia and specialization see Rhodes, 1993). The reverse appears to be more likely, as the benefits are numerous. A reasonably specialized system employs an architecture of rapid response units (or rather, populations of units) which leads to greatly improved processing skills. Such forms of dedication facilitate superior patterns of behaviour beyond those mediated by simple and also classi-cally conditioned responses. The complexity of responses possible at this level of interaction are unlimited: consider, for example, the act of decep-tion. The presence of levels of understanding and perception of stimuli allow a greater range of responses than would otherwise be possible if we operated dichotomously. It is therefore a matter for us to consider at which level to pitch our interpretation of laboratory data.

In fact, it appears that a similar system is responsible for our ability to learn to the degree of being 'expert' other classes of highly similar visual objects. Should an individual choose to become an ornithologist or a horticulturist, then an extensive new database of knowledge will be formed. It is ludicrous to suggest that a unique neural mechanism will evolve for each area of expertise; the reliance has to be on neural plasticity rather than having another processing system available to devote to a new information base. Instead, the very system already resident and configured for specialization for face perception would seem perfectly adaptable to other classes of objects. It is indeed tempting to suggest that similar rules for intra-object discrimination apply not just to faces, given that sensible ground rules have already been implemented and tested (cf. face and flower recognition in a prosopagnosic (De Haan *et al.*, 1987)). Specialization would appear to be rather fundamental to our knowledge of visual processing, given the emphasis which is placed on our abilities to 'tell the difference' even when those differences are hard to verbalize.

The very existence of facial simulacra is sufficient to warrant investigation in a different direction. Does face- (or object-) likeness encompass particular qualities which have been examined already and if so, can components of this account for the experimental observations? Levels of interpretation should accurately reflect levels of cognitive processing.

THE ROLE OF FACIAL PROTOTYPES

Introduction

It would be fair to suggest that the raising of face-likeness thresholds is important in the invocation of far more detailed processing of the percept. This is the major trigger in the time-course of face processing, with voice and speech recognition and perception also contributing to the process. If we have registered a face within the visual scene, then what other fundamental information can be gleaned? In accordance with functional models of face perception (e.g. Bruce and Young, 1986; Burton *et al.*, 1990) particular parameters may be extracted only at successive stages over time. In accordance with this notion, faceness will emerge at the outset.

One problem with the idea of directed facial processing is that 'faceness' may have already activated channels which deal, for example, with expression, age or gender perception. Thus, faceness has potentially accounted for a proportion of the results purported to explain experiments designed to examine higher-order visual interpretations. Priming and classification (latency) studies have attempted to tease apart the 'levels' at which such information is extracted. Facilitatory 'priming' occurs when we find ourselves better able to respond to a stimulus because of prior exposure to a related stimulus (e.g. the name of an actress, followed some time later by the appearance of her actor husband's face). Consciously or unconsciously we have been cued to expect a certain stimulus and so cognitively our sensitivity to related stimuli has been raised. 'Classification' paradigms involve determining the ease with which a given stimulus can be attributed to a particular known or learned stimulus class. Together, these techniques provide useful methods by which the perception and recognition of faces may be studied. However, more social psychology-oriented experiments have tended to neglect these results. I will discuss this shortcoming later in this chapter (further discussion of experimental designs can be found in Chapter 5, this volume). Priming studies themselves are not as susceptible to the influences of individual facets, instead tending to focus on, for example, mediation of identity.

In order to address these issues at the required level, I must limit my discussion to particular aspects of the visage. Facial expression, gender, age, ethnicity and distinctiveness are five facets which I suggest we can permit ourselves to consider as basic facial properties. Gender, age and ethnicity are the most basic of the five. Each of these facets are emergent properties of our experience with faces. We can only make a judgement about one of these facets if and only if we can express it in terms of its relationship to our knowledge base. Using this information alone it is possible to elicit or predict other judgements; these properties are constants across *all* human faces. These attributes are more fundamental than subjective attributions of, for example, attractiveness, homeliness, trustworthiness or honesty, friendliness, health, mental disposition or social standing. Where physiognomy and phrenology failed was to believe whole-heartedly in this to the extent that individual facial features or landmarks *embodied* as opposed to *signalled* these qualities. As face processing is a holistic exercise we must consider, at least at the outset, how facial features interact to provide impressions. However, the physiognomists were not as incorrect in their judgements as we might think. Attribution of character and personality based on facial appearance and mannerisms is commonplace; it is an inescapable component of stereotyping and is extremely difficult to negotiate in an objective manner. It is for this reason that personal bias or interpretation can influence judgements of other qualities signalled by the face alone. Many of these qualities can be demonstrated to be based upon the perception of likeness to the Self. In this way, experiments relying on subjective scale ratings (Likert, 1932) of facial qualities can go terribly wrong unless well controlled.

Prototypes

It is considered appropriate that the basis on which to make comparative judgements of the magnitude of expression, gender, age, ethnicity and distinctiveness are facial prototypes (Benson and Perrett, 1993; Benson, 1994b). Prototypes, or 'averages', represent the central tendency of a class of object (here, specifically the face) drawn from an appropriate sample of the range of objects which it is suggested best exemplifies a particular quality. Prototypical representations may embody structural (first- and second-order features (Rhodes, 1988)) or both textural (tonal, especially skin tone or apparent texture) and structural information.

Prototypes are computed as the precise numerical mean of a sample of faces: a number of faces are captured digitally and their common facial shape extracted; faces are then shape-changed so as to align each of the features before blending them together. Prototype perception is more likely to reflect the qualities embodied within the prototype than any of the constituent images, for the simple reason that a more stable representation has been arrived at by averaging out all inconsistencies while preserving any common terms present. Experimentally, a prototype is a more authentic and representative stimulus. It might be expected that subjects' response data are more 'clean' and less likely to have arisen (in part) through erroneous visual cues.

For gender prototypes, male and female typics can be synthesized for a given age or age band. Normally, within-race and age-bracketed prototypes will be generated so as to avoid cross-cultural influences, and the constituents will show a neutral expression. Age prototypes may or may not illustrate gender differences, but will normally include a bracketed or age specific treatment. Facial expression prototypes are synthesized from sets of exemplars emoting the same expression. Clearly, different individuals will emote the 'same' expression to the different degrees, although it is possible to control this (see Ekman, 1992). Distinctiveness prototypes are more problematic because it is possible to represent more information than intended. However, a highly distinctive prototype may be generated for a particular age, sex and ethnic group. Similarly, a typical prototype may be synthesized which is minimally distinctive in terms of its facial features. In short, a prototype of similarly distinctive faces is more likely to be distinctive than typical especially when compared with a typical prototype created from typical exemplars. Prototypes of individuals may be calculated from several instances of their own image taken at different eras; prototypes of individuals embody each of the four other facial qualities, and so care must be taken in establishing the correct methods prior to experimentation unless a pure recognition paradigm is employed. In any case, the visual nature of any one prototype employed will be determined by the need to factor out, for example, gender and/or age.

It is possible to obtain attribute profiles for a given prototype in an experimental situation. Prototypical stimuli are more likely to facilitate consistent responses from subjects than would the exemplars because of the limited possible ranges of information they contain. Prototypes certainly possess faceness, and may also be considered canonical forms of particular facial qualities which emerge at low levels of cognitive processing. Age, gender and ethnicity serve to limit the scope of cognitive search by massive orders of magnitude. If well-defined facial prototypes are used as stimuli, the stages of face processing may be delineated more accurately. Ethnicity itself is an issue which has received consideration. Valentine's (1991) explanation of the 'other-race' effect is one which lends strong support to the application and use of emergent typics for use in the perception of this and other facial qualities.

While distinctiveness is a strong component of facial identity, it need not be considered in great detail at this point as many response decisions can be made without reference to this. Interestingly, typical faces possess a greater degree of faceness than do atypical (distinctive) faces (Valentine and Bruce, 1986). In this particular experiment it was found that while distinctive faces were recognized (identify) more quickly than typical ones, they were more difficult to classify as faces than typicals when shown normally or with jumbled facial features. In terms of typics, although a distinctive prototype is itself a face it is actually more different from other faces and also the typical prototype (a truer, more representative 'average'), and is thus less face-like.

DIFFERENCES BETWEEN PROTOTYPES

When gender and distinctiveness prototypes are considered *intra*-class, it is possible to begin to describe how male and female and distinctive and typical faces differ. It is tempting to suggest that the *differences* between male and female and distinctive and typical faces represent 'gender' and 'distinctiveness' respectively; however, further consideration needs to be given to the make-up of the prototypes. While 'distinctiveness' (whatever distinctiveness is) extracted from a typical and an atypical prototype may represent what is intended, it again possesses at least age, gender and ethnicity information. Age cannot be easily described in this subtractive manner for a number of reasons. 'Age' embodies gender, and at the same time 'ethnicity', 'distinctiveness', measures of skin tone changes, and the cranio-facial deformations especially apparent between the sexes and during puberty through to the late teens and early twenties. In fact, the face never ceases to change, especially as part of the ageing process. In the same way, 'ethnicity' is problematic. However, it *is* possible to gradually partial out each factor through repeated systematic assessment: the degree to which a particular attribute remains present in a stimulus pattern will depend on the cognitive levels being addressed. In considering facial expressions, the linear Cartesian difference between Anger and Neutral is not necessarily 'Anger' *per se*. The difference between Anger and Happy is not 'Happy', 'Anger', or 'neither Happy nor Angry'. This cannot possibly be the case, as I will describe in the next section.

It is worth considering at this point the degree to which the presence of basic facets of gender, age, ethnicity, expression and gender influence higher-order perceptions of individuals. For example, 'profession' may be defined stereotypically and include each basic facet where some play more important roles than others. An individual may be more likely to be perceived as a criminal if the candidate is male, around 30 years old, non-Caucasoid, with distinctive unattractive facial features or markings, and portrayed displaying a dubious facial expression. Presented with such a stimulus pattern, how can a subject possibly begin to dissociate between even these basic properties in an honesty-judgement task?

I have arrived at the possibility where research on facial types and facial information can proceed in a number of ways. The remaining sections in this chapter deal with particular generic examples to illustrate my arguments.

CATEGORICAL PERCEPTION OF FACIAL SIGNALS

Many psychophysical experiments in visual and auditory psychophysiology are interested in establishing whether or not distinct boundaries exist between exemplars within learned or naturally occurring classes of objects. It is intended that artificial laboratory situations provide better control over sensory processing yet usefully mimic natural processing. One way in which this can be achieved is to vary a stimulus along one or a strictly limited number of dimensions. Subjects are required to make dichotomous responses to stimuli chosen from a continuum which differ only by a small amount, the idea being that at some point a perceptual switch from preferring or describing perception in a particular way of one of the stimuli to the next will take place. This has been termed *categorical perception* (a good reference text is Harnad, 1987). It has been suggested that instead of encoding all possible manifestations (or a large number of them) for particular classes of stimuli we interpolate between well-established and known categories (or exemplars of categories) in order to determine the relative strengths of the stimulus pattern and thereby respond appropriately.

Consider the categorical perception of facial expressions (Etcoff and Magee, 1992). In their experiment, Etcoff and Magee presented subjects with facial stimuli drawn from particular subsets of faces within each of which one facial expression gradually changed into another. With the exception of 'Surprise', they reported that each of the expressions were perceived categorically, i.e. that there might exist distinct classes of expressions into which a given (degree of) expression would fall and thence be perceived, as opposed to facial emotions being seen as belonging to a continuous range of expressions. In a sense, the design of such an experiment is flawed because we do not emote a fixed set of facial expressions and therefore we cannot consider them in isolation. On the other hand, such an experiment has sought to validate the hypothesis of the existence of universally recognized facial expressions. While the authors' approach was valid for considering *categorical expressions*, it is unlikely that it provided the resolution necessary to describe the presence or absence of facial emotion categories and boundaries as precisely as we would like. Further, not all conditions were tested by the authors. Those used were chosen to reflect the extremities (positive and negative) of the universal emotions. It is not clear whether this approach helps us tell if the data can be interpreted in terms of perceptual categories or some cognitive labelling system. In support of this finding, one would like to be able to demonstrate that none of the other expressions considered are responsible for the reported categorical boundaries.

The basic expressions are: happiness, sadness, anger, contempt/disgust, fear and surprise (Ekman and Friesen, 1971; Izard, 1971). Here, I have to consider neutral as a facial expression in its own right. Neutrality provides the basis from which all other expressions can be represented and perceived in a relative manner (which is testable under the categorical paradigm). We are capable of displaying a large number of facial expressions, each of which can vary in strength and can also be influenced by another expression (i.e. feeling) at that time. For example, happiness may be commensurate with contempt and surprise in a given context. A subject posing this expression may not be able to express contempt in a particularly convincing manner and so while the stimulus is defined as the happy + contempt + surprise stimulus, the contempt component will be lacking to the detriment of the experiment. As Waters (1987) has quite correctly suggested, particular combinations of facial expressions are impossible because of the configuration and operation of groups of facial muscles. Nevertheless, combinations of expressions *are* possible.

Let me return to single expressions for a moment. Taking a large sample of subjects trained in posing facial expressions (see the discussion of the 'Facial action coding system' (FACS) in Ekman and Friesen, 1976; 1978) and from this synthesizing the canonical form of happiness, etc. (presumably for male and female posers separately) we can go some way towards standardizing the stimulus set. This is insufficient, however. The quality of each expression needs be measured for good reason. This is because, for example, the difference between happiness and neutral, and sadness and neutral, i.e. the magnitude of 'happiness' and 'sadness' should be experimentally equivalent. The extremities of continua must be perceived with the same clarity or recognizability if perceptual categories are to be examined. This may sound rather pedantic, but in any experiment such as that reported by Etcoff and Magee it is imperative that the visual qualities of each category are as well defined as possible. If they are not, then the response distributions will be unnaturally skewed and it will be extremely difficult to establish whether as many categories as there are basic expressions exist or whether there are fewer categories some of which can accommodate two expressions, e.g. the positive–negative happy–sad category. The effectiveness of labelling each stimulus should also be questioned; as an example, the strengths of each of the surprise conditions illustrated in Etcoff and Magee (1992: 231) are very different. I would suggest then that it is imperative that the perceived (and computed) 'energy' conveyed by each basic emotion be identical. How this may be measured is the subject of discussion in the following sections.

As I have said, we are capable of emoting and perceiving a wide range of facial expressions. Each expression can be produced by the same face, and every face is capable of producing such an expression. For this reason, I suggest that the means by which each stimulus is parameterized in terms of the influence afforded to it by *each* possible condition should be considered. It is entirely possible that the *physical* carriers of emotion information contribute to the fuzziness of the expression categories just as much as do the inconsistencies in our attribution of *labels* of expression categories.

Etcoff and Magee (1992) used facial outlines (line-drawings) as their stimuli. It is to their credit that they succeeded in determining the categorical perception of some facial expressions using only featural and configural information. The presence of textural or tonal skin information plays a crucial role in many aspects of natural face perception and recognition (Davies *et al.*, 1978). It is important to determine to what extent such information alone is responsible for any effects observed in categorical experiments. Again it is clear that it is important to pitch discussion of results at the correct level – visual cues may be signalled by a necessary minimum of information (Shepard, 1984) which are not actually being constrained and addressed by the design of the experiment.

In an attempt to accommodate these problems, the morph transformation (Benson, 1994a) may be employed to provide discrete interval transformation between natural photographic facial images. Morphing differs from the basic facial warp transformation (Benson and Perrett, 1991b) in that any differences between originating and final tonal information are correctly interpolated between (over and above fundamental featural shape changes). Warping comprises simply deformation of the (image) surface configuration. Morph transformation between happy and sad images, for example, can be used in a commensurate experiment and thus the effect of presenting the same stimulus pattern using different representation modalities can be examined. Where discrepancies in the results exist, the effective role of texture versus shape information can be discussed.

Linear interpolation between two classes or types provides a number of intermediate stimuli which are equidistant in terms of the differences between them and their neighbours along the continuum. Let s be the number of transitional steps between two typics. The continuum will therefore contain $s + 1$ stimuli; let $t = s + 1$. If there are n typics to be considered, then there are a total of

$$\frac{n^2 + n}{2}$$

[1]

permutations of typic continua to be tested.[1] A total of

$$n + (t - 2)\frac{n^2 + n}{2}$$

[2]

stimuli need be rendered for the experiment.

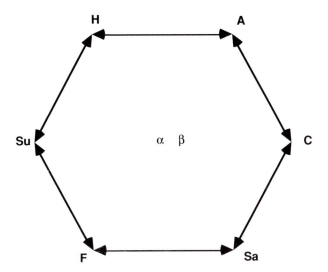

Figure 10.1 Flattened hyper-hull describing interactions within facial expression space

Note The abbreviations are *H*appiness, *A*nger, *C*ontempt/*D*isgust, *Sa*dness, *F*ear, *Su*rprise. Under normal categorical paradigms, the edges of the space (shown with bi-directional arrows) plus H-C, H-Sa, H-F, A-Sa, A-F, C-F, and C-Su would be tested. In reality, an infinite number of other combinations (interactions) between nodal expressions is possible; it is impossible to represent this on paper due to the folding problems introduced by the large number of dimensions present. This figure can only give a flavour of the kinds of tests which are required to obviate the need to assess the role of every possible combination of canonical expressions. α represents a hypothesized 'average' expression which is neither *H, A, C, Sa, F* or *Su*, but is equally weighted, or contributed to, by these nodal expressions. β represents an expression in the space which is more *A, C,* and *Sa* than it is *F, Su, H* or α. Sampling along a linear continuum, say between *H* and *Su*, may help resolve whether or not hybrid expressions exist in particular cultures or whether data genuinely reflect alternating or dual perceptual states.

As already mentioned, facial expressions are unlikely to occur only in their pure and potentially categorical form due to the large number of possible interactions with the other basic expressions. A more rigorous way in which to assess the relative importance and hence the true categorical nature of facial expressions (or any generic class of typics) is to select each stimulus from the uniform distribution provided by the convex hyper-hull defined as follows (and see Figure 10.1). Each theoretical node on the hull exerts a modulatory influence on a chosen point within the space. As an example, the centroid α of the space might be taken to represent neutrality (this can be verified objectively and qualitatively), in which case each of A, C, Sa, F, Su and H (see figure abbreviations) will contribute equally to the synthesis of the 'average' expression in this space. A neighbouring point, β, to the right of α would be influenced more by A, C and Sa than F, Su and H. That is, the weighted contribution of each of A, C and Sa towards the appearance of β is both relatively and proportionally greater than that of F, Su and H.

It will be clear to the reader that the flattened representation of the hull's *expression space* is only informative in a restricted sense. The 'distance' separating H from A, C, Sa, F and Su must be equal to any other typic nodal separation, i.e. unitary in normalized space. If this is not the case then each logical node type need be redefined each time a sample measure from the space is made: in experiments where the dimensions of the space are known to be constrained statistically or procedurally within the hull by scale and rotation relationships then the space may, of course, be flattened. One way to think of this is to assume that the edges of the hull (or polygon in this instance) define the rigidity of the stimulus space and it is therefore a space within which an image or outline can be warped only in a fixed number of dimensions. If this is the case, then H and Sa are opposites in the expression space, as are A and F, for example (I do not suggest this is actually the case; rather I use this to illustrate my point).

This model promotes two appealing features. First, the categorical perception paradigm may be employed at various resolutions in order to quickly establish the presence or absence of cognitive categories within or between classes of objects (preferably typics) and can be correctly assessed while drawing upon the entire gamut of stimuli. Because of the nature of the space one need not specify the number of possible permutations (according to n and t as I have shown in [2] for the degenerate case). The implication of this is quite simple. Iteration by way of repeated sampling from the distribution of *possible* stimuli can be guided by subjects' responses: that is, a *data-driven* experimental design. The stimulus density function (sample resolution) emerges automatically from such a methodology and so the number of experimental stimuli need not be a factor at the outset. This approach better defines *where* the boundaries of cognitive categories actually lie within the class space, should they exist at all. One can therefore relate the findings of Etcoff and Magee (1992) to either the hull's inner space or the edges of the hyper space (strictly speaking, only in the restricted unfolded space shown in Figure 10.1).

Second, data from experiments employing this approach can be collated and displayed within precisely the same framework. An extension to Figure 10.1 would be to include tonal information to represent the scope of any node expressed at any point in the hyper space. Each point examined within the space can be represented as coded hue-saturation-value (HSV) or hue-lightness-saturation (HLS), or subtractive cyan-magenta-yellow-black (CMYK) or additive red-green-blue (RGB) channel values and this information used to interpolate between other nodes employing Gouraud shading (Gouraud, 1971) to complete the inference between known and unknown (untested) locations. As such, the model is predictive as well as representative. The real power of optional coding using tonal detail within the standard Commission Internationale de L'Eclairage (CIE) defined colour space is that percentages, ratios or discrete encoding can be employed hand-in-hand with the semantics of the statistics and measures made in the experiments. Therefore, *additional* information for summary, interpretation and perusal may be displayed in the same graphic.

Using a data-driven experimental paradigm is one way in which we may attempt to arrest and distil complications acquired through requiring subjects to attribute labels to stimuli in perceptual tasks such as those described here. In requesting labelling of facial expressions it is not necessarily clear whether subjects are offering (the desired) insight into their perceptions or forcibly assigning one of the available labels (are we confident the stimuli are correctly designed?), attributing notional mental states to the individual displaying the expression (should we have completely computer-synthesized non-actor expressions?), or even referring to action patterns (the subjects are fear-stricken and look as if they are about to flee in the next instant).

MEASURING FACIAL 'QUALITIES'

It is worth considering how prototypical images can be assessed as part of the design of an experiment. Recent years have seen the development of two approaches for measuring similarity between facial images (the techniques may be applied as easily in other domains). Features and facial structure (multidimensional scaling (Rhodes, 1988); taxonomic classification ('SNOB') (Wallace and Boulton, 1968; Katsikitis et al., 1990; Pilowsky and Katsikitis, 1994); dilation and rotation (Benson and Lothian, 1994[2])), and image 'texture' patterns (principal component analysis, or PCA (Sirovich and Kirby, 1987; Turk and Pentland, 1991; Craw and Cameron, 1991; 1992); see also Craw, Chapter 9, this volume). The latter studies operate most efficiently when prototypical transformations of exemplars have been derived, and it is therefore interesting to notice this particular parallel between machine and human image processing. Whatever the approach, measures of similarity between prototypes, for example, representing happiness and sadness, should provide similar indications of difference energies present when compared with the neutral condition. In this way, it is possible to systematically account for quantitative and qualitative differences in stimulus media and the perception thereof.

FACIAL IDENTITY

As a specific example of problems with the interpretation of components of the facial image I will briefly consider identity, i.e. those qualities which signal the visual presence of the individual. Identity is underpinned by age, gender, ethnicity and distinctiveness (itself a composite attribute).

Consider the possibility that perception and recognition of faces can be modulated using facial feature caricaturing (Perkins, 1975), such that

$$\forall(F) \rightarrow P$$
$$\exists(F') \rightarrow P'$$

[3]

The predicate hypothesis states that, for all faces, and hence for a given face, F, we will observe some measurable perception, P, of that face. Distinctiveness-modulation of that face (after some normalization process to effect an appropriate deformation of the stimulus) generates a modified face, F'. Thus for every caricature F', we will observe a modulated perception, P', of the stimulus. If the face is typical in nature, then caricature exaggeration or diminishment of the features and structure will be ineffective (there is nothing atypical or distinctive about its appearance).

It is important to realize that under the transformation $F \rightarrow F'$, if one facet transformation is null (or more precisely, *unitary*) then transformation is still being made. This merely represents a constant factor in the parameterization of a particular facial identity.

Fortunately, this is testable. Every published objective facial caricature experiment to date upholds this premise in one guise or another (Rhodes *et al.*, 1987; Rhodes and McLean, 1990; Rhodes and Moody, 1990; Benson and Perrett, 1991a; Ellis, 1992; Carey, 1992; Mauro and Kubovy, 1992; Benson and Perrett, 1994; Calder *et al.*, 1995). What these studies have achieved is a demonstration of how face recognition may be enhanced or diminished using perceptual and recognition memory paradigms according to individuating featural characteristics. Caricatures have been rendered by comparing an individual's face with an abstracted prototype, much in the same way that a caricature artist would sketch a portrait. In the case of the artist, the process must involve some notion of a cognitive typic. Where there are significant differences in feature shape or configuration (up to a point which might already be considered perceptually distinctive) these differences can be exaggerated a little in order to make the face more recognizable. Computationally-defined caricatures are effective in conferring perceptual and recognition advantages over veridical stimuli when displayed as line-drawings or natural photographic quality images; however, it has been demonstrated that different paradigms are appropriate for each stimulus type.

The definition of 'feature' is necessarily limited in the scope of these studies. A feature is something which plays an important interactive role in the make-up of an individual's facial appearance. In the general case, one feature may be present while it is not considered a universal trait; this would be signalled as a special binary condition tagged with a localized description. Caricature research has therefore attempted to address the general conditions of identity. It transpires that these generalized universal properties of faces are at least sufficient to elicit perceptions. Whether they are indeed the necessary components remains to be seen. In support of this theory, many studies have examined the active role of various facial features in isolation and it has transpired that some are more important than others and depending on the type of task employed (Ellis *et al.*, 1979; Young *et al.*, 1985; De Haan and Hay, 1986).

One might care to argue that because distinctiveness is a compound attribute, when it is exaggerated what is actually being manipulated are a great many other facets. However, age, gender, ethnicity and expression *are* indicative of an individual's visage. These facets *are* what we call facial distinctiveness. Age governs facial shape and skin texture patterns. Gender may present itself in various 'strengths' ranging from highly feminine (perhaps a 'caricature' of femininity), through typically feminine, androgyny, to masculinity and even an overtly masculine appearance. Ethnicity is extremely complex given the dynamics of demographic expansion. Facial expression may reveal itself as an explicit (posed or reaction) or implicit (facial asymmetry) attribute. Together, these components make up facial distinctiveness and to enhance one facet in distinctiveness experiments is to enhance them all, unless the prototype description embodies an account of the factor(s) not intended for manipulation.

Exceptions to such 'rules' will always exist. It is entirely possible that a 'long narrow face' must be considered a distinctive 'feature' while it is not accountable for by facets such as gender, ethnicity, or entirely by old age. In this case, it is design-driven that this impression of distinctiveness does not interact with subjects' responses possibly providing unintentional enhancement or diminishment of data.

The issue of familiarity is one which I have not yet addressed in the context of facial identity. There is good reason to believe that unfamiliar faces are processed differently from familiar ones (e.g. Ellis *et al.*, 1979; Flin, 1980; Klatzky and Forrest, 1984; Young *et al.*, 1985; Bruce *et al.*, 1987). Identity studies, at least, are beginning to suggest that the problem may be accountable in terms of particular facial attributes through the use of distinctiveness enhancement (Rhodes and Moody, 1990; Mauro and Kubovy, 1992). In a sense, familiarity should not be a confounding issue in identity judgements since although we appear to encode a more holistic impression of a novel face as opposed to the apparently more refined (and possibly emergent) coding for highly familiar faces, the *caricature* recognition process should access the same subsets of facial information. At the time of writing it remains to be seen to what extent this is true, or even which facets are 'active' during unfamiliar face processing. If true, the multidimensional encoding space (Valentine, 1991) supporting memories for faces needs to be as flexible as possible.

Caricatures work because they make use of emergent typics and tap into our visual recognition memory at a facilitatory level. If caricatures were not implementations of veridical stimuli enhanced in the appropriate 'direction' within face space, i.e. made even more distinctive and less like any other face, then perception and recognition would not be modulated in a positive way. Enhanced facets seen in caricature form have demonstrated the importance of facial distinctiveness which plays a crucial role in discrimination between faces and in the recognition of individuals. The question of which facets account for the observations is presently untested.

A FACIAL ALGEBRA

It does not matter whether one can actually visualize 'gender' or 'attractiveness' or 'age' or any such facial quality. What is important is to be able to demonstrate that any of these qualities are either related or dissociable. Having partialled these out we would be in a position to specify a functional facial algebra. It should be possible to manipulate single facets without affecting others, thereby going some way towards describing the variance in a given population sample of exemplars and typics. This is important because it is one way in which our understanding of the bounds of facial attribute perception is defined.

It would be nice to be able to take the differences between prototypes and apply the result to some other face but, as I have suggested, the difference between masculinity and femininity, for example, is not gender *per se*. Gender has some compelling semantic associated with it which is why female faces look female in the first place and not male. That is to say, there is some particular quality to female faces which is not shared by male faces and so it is unlikely that the perception of gender is categorical in nature. It is more likely that individual features or subtle combinations of features are responsible after all our observations easily lead us to suggest that a nose has a feminine feel to it, or a jaw is particularly masculine; the gender of particular features may be perceived categorically but not the face as a whole, as there are complicated feature interactions involved.

I return to my stereotypical criminal: male, 30 years old, non-Caucasoid, unattractive, and with a curious facial expression. What interactions are likely? It might be that being an androgynous (as it turns out) male and 30 *is* attractive, yet it is the expression (which might actually be facial asymmetry as opposed to a genuine expression) which renders the host unappealing. Ethnicity may be irrelevant. But how are we to ever know this without having considered exactly which facets are contributing to the perception required of us by the honesty-judgement task? Worse still, if we the observers are actually affected by the appearance of such a visage (as are autonomic nervous systems (ANS) of the expression posers reported in Ekman *et al.* (1983) and Ekman (1992) (see also covert recognition of faces in Tranel and Damasio, 1985)), then it is highly likely that judgements will be more obfuscated than originally anticipated. One further piece of knowledge to the effect that the male is an international film actor could instantly devalue any judgements conferred.

If we briefly turn our attention to attractiveness we again see that like distinctiveness, attractiveness cannot be a categorical property of faces. Attractiveness is an emergent property. Attractiveness is embedded within gender, just as much as it is a part of age as it is of expression and ethnic group. It would be quite wrong to suggest that a face is attractive unless a number of other factors have been taken into consideration. An 'attractive' female face (devoid of cosmetics and flattering or persuasive lighting) may be considered attractive specifically because it is female and of a particular age. It may be attractive because it is atypically female, and therefore it is a distinctive gender quality appropriate for a particular age which accounts for our perception of attractiveness. Faces are not attractive because of something they have, called attractiveness, which other faces do not possess. Attractiveness is perceived by degree *because* of the underlying properties it displays. These properties, or facets as I have referred to them here, are categorical or narrow-banded, well-defined (at least in the exclusive case) properties and are therefore quantifiable in terms of prototypes derived from a sample of the population of faces. An 'attractive' face has just as much right to be deemed so if it is symmetrical (typical) around the vertical mid-line as if it is asymmetric (distinctive). Because of these contributing factors it is extremely unlikely that Likert-ratings are actually measuring 'attractiveness'. Asking subjects to measure or rate 'attractiveness' by selecting a point on a scale does not take into account several factors, including the most basic of individual differences (self-perception, perceived and observer age, etc.). Further, because rating scales do not require that there is a single attractiveness dimension, it is not at all clear what subjects might be providing ratings of. Neglectful of this, much research in social and visual psychology has succumbed to the lure of attractiveness only to be confounded by more basic principles involved in the perception of faces.

SHOULD WE RECONSIDER FACE PERCEPTION?

We require our subjects to respond to the presentation of facial images according to the rules of our game. Our game might be to respond as quickly and accurately as possible whenever a face is shown. Subjects might be required to name the individual or to identify their gender. Quality judgements may be required such as impressions of how much or how little of a nominated attribute a presented face conveys to a subject.

The appeal of allowing face experiments to evolve using computer synthesized and manipulated images can be readily appreciated when one considers the experimental materials and hypotheses. First, natural images are being used. Second, providing the range of responses is restricted and/or the type of stimuli used are well-defined, then if manipulations are made in positive and negative 'directions' one might expect to observe commensurate changes in subjects' responses. If the hypotheses are borne out, then the correct manipulation has been made: the relevant perceptual feature domain has been identified. For example, facial distinctiveness enhancement should make recognition more easy. The positive results found in studies of caricature suggest that the objective manipulation is relevant to decision making, and so is involved in the stimulus encoding process. As the nature of the judgement changes its pitch, so must the nature of the stimulus be attenuated.

Distinctiveness is only one aspect of facial identity. Gender is the most significant semantic in constraining the search space.[3] From gender typics it is possible to objectively understand the differences between male and female faces. Gender *enhancement* further reveals differences conferred by subjects' preferences (Benson and Perrett, 1992). It is therefore possible to account for a small proportion of the observations found in identity experiments by gender data and thence suggest that gender is a negative, positive or neutral component of identity: new questions may be posed. How much of the caricature advantage can be accounted for by gender alone? Further, how much of attractiveness can be accounted for by gender? And significantly, how much gender-'bending' can we introduce before all we have served to do is to delineate the boundaries of our perceptions? We all want to know what 'attractiveness' is. We are all happy to say 'yes' or 'no' to images of faces. Surely if we want to be able to extol such attributes it is fundamentally important to understand *why* it is that particular nuances of visual stimulation drive us to voice these opinions.

I have provided several reasons why there is still far more to our knowledge of face processing to be uncovered than we have yet considered. Present analyses are too often focused at higher-level impressions obtained in perceptual studies. It should not come as too great a revelation that main effects or related results can actually be expressed in terms of other facets, each of which measurably contribute to the holistic facial algebra. Prototyping emerges at a cognitive level, so we should aim to match the process objectively in experiments. What can be accounted for using the appropriate prototypes provides a valid and powerful means by which the appearance and role of specific facial attributes can be identified. The pre-eminent issues raised by the question of faceness strongly suggest there remains a great deal to be considered in the visual cognition of facial information. Both gender and age may be indicated by other factors such as voice, gait pattern, mobility and posture, characteristics of the hands, and even preserved dermal elasticity. Thus, the face does not *exclusively* communicate the useful or even natural perceptual tokens signalling gender or age, yet we continue to place much emphasis on its appearance, often going to great lengths to cosmetically treat this primary social interface for reasons of a purely personal nature. Ethnicity, distinctiveness and expression *are* conveyed by dominant characteristics present in the facial image. Combinations of these visual cues contributing to primary sensations of faceness or likeness are clearly fundamental to our understanding of higher-order face perception and recognition. Far from being circular, the argument bearing on facial qualities can always be reduced to a number of operational basics: the experimental difficulty appears to lie in understanding the stimulus pattern and thence effectively tapping into early face processing. An adequate algebra is fundamental to our understanding of how the face is constructed and therefore how we perceive its qualities.

NOTES

1 The sum to n terms of an arithmetic series is

$$\frac{n}{2}(2a + (n - 1)\, d)$$

[1.1]

where n is the number of terms in the series, a is the first term, and d is the difference between terms. Simplification of this expression yields the formula given in [1], where $a = 1$, $d = 1$. Note that n must equal $n - 1$ because continua are bidirectional and need only be generated once.

2 Unpublished study and on-going researches (*Use of Procrustes Statistic Employing a Feature Configuration Semantic as a Classifier of Facial Types*). The significance of this research is that very few landmarks describing feature size and spatial arrangement are required in order to reliably capture a measure of similarity. The statistic accounts for the unknown differences between given

exemplars and prototypes. It is interesting to note that the SNOB system and that advocated in this work both require only twelve measurements (from approximately sixty landmarks) or thirteen landmark points in order to effect classification. While the FACEM pre-processor to SNOB ignores facial asymmetry (Katsikitis *et al.*, 1990), the Procrustes technique does not. Both approaches make implicit assumptions about facial symmetry in so far as it would appear to be irrelevant to most discussions which consider facial similarity.

3 A conservative estimate of the 1994 world population statistic shows a difference of 61 per cent males compared with 39 per cent females. These figures reflect a global average only; the average male–female ratio is approximately 1.58:1. Different countries show different male–female ratios; differing populations and projected population increases were taken into account. Sources used in the calculation were *Compact Peters Atlas of the World, 1991*, Harlow, Essex: Longman Group UK Ltd; and *The Times Atlas of the World, 1992*, London: Times Books.

ACKNOWLEDGEMENTS

This work was supported by the United Kingdom Medical Research Council. I thank Colin Blakemore, Ian Craw and Malcolm Young for their encouragement in exploring alternative theoretical avenues in face perception, some of which have been discussed in this chapter. I also thank Bea de Gelder for her interest in and comments on this chapter.

BIBLIOGRAPHY

Benson, P.J. (1994a) Morph transformation of the facial image. *Image and Vision Computing*, 12(10), 691–696.

Benson, P.J. (1994b) On facial image composite prototyping as a descriptive and diagnostic tool. *Journal of Audiovisual Media in Medicine*, 17, 27-30.

Benson, P.J. and Perrett, D.I. (1991a) Perception and recognition of photographic quality facial caricature: implications for the recognition of natural images. *European Journal of Cognitive Psychology*, 3, 105-135.

Benson, P.J. and Perrett, D.I. (1991b) Synthesising continuous-tone caricatures. *Image and Vision Computing*, 9, 123-129.

Benson, P.J. and Perrett, D.I. (1992) Face to face with the perfect image. *New Scientist*, 1809, 32-35.

Benson, P.J. and Perrett, D.I. (1993) Extracting prototypical facial images from exemplars. *Perception*, 22, 257-262.

Benson, P.J. and Perrett, D.I. (1994) Visual processing of facial distinctiveness. *Perception*, 23, 75-93.

Bruce, V. and Young, A.W. (1986) Understanding face recognition. *British Journal of Psychology*, 77, 305-327.

Bruce, V., Valentine, T. and Baddeley, A. (1987) The basis of the 3/4 view advantage in face recognition. *Applied Cognitive Psychology*, 1, 109-120.

Burton, A.M., Bruce, V. and Johnston, R.A. (1990) Understanding face recognition with an interactive activation model. *British Journal of Psychology*, 81, 361-380.

Bushnell, I.W.R., Sai, F. and Mullin, J.T. (1989) Neonatal recognition of the mother's face. *British Journal of Developmental Psychology*, 7, 3-15.

Calder, A.J., Young, A.W., Benson, P.J. and Perrett, D.I. (1995) Self priming from distinctive and caricatured faces. *British Journal of Psychology* (in press).

Carey, S. (1992) Becoming a face expert. *Philosophical Transactions of the Royal Society of London*, B335, 95-103.

Craw, I.G. and Cameron, P.J. (1991) 'Parameterising images for recognition and reconstruction', in P. Mowforth (ed.), *Proceedings of the British Machine Vision Conference*. London: Springer-Verlag.

Craw, I.G. and Cameron, P.J. (1992) 'Face recognition by computer', in D.C. Hogg and R. Boyle (eds), *Proceedings of the British Machine Vision Conference*. London: Springer-Verlag.

Davies, G.M., Ellis, H.D. and Shepherd, J.W. (1978) Face recognition accuracy as a function of mode of representation. *Journal of Applied Psychology*, 63(2), 180-187.

De Haan, E.H.F. and Hay, D.C. (1986) 'The matching of famous and unknown faces, given either the internal or the external features: a study on patients with unilateral brain lesions', in H.D. Ellis, M.A. Jeeves, F. Newcombe and A.W. Ellis (eds.), *Aspects of Face Processing* . Dordrecht: Martinus Nijhoff.

De Haan, E.H.F., Young, A.W. and Newcombe, F. (1987) Faces interfere with name classification in a prosopagnosic patient. *Cortex*, 23, 309-316.

Ekman, P. (1992) Facial expressions of emotion: an old controversy and new findings. *Philosophical Transactions of the Royal Society of London*, B335, 63-69.

Ekman, P. and Friesen, W.V. (1971) Constants across cultures in the face and emotion. *Journal of Personality and Social Psychology*, 17, 124-129.

Ekman, P. and Friesen, W.V. (1976) Measuring facial movement. *Environmental Psychology and Nonverbal Behaviour*, 1, 56-75.

Ekman, P. and Friesen, W.V. (1978) *Facial Action Coding System: A Technique for the Measurement of Facial Movement*. Palo Alto, California: Consulting Psychologists Press.

Ekman, P., Levenson, R.W. and Friesen, W.V. (1983) Autonomic nervous system activity distinguishes between emotions. *Science*, 221, 1208-1210.

Ellis, H.D. (1992) The development of face processing skills. *Philosophical Transactions of the Royal Society of London*, B335, 105-111.

Ellis, H.D., Shepherd, J.W. and Davies, G.M. (1979) Identification of familiar and unfamiliar faces from internal and external features: some implications for theories of face recognition. *Perception*, 8, 431-439.

Etcoff, N.L. and Magee, J.J. (1992) Categorical perception of facial expressions. *Cognition*, 44(3), 227-240.

Flin, R.H. (1980) Age effects in children's memory for unfamiliar faces. *Developmental Psychology*, 16(4), 373-374.

Gouraud, H. (1971) Continuous shading of curved surfaces. *IEEE Transactions on Computers*, 20(6), 623-628.

Harnad, S. (ed.) (1987) *Categorical Perception*. Cambridge, UK: Cambridge University Press.

Izard, C.E. (1971) *The Face of Emotion*. New York: Appleton-Century-Crofts.

Johnston, M.H. (1994) Brain and cognitive development in infancy. *Current Opinion in Neurobiology*, 4, 218-225.

Katsikitis, M., Pilowsky, I. and Innes, J.M. (1990) The quantification of smiling using a microcomputer-based approach. *Journal of Nonverbal Behaviour*, 14, 3-17.

Klatzky, R.L. and Forrest, F.H. (1984) Recognising familiar and unfamiliar faces. *Memory and Cognition*, 12(1), 60-70.

Likert, R. (1932) A technique for the measurement of attributes. *Archives of Psychology*, 140.

Mauro, R. and Kubovy, M. (1992) Caricature and face recognition. *Memory and Cognition*, 20, 433-440.

Morton, J. and Johnston, M.H. (1991) CONSPEC and CONLERN: a two-process theory of infant face recognition. *Psychological Review*, 98, 164-181.

Perkins, D. (1975) A definition of caricature and caricature and recognition. *Studies in the Anthropology of Visual Communication*, 2, 1-24.

Pilowsky, I. and Katsikitis, M. (1994) The classification of facial emotions: a computer-based taxonomic approach. *Journal of Affective Disorders*, 30, 61-71.

Rhodes, G. (1988) Looking at faces: first-order and second-order features as determinants of facial appearance. *Perception*, 17, 43-63.

Rhodes, G. (1993) Configural coding, expertise and the right-hemisphere advantage in face recognition. *Brain and Cognition*, 22(1), 19-41.

Rhodes, G. and McLean, I.G. (1990) Distinctiveness and expertise effects with homogeneous stimuli: towards a model of configural coding. *Perception*, 19, 773-794.

Rhodes, G. and Moody, J. (1990) Memory representations of unfamiliar faces. *New Zealand Journal of Psychology*, 19, 70-78.

Rhodes, G., Brennan, S.E. and Carey, S. (1987) Identification and ratings of caricatures: implications for mental representations of faces. *Cognitive Psychology*, 19, 473-497.

Shepard, R.M. (1984) Ecological constraints on internal representation: resonant kinematics of perceiving, imagining, thinking and dreaming. *Psychological Review*, 91, 417-447.

Sirovich, L. and Kirby, M. (1987) A low-dimensional procedure for the characterisation of human faces. *Journal of the Optical Society of America*, 4(3), 519-524.

Tranel, D. and Damasio, A.R. (1985) Knowledge without awareness: an autonomic index of facial recognition by prosopagnosics. *Science*, 228, 1453-1454.

Turk, M. and Pentland, A. (1991) Eigenfaces for recognition. *Journal of Cognitive Neuroscience*, 3(1), 71-86.

Valentine, T. (1991) A unified account of the effects of distinctiveness, inversion and race in face recognition. *Quarterly Journal of Experimental Psychology*, 43A(3), 161-204.

Valentine, T. and Bruce, V. (1986) The effect of distinctiveness in recognising and classifying faces. *Perception*, 15, 525-535.

Wallace, C.S. and Boulton, D.M. (1968) An information measure for classification. *Computer Journal*, 11, 185-194.

Waters, K. (1987) A muscle model for animating three-dimensional facial expressions. *Computer Graphics (ACM SIGGRAPH)*, 22(4), 17-24.

Young, A.W., Hay, D.C., McWeeny, K.H., Flude, B.M. and Ellis, A.W. (1985) Matching familiar and unfamiliar faces on internal and external features. *Perception*, 14, 737-746.

Name index

Subject index